Olga Lozynska
Victoria Vysotska
Oksana Markiv

Artificial Intelligence for Cyber Countering Disinformation: monograph

Olga Lozynska
Victoria Vysotska
Oksana Markiv

Artificial Intelligence for Cyber Countering Disinformation: monograph

Disinformation and fake news sources Identification based on NLP and machine learning methods

LAP LAMBERT Academic Publishing

Imprint
Any brand names and product names mentioned in this book are subject to trademark, brand or patent protection and are trademarks or registered trademarks of their respective holders. The use of brand names, product names, common names, trade names, product descriptions etc. even without a particular marking in this work is in no way to be construed to mean that such names may be regarded as unrestricted in respect of trademark and brand protection legislation and could thus be used by anyone.

Cover image: www.ingimage.com

Publisher:
LAP LAMBERT Academic Publishing
is a trademark of
Dodo Books Indian Ocean Ltd. and OmniScriptum S.R.L publishing group

120 High Road, East Finchley, London, N2 9ED, United Kingdom
Str. Armeneasca 28/1, office 1, Chisinau MD-2012, Republic of Moldova, Europe
Managing Directors: Ieva Konstantinova, Victoria Ursu
info@omniscriptum.com

Printed at: see last page
ISBN: 978-620-2-42987-0

Content

List of conventions, abbreviations and terms

AI – Artificial Intelligence.

IT – Information Technology.

SMM –Social Mass Media.

GPT – Generative Pretrained Transformer.

CV – Computer Vision.

ML – Machine Learning.

DL – Deep Learning.

DB – Database.

SVM – Support Vector Machine.

NV – Naive Bayes.

MNB – Multinomial Naive Bayes.

DT – Decision Tree.

RF – Random Forest.

LR – Logistic Regression.

BM – Bayes Modelling.

NBTree – Naive Bayes Tree.

MMNBTree – Multinomial Naive Bayes Tree.

MDS – Multidimensional Scaling.

TD-IDF – Term Frequency-Inverse Document Frequency.

CNN – Convolutional Neural Network.

RNN – Recurrent Neural Network.

LTSM – Long Short-Term Memory.

Bi-LSTM – Bidirectional Long Short-Term Memory.

BERT – Bidirectional Encoder Representations from Transformers.

GloVe – Global Vectors.

ChatGPT – Generative Pre-trained Transformer.

NLP – Natural Language Processing.

SA – Sentiment Analysis.

CL – Computational Linguistics.

EDA – Exploratory Analysis.

PSB – Preliminary Investigation Bodies.

AWP – Automated Workplaces.

XGBoost – eXtreme Gradient Boosting.

GloVe – Global Vectors for Word Representation.

NLTK – Natural Language Toolkit.

GRU – Gated Recurrent Unit.

BoW – Bag-of-Words.

KNN – K-Nearest Neighbours.

NLTK – Python Natural Language Toolkit.

GITCS – Global Closed Information and Telecommunication System.

BPMN – Business Process Model and Notation.

Fake – information that is deliberately fabricated, created, or spread with the intent to deceive.

Fake news – false stories that appear to be news spread on the internet or using other media, usually created to influence political views or as a joke.

Disinformation – false information that is intentionally spread to mislead or manipulate people.

Misinformation – false or inaccurate information that is not intentionally deceptive.

Propaganda – information, especially of a biased or misleading nature, used to promote a political cause or point of view.

Narrative – a story or explanation used to frame a specific event or situation, often with the goal of influencing public opinion.

Dataset – a collection of related sets of information that is composed of separate elements but can be manipulated as a unit by a computer.

Cybersecurity – the state of being protected against the criminal or unauthorised use of electronic data or the measures taken to achieve this.

Accuracy – a metric that measures how often a machine learning model correctly predicts the outcome.

Recall – a metric that measures how often a machine learning model correctly identifies positive instances (true positives) from all the actual positive samples in the dataset.

Precision – a metric that measures the accuracy of optimistic predictions made by a model.

F1 score – a metric used in machine learning to evaluate the performance of a classification model, particularly when dealing with imbalanced datasets or when both precision and recall are equally important.

Authentic Behaviour – acting in a way that is true to oneself, aligning actions with core values, beliefs, and personality.

Inauthentic Behaviour – activities that manipulate the platform or mislead users about the content's origin, popularity, or purpose, including creating fake accounts, artificially boosting content, and other deceptive practices.

Stemming – is one of several text normalisation techniques that convert raw text data into a readable format for natural language processing tasks.

Tokenisation – the process of breaking down a text document into smaller units called tokens, which can be words, phrases, or even characters.

Laplace Smoothing – a technique used to adjust probability estimates, particularly in situations where some outcomes have not been observed in a training dataset.

Bigram Probability – count how many times the first word of the pair appears on its own.

Internet Safety – also known as cyber safety, refers to the practices and precautions individuals and organisations take to protect themselves and their information while using the internet.

Hate Speech – a form of expression, whether through words, writing, or behaviour, that attacks or denigrates a person or group based on characteristics like race, religion, gender, or other identity factors.

Censorship – the suppression or prohibition of any parts of books, films, news, etc. that are considered obscene, politically unacceptable, or a threat to security.

Inappropriate Content – online material that is unsuitable or offensive, often due to its content, context, or target audience.

Introduction

In the digital age, disinformation is the deliberate dissemination of false or distorted information with the aim of manipulating public opinion. It poses a serious threat to political, social and economic stability [1]. Given that the bulk of information is disseminated through social networks, blogs and news resources, there is an urgent need to create automated tools that can quickly and effectively identify sources of disinformation in large-scale information flows.

Social networks are the main channels for the dissemination of information, but at the same time, they are platforms for the mass dissemination of disinformation and propaganda. Therefore, the creation of practical tools for monitoring and countering such threats is crucial for protecting the information space.

The scale and dynamics of information flows are of particular complexity. Disinformation campaigns are often carried out in a coordinated and organised manner, using botnets that masquerade as ordinary users. Modern automated tools and big data analysis methods are needed to identify such accounts, their connections and sources of information dissemination.

Artificial intelligence and machine learning technologies are significantly improving the efficiency of fake news and chatbot detection processes. They can be used to analyse texts for signs of falsification, recognise suspicious behaviour on social networks, and detect falsified images and videos.

Although the problem of disinformation is global and affects many countries, addressing it at the national level can make a significant contribution to the worldwide fight against information threats.

Chapter 1 describes the study of fake news identification based on Natural Language Processing, extensive data analysis and deep learning technology. This system automatically checks news for signs of fake news, such as manipulative language, unverified sources and unreliable information. Visualisation of data and result analysis: the user interface that displays the results of news analysis in a convenient and understandable format. The research demonstrates better indicators of news analysis based on Long Short-Term Memory with eight epochs compared to similar works with 3-4 epochs (99% vs 85-96%) because a neural network was developed for news classification using a bidirectional recurrent neural network LSTM and Bidirectional layers in the model. Deep learning models, such as bidirectional LSTM, have high accuracy in recognising patterns in textual data, allowing for better results.

Chapter 2 considers developing a natural language processing system to extract relevant information from criminal reports or fake/propaganda. A detailed description of the developed system was made. The technical requirements were formed. System development is divided into three steps: data preparation, word embedding, and classification. The structure of the product under development has been described. It used libraries and ways of implementing the methods. The structure of the neural network and initial parameters of the network are described in detail based on knowledge rather than machine learning methods: this means that it is necessary to specify patterns, and not to have a purpose to learn and generalise them.

Chapter 3 presents a new method of propaganda analysis to identify signs and change the dynamics of the behaviour of coordinated groups based on machine learning at the processing disinformation stages. In the course of the work, two models were implemented to recognise propaganda in textual data - at the message level and the phrase level. Within the framework of solving the problem of analysis and recognition of text data, in particular, fake news on the Internet, an essential component of NLP technology is the classification of words in text data. In this context, classification is the assignment of textual data to one or more predefined categories or classes. For this purpose, the task of binary text classification was solved. Both models are built based on logistic regression. In the process of data preparation and feature extraction, such methods as vectorisation using TF-IDF vectorisation, the BOW model, POS marking, word embedding using the Word2Vec two-layer neural network, as well as manual feature extraction methods aimed at identifying specific methods of political propaganda in texts, are used. The analogues of the project under development are analysed, and the subject area (the propaganda used in the media and the basis of its production methods) is studied. The model's score for propaganda recognition at the phrase level was 0.74, and at the message level: 0.99. The implementation of the results will significantly reduce the time required to make the most appropriate decision on the implementation of counter-disinformation measures concerning the identified coordinated groups of disinformation generation, fake news and propaganda.

Chapter 4 introduces the availability of effective methods of identifying fake news and countermeasures. Authors use machine learning methods to detect disinformation. A dataset for detecting fake news has been developed. The most frequently used words in fake news, collected from August to November 2024, were studied.

Chapter 5 proposes a structure based on a graph of knowledge for the chronology of homicide investigations. The knowledge graph construction needs to analyse the relationship between the statistics of their crime reports for the following disclosure of criminal offences, particularly the disclosure of murders. Modelling the topic of crime demonstrates a more nuanced model of criminal incidents, which entails a massive loss of information obtained from unified reporting about the related criminal offences. We have proposed two performance indicators to assess crime theme models and demonstrated that choosing a thematic model has important implications for identifying crime hotspots. We have shown that more coherent topics that are simultaneously concentrated on a higher specific subject area can be achieved, allowing for more targeted police intervention, given limited resources.

Chapter 6 describes the features of using Laplace smoothing to identify disinformation in texts, especially in social media chats. An example of implementing a bigram model with Laplace smoothing in Python to detect fake news is proposed. This approach reduces the probability of errors if new or different words appear in fake news compared to the training models. A step-by-step algorithm for identifying disinformation using Laplace smoothing is described, taking into account disinformation criteria, which reduces the probability of inappropriate results from text information analysis of the disinformation dataset. It allows improving the accuracy of classifications, and as a result, using this approach, it is proposed to develop a clearer architecture for identifying disinformation with bigram analysis in the context of fake news.

Chapter 7 describes the features of disinformation detection in product placement and the use of the spaCy library for such analysis, for example, to search for context related to product placement. The need to create and constantly fill the disinformation dataset in accordance with current requests has been emphasised, taking into account further analysis of the assessment of the information dissemination of disinformation. It is essential to analyse the inauthentic behaviour of chat participants in this context by forming and updating criteria. The features of identifying product placement disinformation using software tools for automated processing of disinformation have been described.

Chapter 8 presents an approach to detecting fake news in the digital environment through text analysis using machine learning and natural language processing methods. The proposed method is based on a hybrid text representation combining frequency features and contextual embeddings obtained using the IBM Granite model. A complete data processing cycle was developed, covering the stages of exploratory analysis, text pre-processing and tokenisation, forming vector representations, training a logistic regression model, and obtaining key metrics. The main stages of text pre-processing included converting all characters to lowercase, removing URLs and HTML tags, cleaning from non-letter characters and excess spaces, eliminating duplicates to avoid re-training, and unifying the values of specific fields. A combination of TF-IDF with contextual embeddings was used to vectorise the cleaned texts. It allowed the model to simultaneously consider the statistical significance of terms and their semantic context within the messages. The constructed logistic regression model, combined with a hybrid representation of text data, demonstrated high efficiency, achieving an overall accuracy of 82% and balanced F1-measure values for the "true" and "fake" classes. An analysis of TF-IDF feature weights based on logistic regression coefficients was applied to identify the most relevant terms. The study showed that the model tends to associate truthful information with Ukrainian-language, neutral vocabulary. At the same time, texts with signs of disinformation often contain Russian-language elements characteristic of propaganda or manipulative messages. Further research will be aimed at expanding the dataset and creating new ensemble models to identify sources of disinformation.

Chapter 9 focuses on employing information technology to censor inappropriate content in text and images on web pages. These research directions aim to improve the accuracy, effectiveness, and ethical standards of hate speech detection systems, thereby enhancing their ability to identify and mitigate harmful content across online platforms. The proposed solution is valuable for parents seeking to safeguard their children, educational institutions striving to foster a more conducive learning environment, and individuals prioritising ethical internet usage. It also supports users who wish to limit their exposure to misinformation, including fake news, propaganda, and disinformation. Through the implementation of a browser extension, this system will contribute to a safer internet, reducing users' vulnerability to harmful content and promoting a more positive and productive online environment. The primary objective of this work is to develop a browser extension that automatically detects and censors inappropriate text and images on web pages using artificial intelligence technologies. The extension will enable users to personalise censorship settings, including the ability to define custom prohibited words and toggle the filtering of text and images. Accuracy estimates for various classifiers, such as Random Forest (0.879), Logistic Regression (0.904), Decision Tree (0.878), Naive Bayes (0.315), KNN (0.832) and LSTM (0.8862) were performed.

The monograph is intended for specialists in cybersecurity, machine learning, linguistics, and artificial intelligence systems, as well as for those obtaining an educational and scientific level of higher education in information technology for knowledge processing. The authors consider tools of natural language processing (NLP), machine learning, and deep learning, as well as big data analysis. The monograph presents the results of experiments using various models, including TF-IDF, transform embeddings, SVM and knowledge graphs. The research covers the identification of fake sources in social networks, the development of a set of criteria for detecting sources of disinformation, and the detection of hostile rhetoric, sarcasm and inauthentic behaviour of users in chats. The monograph is supported by the National Research Fund of Ukraine "Information system development for automatic detection of misinformation sources and inauthentic behaviour of chat users", project registration number 33/0012 from 3/03/2025 (2023.04/0012).

Chapter 1. Fake news identification based on NLP, Big Data analysis and deep learning technology

The chapter is written based on scientific publications and research [1-25].

1.1. Known methods for fake news identification

In today's world, due to the rapid growth of the Internet, people have access to much information [1-3]. However, not all information that can be found is reliable [4-5]. Especially in the news field, news agencies create more and more news on different topics to attract readers' attention [6-10]. So, to improve community awareness of the information reliability of news articles with intriguing headlines, the system "Identification of fake news» has been proposed to be developed. The purpose is to develop information technology to recognise fake news. Problems are obtaining data (lack of reliable and representative data sets due to the rapid spread of fake news and its variety); selection of features (the difficulty of identifying characteristics that are discriminating for distinguishing fake news from actual news, especially in the context of constantly changing methods of creating fakes); model training (challenges associated with training models on data that may contain distortions due to classification ambiguity); efficiency and accuracy (ensuring high accuracy and efficiency of the model in quickly recognising fake news to avoid the spread of false information); ethics and transparency (development of a model that takes into account ethical aspects, in particular, avoiding biases and preserving the privacy of users during the processing of personal data); general openness (ensuring the availability and transparency of the model for auditing and verification to ensure consumer confidence in the results of identifying fake news). An automated fake news detection system uses NLP and machine learning technologies to analyse news text. This system automatically checks news for signs of fake news, such as manipulative language, unverified sources and unreliable information. Visualisation of data and result analysis: the user interface that displays the results of news analysis in a convenient and understandable format. Users can view each news item's credibility level and receive a detailed analysis breakdown. Notifying users of suspicious information: the notification service informs users of suspicious or fake information that may appear in their news feed or search results. The tools will help users verify the authenticity of the information they consume and weed out fake news from their digital environment. The innovation lies in creating a system allowing users to verify the integrity of news using machine learning tools. The growing number of fake news and disinformation in the digital space makes it urgent to develop systems capable of detecting and combating this problem. In works [11-13], the research is based on classical methods of machine learning, such as a support vector machine classifier or k-nearest neighbours, etc. The following two are consistent with the deep learning method, a subset of machine learning methods based on artificial neural networks with representation learning, particularly LSTM as a recurrent neural network. Theoretically, LSTM should achieve the best accuracy in fake/non-fake detection in text news. However, the accuracy of the results obtained by the authors in these studies is further interesting, as are the values of this metric. Work [11] demonstrates news analysis based on methods such as Multidimensional Scaling and an SVM classifier with over 90% accuracy of fake identification. The emphasis is on applying the Sentiment analysis method after pre-processing to form input data for classifiers. The accuracy of the obtained tasks is not sufficient. Work [12] demonstrates news analysis based on the classical method of machine learning, as SVM, combined with the NLP method as TF-IDF and based on a hybrid model of deep learning as CNN with LSTM. The last option provides an order of magnitude better accuracy in identifying fake news (92.3% versus 84.29%). The accuracy is also improved because it was conducted on old data for the year 2021 regarding COVID-19 Fake News. The older the data, the more accurate the result, because history has already been specified for this period. It is more challenging to research new news data during an information war among current information, when even an average person cannot consistently and often determine what is fake and what is reliable. The problem today is the prompt formation of such datasets for training systems and their timely and periodic renewal in a short period (for example, weekly or daily), that is, the implementation of the best data collection pipeline. The second problem is the selection of the best NLP methods (in addition to classic pre-processing, noise removal, duplicating, marking, formation of dictionaries of noun groups and not only alphabetic-frequency dictionaries of words, lemmatisation, tokenisation, separation of proper names, etc.), but even conducting a semantic or ontological analysis to identify relationships between entities and distribute weights between them. Theoretically, the sentiment analysis method should better detect a fake because propaganda and fakes are usually written in a negative tone. However, in work [11], it did not significantly affect the improvement of accuracy (90%) compared to others [12-15], where accuracy is better without using the sentiment analysis method (Table 1.1).

Table 1.1. Comparison of research results in [11-16]

Name	**Articles**					
	[12]	*[13]*	*[14]*	*[15]*	*[16]*	*[17]*
	Machine learning	Deep learning	Machine learning	Deep Learning	Machine learning	Machine learning
learning methods	MDS and SVM classifier	SVM + TF-IDF and CNN+ LSTM as a hybrid model	decision tree, KNN, logistic regression, random forest, Bayes classifier, multilayer perceptron	CNN - 3 epochs, LSTM – 4 epochs.	logistic regressio n	logistic regressio n
NLP	Pre-processing , the given characteris tics of text (getting params for each news article), and Sentiment analysis	Data pre-processin g: Studied features based on TF-IDF features	standard libraries from Python, such as pandas, sklearn, NumPy, seaborn, matplotlib, etc.	TF-IDF character istics. GloVe (Global Vectors).	Word2ve c library, modified Porter stemmer method, TF-IDF algorith m and TfidfVec torizer method.	TF-IDF
dataset	[18]	[19]	[20-23]	[24]	The author's	articles 31972

					dataset of news in russian and Ukrainian languages	non-propagandistic and 4201 propagandistic
accuracy	90%	84.29%. (SVM+ TF-IDF) and 92.3%. (CNN+ LSTM)	DT 0.9903/ 0.98 as fakes/non-fakes identification (difference 0.013), KNN 0.999/0.83 (0.169), LR 0.9988/ 0.9965 (0.0023), random forest 0.933/ 0.991 (0.058), Bayes classifier 0.913/ 0.998 (0.085), multilayer perceptron 0.995/ 0.998 (0.0034)	94-96% The work focuses on researching the time spent learning the model. Authors have ~391s for CNN and ~391s for RNN.	The training data is 0.9899, and the test data is 0.4856	training, data is 0.9433254618697041, and for test data is 0.7332361516

Deep Learning methods should theoretically give better accuracy results. Still, in paper 3 (where classical learning methods are applied), the accuracy is better than in papers 2 and 3 (where deep learning methods are used). Conclusion - if you do not choose the best NLP methods for preliminary processing of datasets and/or do not form/select a complete/accurate dataset (or rather several, as it was done in work [13]), the accuracy of identifying a fake will not significantly improve. So, there are errors in the input data (incomplete or inaccurate datasets) and models of the previous NLP method of news processing. It, in turn, affects the accuracy of training models and subsequent determination (identification) of fake/non-fake news. Work [13] demonstrates the processing of several datasets using classic machine learning methods such as multilayer perceptron, logistic regression, random forest, the Bayes classifier, the decision tree and the k-nearest neighbours. All obtained accuracies range from 0.913 to 0.999. However, preliminary processing of news texts was performed using classic methods (including NLP) and standard Python libraries such as Pandas, Sklearn, Numpy, seaborn, Matplotlib, etc.

Research [14] demonstrates using CNN with three epochs and LSTM with four epochs (based on TF-IDF characteristics). A 94-96% accuracy was obtained. In work [14], the emphasis is on studying the model of the time spent studying. For example, let's find the average value of the indicator for each of the algorithms. We have ~391s for CNN and ~391s for RNN.

In [15], compared to previous works [11-14], fake news is analysed in russian and Ukrainian languages, not in English. Therefore, the emphasis of the research is on the peculiarities of NLP processing of text content in the Slavic language for identifying fakes and propaganda based on the Word2vec library, modified Porter stemmer method, TF-IDF algorithm and TfidfVectorizer method. A logistic regression method was used for machine learning (accuracy for training data is 0.9899, and for test data is 0.4856). The complexity of processing and analysis of Slavic languages, strong Sinomization and the novelty of information noise in such messages explain a significant decrease in accuracy. In [16], propaganda is identified based on the analysis of political news in 35,993 English-language articles (including headlines) based on a logistic regression and TF-IDF (31,972 non-propagandistic and 4,201 propagandistic articles). The accuracy for training data is 0.9433254618697041. But for test data, it is 0.7332361516. The model successfully classified 1917 non-propaganda articles and 205 propaganda articles (2012), but 585 and 146 non-propaganda articles were misclassified (731). As we can see, the accuracy of training data when identifying Slavic and Germanic languages is similar (0.9899 and 0.9433), with the same methods of NLP (TF-IDF) and machine learning (a logistic regression). Still, for test data, there is a significant difference (0.4856 and 0.7332) – for English-language texts, the accuracy is almost twice as high as for Slavic languages.

Each of the six papers (Table 1.1) shows different accuracies of identifying fake news based on learning on different datasets (including different amounts and generated in other periods) and various methods of NLP, analysis, and machine learning (including Deep Learning). If we take one dataset, one NLP method and all the machine and deep learning methods listed in [15], then it is possible to state which machine and deep learning methods are the best based on the results of calculating the accuracy and loss metrics.

It is also advisable to analyse the time spent on identifying fakes for each of the methods because, for various tasks, it is better to sacrifice accuracy to reduce identification time, and for others, the opposite. During the analogues' analysis, resources were identified NewsGuard (uses a team of journalists and technology to evaluate the credibility of news sources online; they create news site rankings in different categories to help users distinguish reliable sources from those spreading fake news); Snopes (an online resource that specialises in identifying and debunking myths and pseudo-facts; carefully verifies information and provides users with reliable data to make informed decisions); British organisation Full Fact (specialises in fact-checking and identifying false information in news, politics and public discourse; use a combination of automated and manual methods to fact-check); Bellingcat (a non-profit project that uses open sources and Internet investigations to identify and document various situations, including disinformation and fake news). Use of language and text style: Analysis of the presence of manipulative techniques, sensational headlines, emotional load, aggressive tone, etc., information source (checking the authority and reliability of the sources from which the information is taken); fact-checking (analysing the veracity of statements and facts presented in an article by checking with trusted sources or databases); contextual analysis (understanding the context and circumstances in which information is given to identify possible attempts at manipulation). The evaluation of characteristics compared to analogous processes may include analysing qualitative and quantitative metrics for each characteristic and comparing them to similar peers (Table 1.2). A numerical scale of 1 to 10 will be used for grading.

Table 1.2. Construction of a comparative table for comparing the system with analogues

Features	Products		
	System	NewsGuard	Snopes
Platform	Web	Web	Web
User interface	7	6	5
Reliability	7	8	6
Precision	7	6	6

The use of advanced machine learning technologies allows for more accurate and effective detection of fake news compared to analogues. Conclusions about the feasibility of developing the system are problem relevance (the growing number of fake news and disinformation in the digital space makes it urgent to create systems capable of detecting and combating this problem), and market potential (the popularity of news portals and social media creates a significant demand for tools that help users distinguish between fake and authentic information). The system's primary functioning process can be displayed in the following sequence: receiving the text for analysis from the user, text analysis, and notification of the analysis result.

1.2. Methods and tools

Methods and tools of product development are machine learning (to classify news, it needed to use deep learning methods, such as LSTM and bidirectional LSTM); NLP (includes text pre-processing, tokenisation, lemmatisation, stop-word removal, and text sequencing); programming language (Python, due to its broad support and availability of libraries for machine learning and NLP); TensorFlow and Keras (for building and training deep learning models); NLTK (for text processing as tokenisation, stop words); Gensim (for simple text pre-processing); Scikit-learn (to divide data into training and test sets); Matplotlib, Seaborn, Plotly (for visualisation of data and results). Analogues are NewsGuard (uses a team of journalists to evaluate the news; disadvantages are subjectivity and limited scope); Snopes (uses fact-checking based on manual analysis; disadvantages are subjectivity, takes much time); Full Fact (uses fact-checkers to verify news; disadvantages are subjectivity, limited scope); Bellingcat (uses open sources and a combination of manual and automated analysis; disadvantages are high expenditure of time and resources). Advantages of the selected methods and tools are automation (the use of machine learning models allows automatic processing of large volumes of data without the need for human intervention); scalability (machine learning algorithms can process large data sets in real-time, allowing the system to be more scalable compared to manual methods); objectivity (algorithms reduces the subjectivity inherent in manual analysis); accuracy and speed (deep learning models, such as bidirectional LSTM, have high accuracy in recognising patterns in textual data, allowing for better results); interactivity (the web interface provides users with convenient access to analysis results, which improves the user experience). Details of methods and means are NLTK and Gensim (used for text pre-processing, including tokenisation, lemmatisation, removal of stop words and other unwanted characters; NLTK provides tools for working with text such as tokenisers and stop word corpora; Gensim offers simple tools for pre-processing and building Word2Vec models); TensorFlow and Keras (used to develop and train deep learning models; BiLSTM allow the model to consider the context to both the left and right of each word; Embedding Layer converts text data into numeric vectors that deep learning models can process); Matplotlib, Seaborn, Plotly (used for data visualisation, which helps to understand data distribution and simulation results). The software consists of the following components: import the necessary libraries; data collection module (downloading and combining real and fake news datasets; adding columns with labels to classify news); data processing module (text pre-processing, including text cleaning, stop word removal, lemmatisation and tokenisation; preparation of textual data for further analysis); analysis module (creation and training of a deep learning model based on bidirectional LSTMs; using models to classify news as fake or real); user interface (Web interface for interaction with users and display of analysis results; below is the code to implement each of these components).

1.3. Experiments, results and discussion

The dataset shown in Fig. 1.1 shows 23481 fake news and 21417 real news [24]. Results analysis of the overview of the number of different topics and combining individual words into lines for further training are shown in Fig. 1.2-1.3.

title	text
As U.S. budget fight looms, Republicans flip t...	WASHINGTON (Reuters) - The head of a conservat...
U.S. military to accept transgender recruits o...	WASHINGTON (Reuters) - Transgender people will...
Senior U.S. Republican senator: 'Let Mr. Muell...	WASHINGTON (Reuters) - The special counsel inv...
FBI Russia probe helped by Australian diplomat...	WASHINGTON (Reuters) - Trump campaign adviser ...
Trump wants Postal Service to charge 'much mor...	SEATTLE/WASHINGTON (Reuters) - President Donal...

title	text
Donald Trump Sends Out Embarrassing New Year'...	Donald Trump just couldn t wish all Americans ...
Drunk Bragging Trump Staffer Started Russian ...	House Intelligence Committee Chairman Devin Nu...
Sheriff David Clarke Becomes An Internet Joke...	On Friday, it was revealed that former Milwauk...
Trump Is So Obsessed He Even Has Obama's Name...	On Christmas day, Donald Trump announced that ...
Pope Francis Just Called Out Donald Trump Dur...	Pope Francis used his annual Christmas Day mes...

Fig. 1.1. Data from the "True.csv" file (23481) and "Fake.csv" file (21417)

Parameters for model training are total_words = 224052, embedding_dim = 256, lstm_units = 128, dense_units = [256, 128, 64], dropout_rate = 0.3. The learning model consists of a layer for text embedding, a bidirectional (LSTM) layer for traversing the text in two directions, and dense layers for classification. Dropout was also used to reduce model overtraining (Fig. 1.4). The dataset was used for model training and validation based on eight epochs. After training the model, the following results were found. The model shows instability during training (Fig. 1.5-1.6). The confusion matrix and the classification report show that the model cannot identify the news correctly. The results shown above show that the model needs to provide more accuracy to be used, so experiments were carried out to improve it. The following experiments were performed using the improved model.

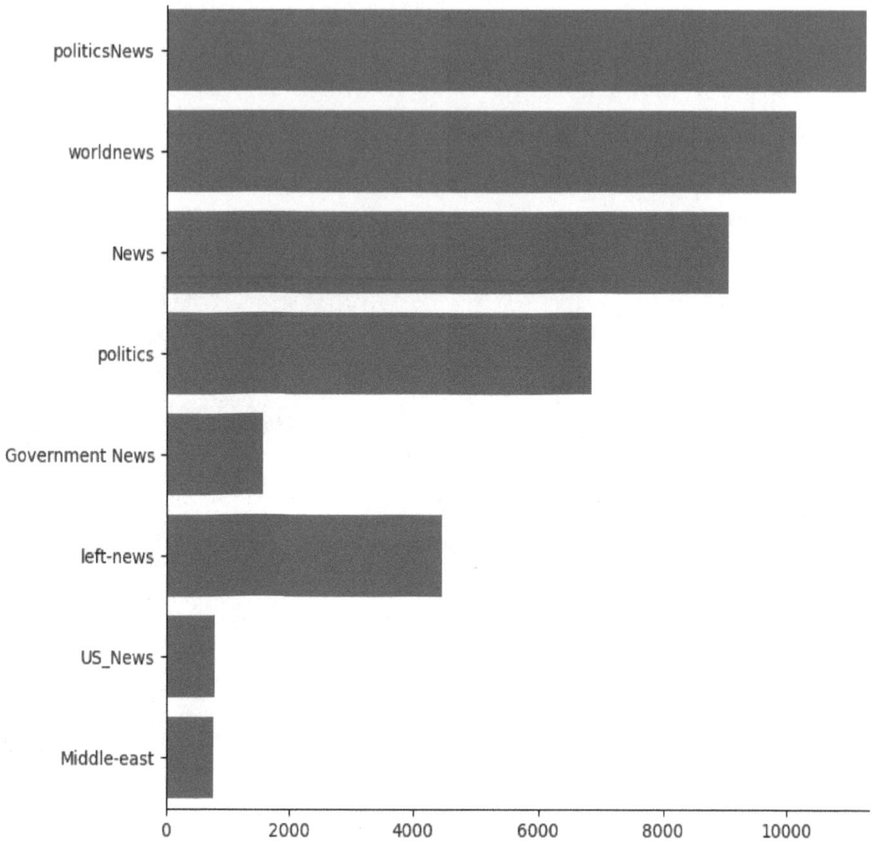

Fig. 1.2. Overview of the number of different topics and news on this topic

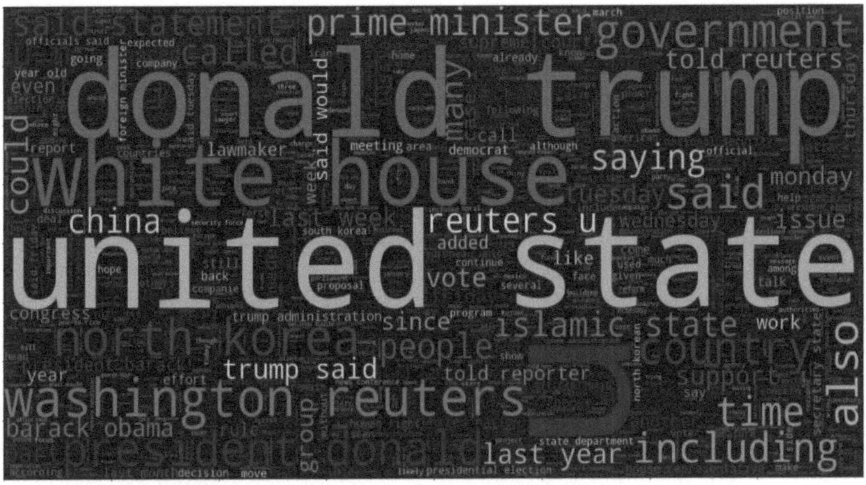

Fig. 1.3. The most frequent words in the fake and real news dataset

```
44s 639ms/step - accuracy: 0.8857 - loss: 0.3197 - val_accuracy: 1.0000 - val_loss: 0.0020

42s 662ms/step - accuracy: 0.9992 - loss: 0.0039 - val_accuracy: 1.0000 - val_loss: 1.5584e-04

41s 634ms/step - accuracy: 0.9999 - loss: 6.4474e-04 - val_accuracy: 1.0000 - val_loss: 7.4196e-05

41s 633ms/step - accuracy: 1.0000 - loss: 3.1450e-04 - val_accuracy: 1.0000 - val_loss: 4.2458e-05

41s 633ms/step - accuracy: 1.0000 - loss: 6.1151e-04 - val_accuracy: 0.9997 - val_loss: 3.9274e-04

40s 631ms/step - accuracy: 0.9999 - loss: 0.0016 - val_accuracy: 0.9994 - val_loss: 0.0013

41s 641ms/step - accuracy: 1.0000 - loss: 9.5947e-05 - val_accuracy: 0.9997 - val_loss: 5.5482e-04

42s 661ms/step - accuracy: 1.0000 - loss: 1.1088e-04 - val_accuracy: 0.9997 - val_loss: 6.6213e-04
```

Fig. 1.4. Model learning process

For the benchmark, it is necessary to take news samples, one real and one fake, and test the model. After that, it is essential to analyse the obtained results. News items selected for manual testing did not participate in model training. The result obtained is "Real". The model correctly classified the real news as accurate (Fig. 1.7). This shows that the model can recognise news text that matches the expected characteristics of real news. The result received "Fake".

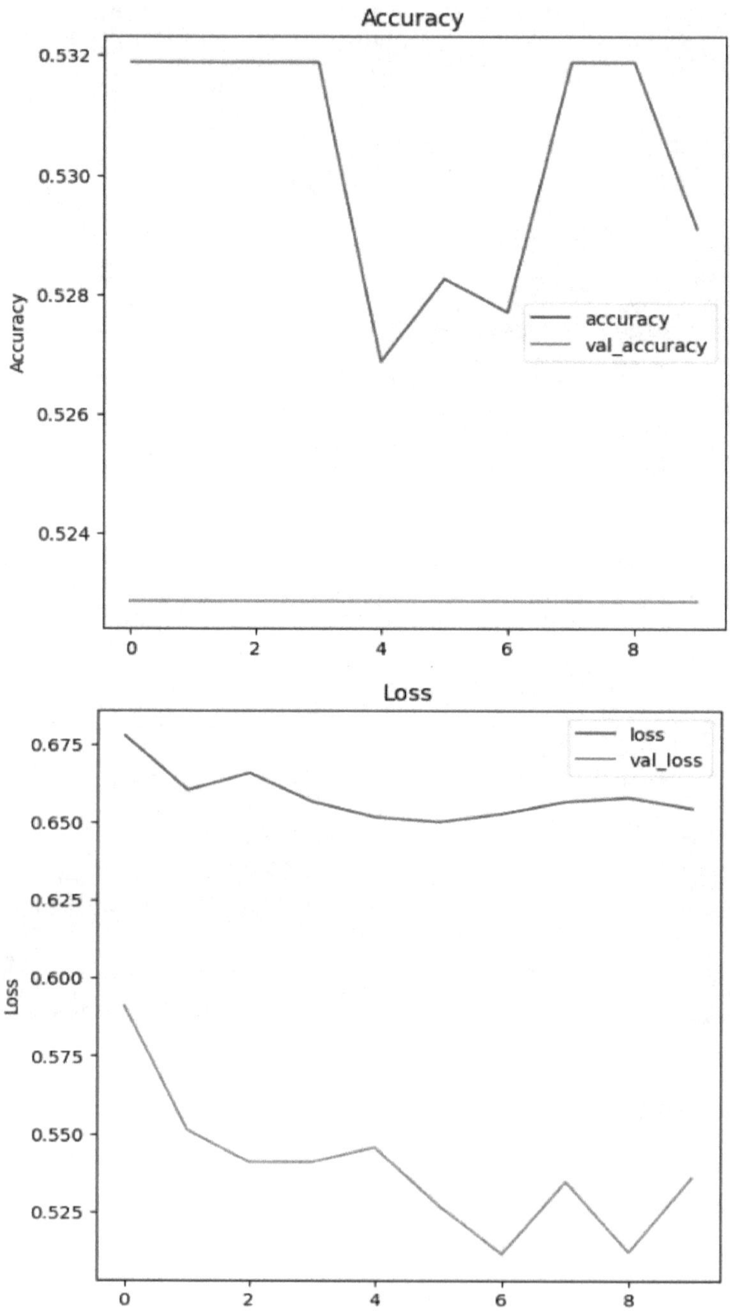

Fig. 1.5. Model training results

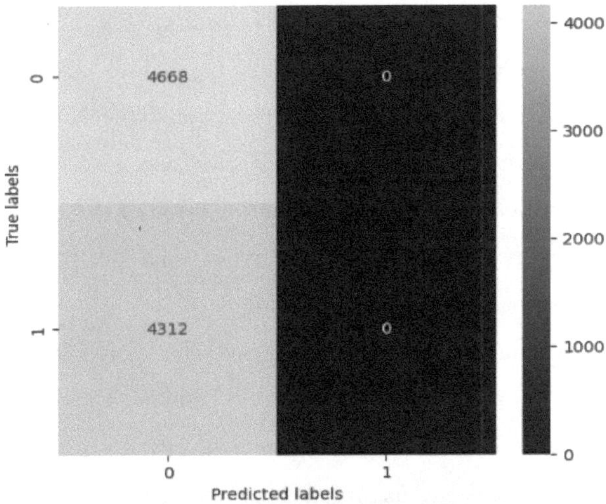

	precision	recall	f1-score	support
0	0.52	1.00	0.68	4668
1	0.00	0.00	0.00	4312
accuracy			0.52	8980
macro avg	0.26	0.50	0.34	8980
weighted avg	0.27	0.52	0.36	8980

Fig. 1.6. Confusion matrix and report about classification

Input Text: 21416,Indonesia to buy $1.14 billion worth of Russian jets,"JAKARTA (Reuters)
two cabinet ministers said on Tuesday. The Southeast Asian country has pledged to ship up
delivered in stages starting in two years. Indonesian Trade Minister Enggartiasto Lukita said
being negotiated . Previously he had said the exports could include palm oil, tea, and coffee
Indonesia and Russian state conglomerate Rostec. Russia is currently facing a new round o
threats of a cut in consumption by European Union countries. Indonesia is also trying to mo
Russia in 2016, wants to expand bilateral cooperation in tourism, education, energy, technol

Prediction: Real

Input Text: were consolidated in federal court, all argued that the privacy rights of non-Yah
company.Now, lawyers representing the plaintiffs are singing a different tune. Last week, th
Yahoo users won t get any payment, but the class lawyers at Girard Gibbs and Kaplan Fox
oppose any fee request up to $4 million.)While users won t get any payment, Yahoo will ch
scanning e-mails. Instead, the company has agreed to make a technical change to when it
advertising purposes after a Yahoo Mail user can access the email in his or her inbox. The
MORE NSA NEWS AT: 21st Century Wire NSA Files",Middle-east,"January 16, 2016",0

Prediction: Fake

Fig. 1.7. Identified authentic and fake news

The model correctly classified fake news as fake (Fig. 1.7). This shows that the model does an excellent job of identifying anomalous and implausible texts often found in fake news. The model demonstrated the ability to accurately classify real and fake news, confirming its effectiveness in recognising texts with different characteristics. The successful determination of the correctness of both types of news testifies to the high quality of data pre-processing and the effectiveness of the machine learning algorithms.

Prospects for further research are dataset expansion, improvement of text processing, model optimisation, and integration with real systems. These areas of further research and improvement will improve the efficiency and accuracy of the fake news recognition system, making it more universal and reliable for real use after making improvements to the model and re-training with other parameters. The model achieved results that can correctly identify fake news. The updated results of model training are shown in Fig. 1.8-1.10. It can be seen that the model's ability to identify fake news correctly has significantly increased compared to previous results. Learning results have become much more stable and higher.

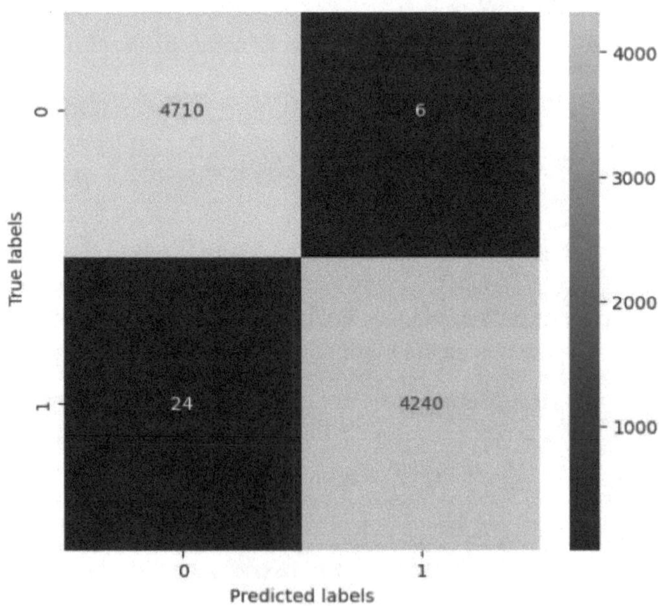

Fig. 1.8. Confusion matrix

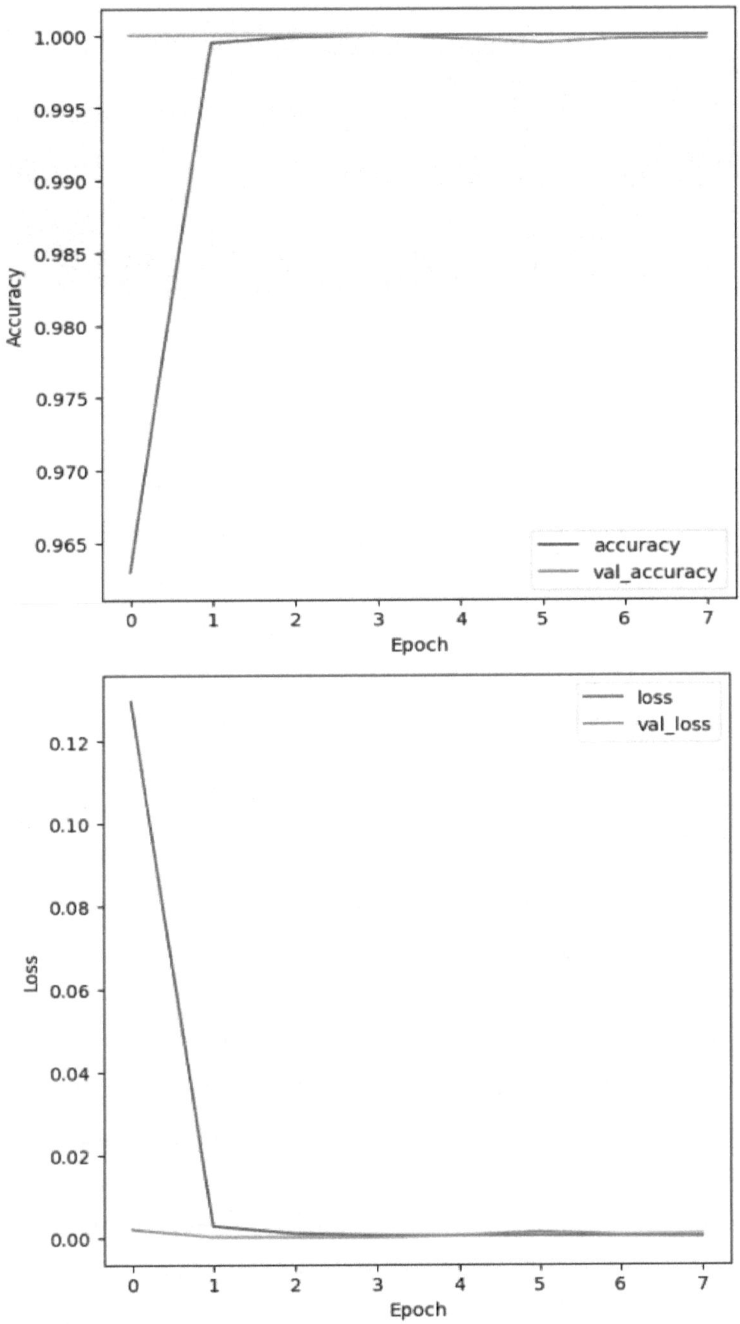

Fig. 1.8. Model training results

	precision	recall	f1-score	support
0	0.99	1.00	1.00	4716
1	1.00	0.99	1.00	4264
accuracy			1.00	8980
macro avg	1.00	1.00	1.00	8980
weighted avg	1.00	1.00	1.00	8980

Fig. 1.10. Report about classification

1.4. Conclusions for Chapter 1

During the execution of the project on recognition of fake news, the following main stages were completed selection of methods and mean (the NLTK, TensorFlow, pandas, NumPy, matplotlib, seaborn, gensim libraries were used for text processing, visualisation and model building; the methods of tokenisation, data cleaning, removal of stop words, and lemmatisation were applied to prepare the text); software development (datasets of real and fake news were collected and combined; data pre-processing including text cleaning and simulation preparation was performed; a neural network was developed for news classification using LSTM and Bidirectional layers in the model; the model was trained on the training sample and tested on the test sample); control example (testing was performed on a control data set; the obtained results showed that the model successfully identifies real and fake news with high accuracy); statistical analysis (an analysis of the results of training and testing of the model was carried out; a confusion matrix and accuracy and error graphs were constructed to visualise the results; the accuracy of the model was assessed, and a classification report was constructed). Analysis of the obtained results is based on the model's accuracy (the model showed high accuracy on the test sample, which indicates its ability to recognise fake news effectively) and metrics (the confusion matrix showed that all the news items were classified correctly). The classification report confirmed high accuracy, completeness and F1 score for both classes (real and fake news).

Prospects for further research are dataset expansion (including more data from different sources to increase the generalizability of the model; using multilingual datasets to extend the application of the model to other languages); text processing improvements (investigating more efficient text cleaning and processing methods, such as using advanced lemmatisers and tokenisers; using pre-trained transformer models (e.g. BERT, GPT) for a deeper understanding of the text); model optimisation (selection of hyperparameters to improve model performance; exploring alternative neural network architectures, such as more profound or more complex recurrent neural networks); integration with real systems (integrated systems development for automatic detection of fake news in real-time on social network platforms; creating web applications or browser extensions to allow users to verify news); content and context analysis (investigating techniques for analysing the context of news to detect more hidden fake news that can be written in a style that mimics real news; semantic analysis inclusion to recognise manipulative and trending news). These prospects will increase the accuracy and efficiency of the model and make it more universal and suitable for use in real conditions.

Chapter 2. NLP Tool for extracting relevant information from criminal reports or fakes/propaganda content

The chapter is written based on scientific publications and research [26-78].

2.1. Literature review and problem statement

"Manual" systems for searching for information about crimes or identifying fakes/propaganda no longer meet modern needs - they are not capable of providing prompt and accurate information. Various information online is currently subject to regional censorship due to political, economic, social, religious, and other factors, for example, for controlling or managing the opinions of the people in that region [26-32]. At the same time, purposeful or random/chaotic fake information is spread on the Internet. It is easy for the average person to get lost and navigate in this mass of content flow with opposite facts and causes of events/phenomena. It is unethical, illegal, and non-expedient to control what is shown or hidden (censored content) among Internet content to the average user in democracies. It is one of the first steps in the transition to totalitarianism. But providing information, for example, to journalists about possible thematic fakes for investigative journalism or warning the average reader about the possibility of misinformation in this content/resource is, on one hand, supporting freedom of speech, and on the other hand, enabling people to choose what to believe and why not. At the same time, it provides an opportunity to gain an understanding of events and orientation in a large flow of information, both for solving everyday problems and adjusting business strategies and more. Significant and mass dissemination of (dis) information against the background of the war in Ukraine, without proper analysis, potentially leads to panic among the relevant population stratum/region. It significantly affects the process of adjusting plans/strategies of business, social services, etc. Against the background of the information war, a lot of time and resources are spent on the relevant collection, analysis, and formation of relevant conclusions on the content of pertinent information. The language of the information also influences this, the translation of which may partially / significantly change the content. The system will not be able to completely replace human activity in this direction. However, it can be a significant helper in quickly forming relevant databases of such content and responding to local changes or the dynamics of changes in the content flow, marking certain content as potentially fake in a certain percentage. The goal is to create an NLP system for identifying relevant content in crime reports or fake/propaganda Internet news. The first task will help solve problems in the field of criminology and police investigations by reducing the amount of manual work of the staff. The second task allows one to gain advantages in the information war.

Propaganda technology in the world was used a long time ago by various influential personalities of each generation to implement human resources in the interests of a specific person, group of persons or state. Before the development of information technologies and digital means of information transmission, this method of manipulating people was used, using postcards and notes with sharp headlines or provocative phrases. They were meant to convince and change the human vision to benefit someone. Nowadays, when information is transmitted at an instantaneous speed around the world, it has become easier and simpler to implement propaganda theses among the population. For this, television is used - a means that is so common among older people, who are easily influenced by unverified information; magazines, newspapers, and telegram channels that constantly issue provocative headlines that cause people to feel aggressive and quickly accept false information as truth. Every piece of information that a person comes across in the news should be questioned, and other sources should be sought that can introduce a person to an alternative opinion and enable them to compare and assess whether it is true or false consciously.

For such a study, it is advisable to use logistic regression of a linear model and a quantitative assessment of forecasts [33]. We also decided to look for certain analogues or similar solutions to implement our task based on searching for specific words and finding their contextual proximity [33-34]. This function is also called semantic analysis [35-37]. With the help of the Word2vec library, it is possible to analyse which words are most often used in the text [38-44]. Figure 2.1 shows the words that are most often used together with the word "migrant" - the word "nine" (Fig. 2.1).

```
('девять', 0.9719222784042358)
('умерший', 0.9719189405441284)
('центральный_азия', 0.9718897938728333)
('выдворять', 0.9718507528305054)
('июль', 0.9716606140136719)
('численность_население', 0.9715338349342346)
```

Fig. 2.1. The result of the work of the Word2vec library

The method works quite well, but it also has drawbacks. First of all, its implementation requires the additional creation of a text file and the addition of all words with the number of their usage, which takes up a lot of memory and is quite inconvenient. Second, each word must be translated into its original form. For example, the terms "went" and "going" should be converted into the word "go". And the last thing is the need to create a bin file, from which you need to get information, which takes up a lot of computer memory. There is an implementation of searching for words in the text using the task of frequency analysis (Fig. 2.2). The research takes place so that the line should be rewritten so that the most frequently used word should be the first in the line, and the rarest word should be the last [44].

```
from collections import Counter

words = []
for _ in range(int(input())):
    words.extend(input().split())

counter = Counter(words)
pairs = [(-pair[1], pair[0]) for pair in counter.most_common()]
words = [pair[1] for pair in sorted(pairs)]
```

Fig. 2.2. Frequency analysis implementation code

So, this method will help find the most frequently occurring words in the text. However, with further analysis and work with these obtained results, a problem arises, such as the presence of excess information and information noise. This method will form tuples from the text, which need to be processed again. The main problem is that it does not use a machine learning model. Having analysed the known approaches to solving this problem, we can conclude that there are few published analogues of the solution to this problem yet: the automatic definition of Russian-language propaganda in online publications and warnings about it, or blocking this.

2.2. The study materials and methods

When reviewing the scientific literature and studying possible methods of previously set tasks for this project, the following methods were chosen: semantic analysis (Fig. 2.3), semantic role labelling, frame semantics, pre-processing, data clean-up method, missing data, filling missing values, and level encoding [32]. There are not enough resources to thoroughly analyse all new/old content. And while the analysis is carried out, the (dis) information itself will become obsolete. But the rapid formation/modification/replenishment of databases/ repositories of tagged content as blocked/unblocked in a particular region, sorted by relevant metrics (time, topic, blocking region, language, etc.) from relevant/relevant to less relevant for further analysis of results of NLP/ML methods/technologies will significantly speed up the process of navigating the chaos of new information on the Internet. Determining the topic/reason for blocking content (censorship) in a particular region will improve the quality of the identification of fakes on the specific subject. To implement the task, we will use logistic regression of the linear model, quantitative assessment of the quality of forecasts, stemming, the TF-IDF algorithm and the division of the model into training and testing [45].

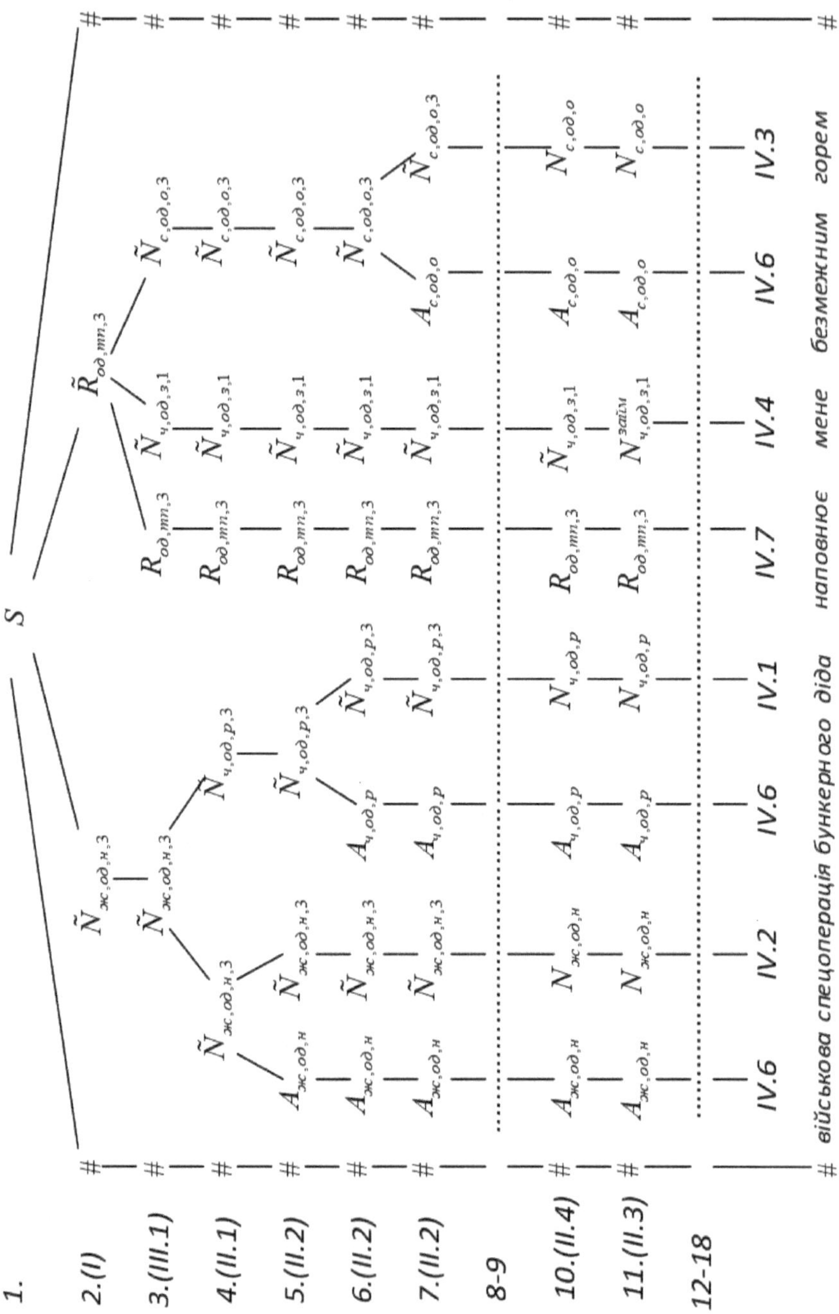

Fig. 2.3. Results of work on test dataset

First, after importing the input data saved in CSV format, it is necessary to correctly generate the text data according to the morphological norms, using the Porter stemmer method, which is correct for this.Porter's stemmer is a well-known algorithm for stemming the selection of the base of a word, thereby cutting endings or suffixes from the base of a word [46-47]. This algorithm works with input data in russian almost flawlessly. With the help of this algorithm, it was possible to modify the input words of the given sentences so that the trained model could work with them correctly. TfidfVectorizer - a method for converting text data into a numerical vector, which allows you to determine the TF-IDF indicator, which is an essential characteristic of assessing the importance of a specific word in a sentence; the significance of this indicator determines the number of its repetitions/uses in a sentence [28]. Next, we classify sentences and determine the probability of a given sentence corresponding to the propaganda class or remaining true. For this, we will use the method of logistic regression [49] for detecting fake news in online media, web resources, and social networks [50-51]. Logistic regression is a type of statistical model that estimates the probability of an event based on a given set of independent variables. Because the outcome is a probability, the dependent variable is bounded between 0 and 1.

2.3. Experiments and results of the system

The process of functioning of such a system:

1. Collection and integration of relevant language content from relevant resources into the data warehouse.
2. Check whether this content is blocked/blocked from a specific resource in a particular region.
3. Marking of each content as blocked/non-blocked in a particular region with appropriate additional metrics (time, resource, frequency of blocked/non-blocked duplicates, the presence in the title/digest/annotation of relevant marked words, such as proper names, etc.).

4. Formation of an intermediate database of labelled, sorted data.

5. Using the top content of NLP methods to calculate the potential of the fake and/or topic as reasons for blocking/non-blocked content in a particular region based on dictionaries and a set of metrics.

5.1. Calculation (in per cent) of the level of fake presence (published without censorship, i.e., marked as non-censored) in the textual content of the publication based on NLP methods, relevant dictionaries, and a set of metrics.

5.2. Also, calculation (as a percentage) of the topic of textual content marked as censorship in a particular region/country based on NLP methods, relevant dictionaries, and a set of metrics.

6. Using machine learning technologies to improve data analysis/labelling / NLP. Pre-training ML models on a proven training dataset.

7. Models/templates of potential fakes are formed to update the list of metrics for sorting marked content in stage 3 and the list of metrics/dictionaries for correct NLP in stage 5.

8. Constant updating of the intermediate database of labelled sorted data and transfer to the archive of obsolete content.

9. Update the training dataset to improve ML models.

General scheme of the process (Fig. 2.4):

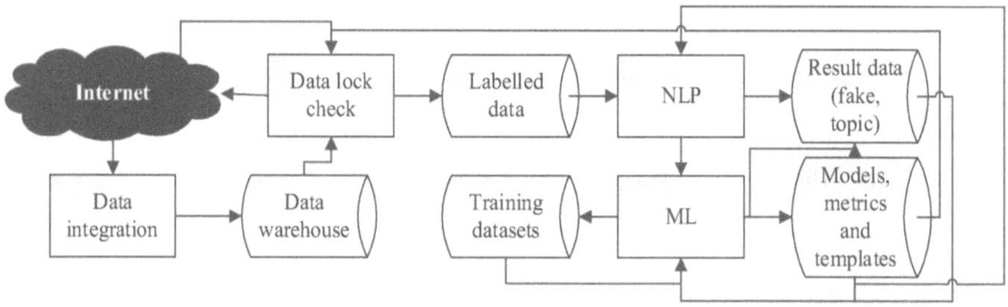

Fig. 2.4. General scheme of the system

Stage 1. *Pre-labelled data → NLP → ML → Models / templates / metrics.*

Stage 2. *Input new data → Data labelled (blocked / non-blocked) → NLP → ML → Content marked (fake / non-fake) or finding a potential reason for blocking (not fake, but this event/topic is banned in a particular region for the average audience).*

General scheme of the NLP process of determining the content topic:

1. Defining the set of keywords of the relevant content and the set of available marker words (proper names, abbreviations, top words of the appropriate topic, etc.).
2. Determine, if possible, the topic of the content.
3. If the keywords are difficult to determine, the topic identification involves the identification of stable phrases.
4. Determine, if possible, the topic of the content.
5. If it is difficult to determine the topic by stable keywords, conduct semantic analysis and possibly construct an ontology.
6. Determine, if possible, the topic of the content.
7. If, according to the results of semantic analysis, it is impossible to do it, mark it and transfer it to the list for the work of the moderator of content.
8. For a specific topic in stages 2, 4, or 6 of the issues, if the content is marked as blocked, check the list of topics blocked in this region previously. If not, refresh the list. If there is a renewed number of blocked contents on this topic, it may be due to censorship in a particular region.

The NLP of the process of defining content as fake / non-fake is a complex process, as it depends not only on the speed/quality of pre-collected / integrated and processed content (blocked / non-blocked in a particular region content topics) but also on an effectively selected machine learning model on trained datasets. Fake is usually not blocked. The purpose of its creation is to spread as quickly as possible around the world and in those regions where accurate information (not fake), potential can be blocked (not guaranteed). If non-fake information is blocked in a particular area, and the opposite information (fake) from this area is spread, the chance to identify the fakes increases. If the non-fake is not blocked and the fake is freely distributed in parallel, NLP methods will not help. They can only mark two sets with opposite explanations for the event/phenomenon. And only in additional statistical studies can it be identified as a set of fakes (potentially), and it is not. The difficulty lies in the content languages themselves. For comparison with English-language content, Ukrainian / russian languages are quite complex for automatic processing, special extraction, and semantics analysis.

Currently, there are many computer linguistic systems for various purposes, including for fakes/propaganda and analysis of criminal reports, even for processing Ukrainian-language textual content. These are traditional commercial projects of a closed type (there are no publications or access to the administrative part), and these are usually foreign projects. There seems to be a lot of publications to understand how the natural language processing and machine learning process works in general, especially for English texts [52-59]. But the peculiarities of these models, methods, algorithms and technologies directly for Ukrainian/ russian language textual content do not lead to almost any positive result [59-78]. Already at the level of morphological analysis, a significant conflict arises between the developed methods and the incoming Ukrainian text - the output is not correct. For example, for a simple Porter algorithm (stemming) without appropriate modification, it will be proper to separate the base of the word from the inflection, which will lead to incorrect identification of the keywords of the texts, which in its situation is a problem for any NLP task where it is necessary to quickly identify a set of keywords (categorization, search, annotation, etc.). Determining the main processes and features of the linguistic analysis of Ukrainian-language texts greatly facilitates the stages of processing the text flow of content as integration, support and content management (Fig. 2.5). In turn, the adaptation of the processes of intellectual analysis of textual content taking into account the functional requirements for the relevant system modules will lead to the possibility of developing types of similar systems based on the principle of modularity (adding identification of components depending on the content of the NLP task and the purpose of the system). The application of the specified technologies/methods/models in the typical architecture of the system, adapted for any NLP task of processing Ukrainian-language textual content, is a necessary prerequisite for the successful implementation of a computer linguistic system project for solving a specific NLP task that requires the use of the appropriate set standard libraries, utilities and open source software that will solve specialized project tasks according to the end user's needs.

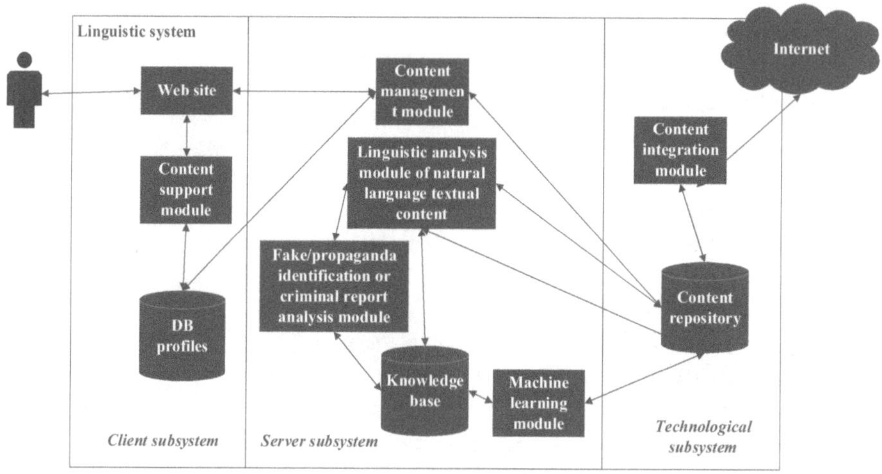

Fig. 2.5. Generalised architecture of a linguistic system for identification of fakes/propaganda or analysis of criminal reports

The Python programming language and the Jupyter Notebook platform were used to implement the methods for executing the program code. The training model was built with text data, so the pandas library and the read_csv method were used to read the input data (Fig. 2.6). When filtering data, it is also important to use stop words, i.e., familiar words, pronouns or prepositions, to remove them from the analysis process for a more accurate result. For this, the nltk.corpus library was used, which contains a collection of stop words for each language (Fig. 2.6). The heading ('text') and ('title') were combined into one column for a more efficient analysis of the sentences (Fig. 2.7). When the main visual work on formatting the text data was done, it became necessary to use the stemming method to highlight the unnecessary words for further analysis and to form a correct sample of sentences.

```
news_dataset = pd.read_csv('D:/Desktop/rus.csv', sep=',', encoding ='windows-1251')
news_dataset.head()
```

0.3s

source	title	text	publication_date	rubric	subrubric
lenta.ru	Синий богатырь	Укронацисты снова съели маленького мальчика за...	2020-08-30T00:01:00+03:00	Экономика	Война
lenta.ru	Загитова согласилась вести «Ледниковый период»	В Российской армии потерь нет.	2020-08-31T20:04:00+03:00	Спорт	Война
lenta.ru	Объяснена опасность однообразного питания	Украинские военные из 115-й бригады отказавшие...	2020-08-31T20:07:00+03:00	Из жизни	Война
lenta.ru	«Предохраняться? А зачем?»	Вербовщика в украинские нацбатальоны задержали...	2020-08-30T00:04:00+03:00	Интернет и СМИ	Война
lenta.ru	Ефремов систематически употреблял наркотики	Шойгу повторил что российские военные не нанос...	2020-08-31T18:27:00+03:00	Культура	Война

```
['и', 'в', 'во', 'не', 'что', 'он', 'на', 'я', 'с', 'со', 'как', 'а', 'то', 'все', 'она', 'так', 'его', 'но', 'да', 'ты', 'к', 'у', 'же',
'вы', 'за', 'бы', 'по', 'только', 'ее', 'мне', 'было', 'вот', 'от', 'меня', 'еще', 'нет', 'о', 'из', 'ему', 'теперь', 'когда', 'даже',
'ну', 'вдруг', 'ли', 'если', 'уже', 'или', 'ни', 'быть', 'был', 'него', 'до', 'вас', 'нибудь', 'опять', 'уж', 'вам', 'ведь', 'там',
'потом', 'себя', 'ничего', 'ей', 'может', 'они', 'тут', 'где', 'есть', 'надо', 'ней', 'для', 'мы', 'тебя', 'их', 'чем', 'была', 'сам',
'чтоб', 'без', 'будто', 'чего', 'раз', 'тоже', 'себе', 'под', 'будет', 'ж', 'тогда', 'кто', 'этот', 'того', 'потому', 'этого', 'какой',
'совсем', 'ним', 'здесь', 'этом', 'один', 'почти', 'мой', 'тем', 'чтобы', 'нее', 'сейчас', 'были', 'куда', 'зачем', 'всех', 'никогда',
'можно', 'при', 'наконец', 'два', 'об', 'другой', 'хоть', 'после', 'над', 'больше', 'тот', 'через', 'эти', 'нас', 'про', 'всего', 'них',
'какая', 'много', 'разве', 'три', 'эту', 'моя', 'впрочем', 'хорошо', 'свою', 'этой', 'перед', 'иногда', 'лучше', 'чуть', 'том', 'нельзя',
'такой', 'им', 'более', 'всегда', 'конечно', 'всю', 'между']
```

Fig. 2.6. View of data and Stop-words

```
news_dataset = news_dataset.fillna('')
# merging the author name and news title
news_dataset['text'] = news_dataset['title']+' '+news_dataset['text']
news_dataset_origin['text'] = news_dataset['title']
print(news_dataset['text'])
```

✓ 0.7s

```
0       Синий богатырь Укронацисты снова съели маленьк...
1       Загитова согласилась вести «Ледниковый период»...
2       Объяснена опасность однообразного питания Укра...
3       «Предохраняться? А зачем?» Вербовщика в украин...
4       Ефремов систематически употреблял наркотики Шо...
                              ...
1560    Стало известно о новых условиях сделки по нефт...
1561    Доктор Мясников назвал неожиданную причину зар...
```

Fig. 2.7. Combine title and text into one column for further analysis

Porter's stemming method selected all words contained in stop words. It removed them from the text field, forming sentences from only essential words that will help filter them in further analysis (Fig. 2.8).

```
port_stem = PorterStemmer()

# %%
def stemming(content):
    stemmed_content = re.sub('[^а-яА-Я]',' ',content)
    stemmed_content = stemmed_content.lower()
    stemmed_content = stemmed_content.split()
    stemmed_content = [port_stem.stem(word) for word in stemmed_content if not word in stopwords.words('russian')]
    stemmed_content = ' '.join(stemmed_content)
    return stemmed_content

# %%
news_dataset['text'] = news_dataset['text'].apply(stemming)
print(news_dataset['text'])
 4.4s

                                            синий богатырь
          загитова согласилась вести ледниковый период
               объяснена опасность однообразного питания
                                           предохраняться
          ефремов систематически употреблял наркотики

vectorizer = TfidfVectorizer()
vectorizer.fit(X)

X = vectorizer.transform(X)
X_train, X_test, Y_train, Y_test = train_test_split(X, Y, test_size = 0.2, stratify=Y, random_state=2)
```

Fig. 2.8. Rejecting stop words and Distribution of test/train data

The next step was to convert the text data into a numeric vector and train the test part of the data (implementation of the stemming method). For this, the TfidfVectorizer and the train_test_split techniques are used (Fig. 2.8). After training the sample, you need to build a logistic regression to determine the accuracy of the training sample (Fig. 2.9a) and determine the accuracy of the test sample (Fig. 2.9b). Now we have the opportunity to derive the result of our calculations, depending on whether the news is propaganda for propaganda or the truth (Fig. 2.9c).

```python
model = LogisticRegression()
model.fit(X_train, Y_train)
# accuracy score on the training data
X_train_prediction = model.predict(X_train)
training_data_accuracy = accuracy_score(X_train_prediction, Y_train)
print('Accuracy score of the training data : ', training_data_accuracy)
```

✓ 0.7s

```
Accuracy score of the training data :  0.9800319488817891
```

```python
X_test_prediction = model.predict(X_test)
test_data_accuracy = accuracy_score(X_test_prediction, Y_test)
print('Accuracy score of the test data : ', test_data_accuracy)
```

✓ 0.3s

```
Accuracy score of the test data :  0.48562300319488816
```

```python
for i in range(100):
  X_new = X_test[i]

  prediction = model.predict(X_new)
  if (prediction[0]==0):
    print('The news sound like true ----------- ' + news_dataset_origin['text'].values[i])
  else:
    print('The news sound like propaganda ----- ' + news_dataset_origin['text'].values[i])
```

✓ 0.1s

```
Output exceeds the size limit. Open the full output data in a text editor
The news sound like propaganda ----- Синий богатырь
The news sound like propaganda ----- Загитова согласилась вести «Ледниковый период»
The news sound like true ----------- Обьяснена опасность однообразного питания
The news sound like true ----------- «Предохраняться? А зачем?»
The news sound like true ----------- Ефремов систематически употреблял наркотики
The news sound like true ----------- «Вы живете в мире созданном блондинкой»
The news sound like propaganda ----- Пенсионер устроил у себя дома отель и попал под суд
The news sound like true ----------- Красно-белые идут
The news sound like propaganda ----- В Арктике обнаружили новый пролив
The news sound like true ----------- «Блат здесь развит еще сильнее чем в России»
```

Fig. 2.9. Determining the accuracy of the training/test data and result analysis.

2.4. Counteraction to russian propaganda

We note that legal mechanisms for counteracting disinformation and propaganda are essential in addition to technical means. The EU's policy in this area is to ensure freedom of speech and the impossibility of banning certain media activities, even if they spread disinformation. Thus, russia and other foreign states continue to misinform European society systematically. Some countries have already introduced criminal liability for spreading fake news and propaganda about russia's war against Ukraine. We consider it necessary to introduce criminal liability in all countries of the European Union for the use of the Z symbol and to ban or restrict the activities of media that spread russian propaganda.

2.5. Conclusions for Chapter 2

A detailed description of the developed system was made. In particular, the technical requirements were formed. System development is divided into three steps: data preparation, word embedding, and classification. The structure of the product under development has been described. It used libraries and ways of implementing the methods. The structure of the neural network and initial parameters of the network are described in detail based on knowledge rather than machine learning methods: this means that it is necessary to specify patterns, and not to have a purpose to learn and generalise them. A second aim of this project was to apply text summarisation to case reports; that is, converting the text from long, detailed reports into a coherent, natural-language summary. There are several ways to achieve text summarisation in NLP, in particular by analysing keywords, marked special words, and emotional words. It is worth thinking about another way to sum up the text, and this is with the help of knowledge graphs previously built. In addition to summarising the text, future work in this project may be related to the study of the SpaCy library and the discovery of other tools. This project is essentially the subtask of a great idea, and it is worth working further towards the ultimate goal. The result of the work is a finished training and data analysis model, which successfully fulfils the main task - filtering russian-language news and further dividing it into potential propaganda and accurate information. Due to the current situation, the model was configured to check data in Russian, but the program can be easily reconfigured to, for example, Ukrainian, English, or German. Among the recommendations, for the convenience of understanding the results, it is desirable to use data sets where at least one column is roughly a headline or something that briefly identifies the analysed news. Advantages of the model: fairly good accuracy of results; the possibility of using a wide range of languages; the ability to analyse extensive data without keeping it on the device. Disadvantages: the need for further improvement in accuracy.

Chapter 3. Disinformation, fakes and propaganda identifying methods in online messages based on NLP and machine learning methods

The chapter is written based on scientific publications and research [79-151].

3.1. Basic principles of disinformation

The emergence of the latest technologies in mass communication creates new challenges for the world as a whole. The most difficult and incomprehensible thing of modern times is disinformation. The current information field is under threat due to fraudulent activities [79]. It is pretty difficult to prevent the danger since the delivery technologies and distortion of information are constantly changing. More and more often, we pay attention to such a phenomenon as "disinformation" and have known for a long time that it has become a component of our information space. The number of states using disinformation campaigns is constantly growing, and information manipulation has turned into a weapon of entire countries that use it to preserve their regimes and influence other states, undermining their stability and even interfering in elections. Global disinformation campaigns inspired by authoritarian governments and activists of radical movements to manipulate the consciousness of the population and individual groups have become a daily practice that threatens the democratic development of states and international stability. As you know, disinformation or misinformation is a psychological influence method that consists of providing the object with content that misleads them about the creation of a distorted reality and the actual state of affairs. It is the distribution of distorted, incomplete or deliberately false information to achieve a propaganda, commercial, military or other aim. According to the Cambridge Dictionary, misinformation is "false information that is disseminated with the intent to mislead people." Although information technology development provides new opportunities in public administration development, informing the population, and the citizens' involvement in the state development, it also increases the risks of disinformation. With the help of algorithmic systems and artificial intelligence, fakes can be more convincing and intended for an audience that is more likely to believe them.

Recently, the most popular source of content in the world has been the Internet. Misinformation can easily spread on SMM due to the lack of editorial control, freedom of posting for any user, and the ability to quickly create and share information for free. Internet users can easily spread viral content, which leads to widespread distribution on many sites. Today, social networks have gained enormous popularity because everyone can create content there. With the Internet overflowing with information, it becomes critical to distinguish between credible and misleading sources. Online media and social networks allow for the rapid exchange of information, including disinformation, both on purpose and accidentally/chaotically. Along with the main advantage of providing quick access to up-to-date and relevant information for everyone, online media are often used to spread intentionally false content, such as, for example, the MH17 crash [80-81]. At the same time, a significant amount of online information is subject to censorship on content with opposing facts and reasons for events/phenomena [82-83]. It doesn't allow for an understanding of events and orientation in the flow of information to solve everyday problems and adjust business strategies, etc. [84-85]. Political propaganda is a targeted and deliberate dissemination of information aimed at influencing public opinion in favour of a particular public position or common cause. Propaganda can take the form of disinformation, i.e. fabrication of false and fake news or use more complex and sophisticated methods. Propaganda, fake news and disinformation are usually generated, shaped and disseminated through the media, and are related to specific political events, such as an election campaign, financial crisis, etc. Therefore, in some cases, it is necessary to know the context of the political climate in the world to recognise propaganda. The widespread and massive dissemination of fakes, propaganda and disinformation against the backdrop of the war in Ukraine, without systematic and thorough analysis, is likely to influence and control public opinion, as well as lead to panic among the relevant region/population, significantly affecting the adjustment of strategies/plans of government agencies, social services, businesses, etc. Blocking disinformation and sources of its dissemination, as well as identifying potential authors based on the analysis of inauthentic behaviour, is usually a functional responsibility of the authorised bodies, especially during an information war. However, disinformation is now generated/distributed so quickly and efficiently through the use of modern information technologies and artificial intelligence that no one can handle this task 100% without using new tools and methods based on ML. There are not enough resources to thoroughly analyse all the latest/old content. And by the time a systematic data analysis is carried out, the disinformation itself will have become outdated. However, the rapid formation/modification/updating of databases/data warehouses of labelled text as unblocked/blocked in a particular region, sorted by parameters based on ML/NLP, will significantly speed up the information chaos navigating process on the Internet. The IS should be implemented based on information security principles to identify, monitor, and report the level of threat and forecast cyber threats. There are different ways of conducting disinformation activities, each of which has its own positive and negative features. The specific choice of one or another method directly depends on the operational situation in a particular area of activity of the special service, the tasks that are set before it, etc. As you know, disinformation is based on the following principles [86-89]:

- "Transfer of responsibility." Shifting responsibility as a disinformation campaign mechanism. The easiest way to avoid negative consequences is to move the responsibility to someone else. Therefore, propagandists often use this technique to prevent condemnation of their actions by the world community.
- "Principle of contrast." The principle of contrast is used when negative information needs to be presented, but the tactic of direct accusations

looks pretty frank. In propaganda, it is used when it is necessary to divert the attention of society from one defeat to another, a more resonant event, which will overshadow the failures.

- "Principle of psychological shock." News about extraordinary events that cause a bright and stormy reaction in society and destroy all levels of psychological protection can be a psychological shock. Thus, after the destruction of this defence, propaganda can impose the theses and opinions it needs.
- "Rhetorical question" in disinformation consists of the application of unappealing fake facts leading to a question that does not need an answer.
- "Grid" is several Telegram channels united by the management system. These information-terrorist channels are united in the so-called nets. The purpose of creating a grid is to quickly distribute information to a specific audience.
- "Classifiers" – a system of distribution of disinformation messages by groups according to predefined characteristics. Classifiers are "keywords" to which variants of disinformation messages (narratives) are selected.

Next, we will consider the mechanisms of disinformation used by the enemy [86-89].

- "Persuasion" is a method of organised influence on a person's psyche through an appeal to their critical judgment, with an opinion in which someone firmly believes.
- "Distraction" – shifting attention from one object to another. It is carried out through the dissemination of information that is an extraneous stimulus to a person engaged in an essential activity at that moment.
- In general, the essence of the psychological "halo effect" can be expressed in two statements: "next to - means together" and "if a person is effective in one field, he will be the same in another".
- "Guided comment" is a message in which a person's thoughts are directed in the right direction. The principle of its operation is as follows: the message is accompanied by the interpretation of the commentator, who offers the

reader several options for explanation. Comments are written according to the principle of "two-sided messages", which contain arguments both "for" and "against" according to the reader's choice.

- "Creating a problem" is a targeted selection of information to increase the significance of some events and reduce the importance of others. How does it work? Increasing the status of the "problem-target": the media covers a "profitable" event, giving it exceptional importance, regardless of its true significance for society. Understating the status of the "problem-target": the mass media provides limited information about the "unfavourable" event, which downplays its status.

- "Detouring from the flank" is the transmission of reliable information, the accuracy of which is known in advance to listeners or readers and can be easily checked by them. Propaganda messages are actually "packaged" in such data. The purpose of using "flanking" is to draw the audience's attention to familiar information to get the opportunity to convey the desired information.

- "Statement of fact" is a presentation of desired information in the media as such, which cannot be doubted. Most often, the news format or the sociological research format is used for this mechanism. To give greater authority to materials utilising the mechanism of "stating the fact", propaganda widely uses the comments of "leaders of public opinion" - popular journalists, well-known political scientists, etc.

- "False analogy" results when comparing properties and relations, the relationship of which has no factual basis in reality. People tend to think in analogies, using cause-and-effect logic. When these connections are replaced by propaganda, a false analogy occurs in which the probability of the conclusion is zero.

- "Preemptive strike" is a pre-emptive injection of disinformation. Its task is to provoke a counter-reaction from the "adversary" and use it in a more advantageous context for himself. This technique is used by propagandists to accelerate the escalation of the conflict and, with the spread of disinformation, to create a provocation by which to "quench" the accurate information.

- "Everyday narrative" is used by propaganda to "teach" the audience misinformation about committed violence, murders, terrorist acts, shelling, etc.
- The "primacy effect": the propaganda success is that misinformation reaches the audience before the truth. When receiving contradictory information that cannot be quickly verified, a person tends to prefer the information that arrived first.
- "Conspiracy" - this method uses propaganda when it is necessary to reduce the relevance and cause an adverse reaction to any event. The aim of "persuasion" is to cause fatigue in the audience from misinformation on a specific "hot" topic to discourage further interest in it.

3.2. Known platforms and projects for automatic identification and analysis of fakes, propaganda, and disinformation

Thanks to the Internet, a new way of spreading news and content in general has appeared. In the past, people relied on traditional mass media such as radio and television, which included more well-known news sources. Nowadays, people increasingly turn to online information sources, such as social media, which allow anyone to post anything without the need for fact-checking or editorial evaluation. Many people are concerned that websites may publish misleading material, passing it off as "real" news. More and more people are involved in social networks thanks to the growing popularity of various gadgets with Internet access and increasing mobile Internet speeds. Indeed, Facebook is used by most people around the world, and many of us get our news from SMM posts. Given the recent attention to SMM's role in spreading fake news about current political and social events, it is critical to understand how the public interacts with misinformation on SMM platforms. Fake news about contemporary social and political issues spreads on SMM at breakneck speed. These hoaxes or fake stories misinform or deceive the audience, either intentionally or unintentionally. These stories are usually created to sway people's opinions, push a political agenda, or confuse people, and can be a lucrative business for online publishers. Sources such as Facebook, Twitter, and other SMM platforms have become essential resources in providing news content. The sheer volume of content and the speed with which it is generated and disseminated on the Internet make it virtually impervious to human verification. Therefore, there is an urgent need to develop technologies that can help people automatically check facts and reliably detect fake news. The study aims to develop information technology for detecting disinformation to increase the state's level of information security. It will help to automatically detect sources of disinformation, as well as the peculiarities of their distribution and reposts based on natural language processing and machine learning technology.

It requires solving the following tasks to achieve the aim's realisation:

– NLP of false text content to identify characteristics of propaganda;

– recognising propaganda at the message level;

– recognising propaganda at the phrase level;

– training models to generate forecasts based on a test sample;

– development of IS (intelligent system) modules for analysing textual content streams to detect propaganda;

– experimental testing of the developed IT for recognising disinformation, fakes and propaganda in textual content based on ML and NLP methods.

The project aims to use artificial intelligence to develop and improve cyber warfare tools, in particular, to combat disinformation on the Internet, namely, to automatically identify sources of disinformation and inauthentic behaviour (bots) of coordinated groups. It is necessary to investigate the phenomenon of political propaganda in the news media to recognise the propaganda presence in textual data. It is also required to develop an algorithm for preparing and extracting features of textual data, as well as to build a machine learning model that will recognise the political propaganda presence in texts using these features. The object of the study is the processes of searching, detecting, and classifying political propaganda, fakes, and disinformation in the media, in particular on the Internet. The subject of the study is methods and tools for recognising propaganda, fakes and disinformation in textual data. The research focuses on propaganda identification using machine learning, fake news, and a disinformation recognition system using NLP at both the phrase and document levels. The problem of political propaganda is becoming increasingly relevant as information becomes more accessible, the practice of digitalising public media spreads, news production and editing become easier, and the influence of SMM grows. For example, the propaganda spread study through SMM confirms that propaganda disseminated in this way spreads faster and to a broader demographic spectrum, and is more resistant to recognition due to the confirmation bias used [90]. In addition, a recent study by Science Magazine showed that gossip and fake news spread about six times faster than reliable and truthful information [91]. It indicates that the phenomenon of political propaganda not only has a detrimental effect on the current political climate but also partially shapes it. At the moment, most projects related to propaganda detection are carried out using statistical research with the involvement of specialists. Still, due to the rapid spread of propaganda through online media, it is pretty inefficient and expensive in terms of resource use. That's why an effective ML model creation to optimise this process is more relevant than ever. For successful analysis and processing of natural text, it is necessary to note certain signs of propaganda that are used to classify the text. It is essential to analyse what kind of structure a text should have to be labelled as possibly propagandistic. The primary methods of spreading propaganda are as follows [92]:

– Distraction. Presentation of irrelevant material that is not related to the issue under the textual content discussion.

– Distortion of the position. Replacing a position with a similar, but not the same, position.

– Whataboutism. The opponent's position is discredited by accusing them of hypocrisy without providing direct arguments.

– Causal simplification. Identification and presentation of only one hypothetical cause of a particular phenomenon when there are several such causes.

– Deliberate vagueness, confusion. The deliberately abstract terms and words are used in such a way that the interpretation of what is said is not clear.

– Appeal to authority. Claiming that a claim is valid because a current authority/expert supports it, usually without providing any evidence.

– White and Black deception. Presenting two alternative options or points of view as the only possible ones, even if other options exist.

– Labelling. A way in which a source of propaganda attaches a negative meaning to the phenomenon it opposes, usually by appealing to something the target audience fears or hates.

– Loaded language. Specific phrases and words are used with strong emotional connotations (negative or positive) to influence the target audience.

– Exaggeration or minimisation. A particular phenomenon is presented either in an excessive way or as something less important than it is.

– Flag waving. Manipulation of the target audience's patriotic views/feelings to justify/promote a phenomenon/idea.

– Doubt. Questioning the credibility and reliability of a particular person or phenomenon.

– Appeal to fear or prejudice. An attempt to promote support for a specific idea by instilling fear and anxiety, or appealing to certain social prejudices of the target audience.

– Slogans. The short, punchy phrases are used to label or stereotype by appealing to the emotions of the target audience.

– Clichés without substance. Words/phrases that prevent reasoned discussion of the situation and critical thinking.

– Common platform. An attempt to convince the target audience to join the cause and make a specific decision, like everyone else or the majority.

– Repeating the same message several times to zombify the target audience.

Propaganda is a complex communicative phenomenon that uses a variety of methods and approaches to achieve its goal. The task of identifying propaganda in texts is actual now, and many studies have been conducted in this area. Several analogues have been selected for analysis, differing in research and modelling methods.

– Framing and Agenda-setting in Russian News: A Computational Analysis of Intricate Political Strategies. The study was conducted by a team of researchers from Carnegie Mellon University, the University of Haifa, and Stanford University in 2018 [93]. The main goal of the study was to investigate the "framing" in Russian news sources during the country's economic downturn and how it relates to the coverage of US-related news in Russian media (since most of them are run by and under the direct influence of government agencies). A strong negative correlation was found between the economic situation in Russia and the news stories focusing on the US. The next step is to examine the context and frame in which this news is presented. The frame in this context defines the way (with what connotations) a particular news item is covered in the media. Then, it is hypothesised that the correlation is causal and that the unfavourable economic situation in Russia is a direct factor that causes increased attention to the United States in the state mass media. Using probabilistic methods (Granger causality and linear regression model), it is established that the causal relationship between these two variables is present in the selected dataset. Then, the Bayesian probabilistic method using the so-called frame lexicons was formed, taking into account a particular word and the frame to which it belongs. For each frame, 250 words were selected that have the highest probability of occurrence in the relevant context. Logistic regression and the bag-of-words model were chosen as the initial, basic solution. To determine which frames relate to the USA, nPMI (Normalised pointwise mutual information) was calculated. Five frames were identified and used in the research. The study also uses Structure Topic Modelling to conceptualise the messages at the level at which the reader would perceive them. Thus, the study examines a method of propaganda aimed at distracting the public from the problematic state of internal affairs in the country by shifting attention to foreign policy.

– The Supervised Learning Algorithms Use in Political Communication and Media Studies: Locating Frames in the Press. The study focuses on the research of framing in contemporary media [94]. It is based on a Spanish news sources dataset for 2015, with a particular focus on the coverage of the refugee crisis. Two frames were selected for classification: human rights and security. The main ML algorithm used in the research to build the model is the SVM (Support Vector Machine) method, which is used to solve classification problems and is based on the assumption that the data are linearly distributed in such a way that a hyperplane can be found that could effectively separate them from each other. However, the linear kernel of the model did not show satisfactory results, so the final version of the algorithm used a support vector method with a radial kernel. The IDF (Inverse Document Frequency) algorithm was used to remove semantically insignificant words from the corpus.

– Fakegrizz is a propaganda detection tool created by the Ukrainian data research platform Texty.org [95-96]. The system is designed as an application for a web browser and as a chatbot for the Telegram platform. Fakegrizz takes a link to a news story as input and, using web scraping, determines whether the text presented by the source contains manipulation or propaganda. The model is built on the principle of transfer learning, which means that a general-purpose model is used, which may not have been trained for a specific task. Still, later, the model's hyperparameters are adjusted to suit the task [97-98]. Instead of focusing on the classification problem and spending resources on labelling data with the appropriate classes, Fakogriz is built on a clustering algorithm that automatically determines the class of data it receives.

We will analyse the works that provide solutions for identifying disinformation. The author and his team [99] demonstrated a model using ML and NLP methods that collects articles using a support vector machine and decides whether the news is real or fake. They used an SVM algorithm for binary classification to organise the articles, and based on this, the model works to classify the articles as genuine or fake. The proposed models used three main modules to refine articles or content: an aggregator, an authenticator, and a suggestion or recommendation system. In this paper, they also used the Naive Bayesian method to check articles for truth or falsity. They obtained a result with an accuracy of 93.50%, which was achieved by combining these three algorithms: the Naive Bayesian method, SVM, and NLP. In a report by the Pew Research Centre of the United States [100], it is said that adults get about 70% of their news from social networks. With the news of Donald Trump's election as president, this information led to an increase in Facebook users. This article examines the linguistic and visual features that play a role. Thus, the authors achieved an accuracy of about 83 per cent. In work [101], the authors observed the influence of people on SMM and found that 62% of American adults depended on SMM for news in 2016, which is 13% more than in 2012. The primary source of information is television. We have seen that this information is either free or has a very low cost, which leads to fake news on this platform. In the publication [102], the authors note that fake news is divided into clickbait, influential and satirical. To stop fake news, techniques such as spam detection, positioning, and benchmarking have been applied. Next, the author considered sentiment analysis, which falls under NLP methods. An example of fake news that was discussed was the "Electroshock" of a Chinese airport security robot that occurred in 2016 and resulted in over 12,000 fake news stories in China that were posted on 244 different websites as sources. In [103], the authors observed that the influence of fake news on our daily lives has increased significantly. They discussed three approaches to detect fake news: Naive Bayes, SVM, and Neural Network. The accuracy of detecting fake news using the naive Bayes method is 96.08% while using the other two methods, such as the neural network and SVM method, the accuracy of detecting fake news is 99.90%. The authors of this article are trying to convey information to readers about how much influence fake news can have on a person's life. They discuss the case of Thailand (2017), which faced a major disaster due to the spread of fake climate news. The authors claim that before using the machine learning method, they apply a normalisation method to clean the data. In [104], the authors studied how to detect fake news from Twitter posts. Authors usually work on Twitter posts, whether they are real or fake. They talk about misinformation about the earthquake in Chile (2010) and the US presidential election. It was proposed that NLP be used to detect fake news. First, they have to classify the news to know whether it is real or fake, and then different types of models are applied to get the result. The authors' primary focus is on improving the effectiveness of detecting fake news, so they included a word length method that involves counting the words in a sentence. The authors used five different machine-learning algorithms and Python as the programming language. The five machine learning methods include Naive Bayesian, Logistic Regression, Support Vector, Recurrent Neural Network, and Long Short-Term Memory. The authors work with textual data, so they used several different ideas to process the dataset, namely count vectors, TF-IDF, and word embedding. The authors also proposed four feature vectors: count vectors, word-level vectors, N-gram vectors, and character-level vectors. As a result, the support vector method turned out to be the best model for detecting fake news. In work [105], the authors note that SMM is a key problem of modern life. Anyone can register as a news publisher on social platforms, spreading information without verification. It very quickly misleads society. Thus, the authors believe that SMM is a platform for spreading misinformation. The authors proposed some signs for detecting fake news – these are signs that stand out from the news article, the news source, and the knowledge environment. Text features are also used to detect fake news. Image processing techniques are used to extract text from images and videos.

The total number of text features evaluated by the author is 141. Lexical features, semantic features, linguistic features, and psycholinguistic features are grouped into groups. The author used a classifier to measure the strength of features. It is a classifier of K-Nearest Neighbours, Naive Bayes, Random Forest and SVM. To measure the performance of each classifier, the author used the area under the ROC curve and the Marco F1 Score. The area under the curve is more relevant for detecting fake news, while the Macro F1 score shows the general function of the classifier. In [106], the authors considered the classification of artificial intelligence systems, artificial intelligence models used by security products, and their capabilities. They provided recommendations that should be taken into account when using generative artificial intelligence technologies in cyber defence systems. Table 3.1 provides an overview of existing approaches to detecting fake news from the point of view of machine learning [107]. Among these approaches, some classifiers gave the desired result. In the article [103], the authors achieved the highest accuracy rate of 99.90% using the support vector method, naive Bayesian method and neural network.

Table 3.1. Overview of existing approaches to detecting fake news from the point of view of machine learning [107]

Research	Precision	Data set	Approach
[99]	93.5%	Various news sites, RSS feeds	Naive Bayes method, support vector method and NLP
[103]	99.9%	Data was collected from 948,373 messages via the Twitter API	Support vector method, neural network and naive Bayesian method
[104]	89.34%	20,360 data points were collected from Chile, the 2010 earthquake dataset	Support vector method, naive Bayes method, logistic regression, long short-term memory and RNN
[105]	89%	News from Buzzfeed	The method of KNN, the technique of support vectors and the naive Bayesian method

All the classifiers considered in the table used some text features, N-gram, F-1 Score, etc. Using these features, the classifiers work better, and the authors try to improve the accuracy of detecting fake news. This table shows which classifiers are better compared to others. So, among all these classifiers, the best ones are the support vector method and the naive Bayes method, which give the highest results. It is challenging to find out the facts of news that are shared by different parties on social networks, which contradict each other. Such news is mainly related to politics. Therefore, among political news, it is challenging to classify whether the news is real or fake. Distinguishing these types of news as real or fake requires more powerful and sophisticated models that can easily and cheaply classify news. Another big challenge in social networks is verifying the authenticity of news authors or publishers. Nowadays, it is very easy to create a page on Facebook, Instagram, or any other social network, as well as a YouTube channel. So anyone can post news on these platforms. It creates a new problem – to know which of the authors is fake and which is real. That is why it is essential to develop a model that can easily verify the authenticity of news authors and publishers. These models will help online news readers decide which authors' news should be read and which should be ignored [107].

To implement the NLP strategy, tools, techniques, and software are used to work with text data and speech [108], the main ones of which are listed in Table 3.2. As part of the NLP technology, machine learning technologies are used to improve the effectiveness of linguistic analysis. Machine learning using neural networks is a deep learning strategy that allows you to recognise complex patterns in text data for classification and the generation of new text data. However, all mentioned technologies are used for different purposes - from basic processing of text data to complex analytical tasks that allow obtaining valuable data from text sources for further use in various industries. Machine learning has implications for NLP at different stages of processing textual data. After parsing, machine learning is used to achieve a better understanding of textual data and to solve various natural language analysis tasks. Namely, machine learning is used for:

1. Creating language models that predict the following words in a sentence or determine the probability of specific textual data.

2. Classification of text data by categories, sentiment analysis, detection of named entities, speech recognition, etc.

3. Training of the model for automatic translation of text data from one language to another.

4. Development of ML algorithms for recognising fake news.

5. Creation and training of NLP models for automatic generation of answers to user questions.

Table 3.2. Tools, techniques and software for text data processing

Type	Name	Explanation
Language models	GPT (Generative Pre-trained Transformer)	A series of models that apply transformers to text data generation and various NLP tasks.
	BERT (Bidirectional Encoder Representations from Transformers)	A model that uses contextualised vector representations to better understand the context of textual data.
Vectorisation of words	Word Embeddings	Methods that convert words or phrases into numeric vectors, such as Word2Vec, GloVe, or FastText. It allows computers to better understand the semantics of words.
Libraries and tools	NLTK (Natural Language Toolkit)	NLP library that includes a variety of textual data analysis, tokenisation, lemmatisation, and more.
	spaCy	NLP library that offers fast and efficient analysis of text data based on modern methods.
	Gensim	A library for thematic modelling of text data and working with vector representations of words.

The strategy of using NLP technology in combination with machine learning covers a wide range of tasks that are relevant to the scientific research topics:

- Language input and output processing: interacting with computer systems through language, including recognising and generating speech to perform tasks.
- Creating intelligent assistants: interacting with people through speech and text data to provide information, perform tasks or answer questions.
- Fact-mining and analytics: extracting key information from text data sources and analysing that data for valuable insights.
- Semantic analysis: understanding the meaning of words and their context, which allows you to analyse text data at a deeper level.
- Information extraction: identification and selection of certain entities (persons, places, dates) or facts from textual data.
- Sentiment analysis: determining whether textual data has a negative, positive, or objective colour.
- Machine translation: text data or speech translation from one language to another.
- Speech generation: generating text data or speech using algorithms and models.

• Speech recognition: converting speech into text data or numeric format for further analysis.

Although NLP has enormous potential, it also has some limitations that, in some way, affect the definition of research problems. The limitations of using NLP are substantiated in detail in [109] and are given below. Significant limitations of NLP:

• Lack of context. In complex analyses of textual data, particularly in large volumes of information, NLP models may have difficulties in determining context or taking into account longer historical context, which can lead to inaccuracies in understanding.

• Non-universality of language: there is a wide variety of linguistic features between different languages, which requires the creation of separate models for each language. Some languages may also have less data available to train NLP models.

• Ethical issues: NLP can raise ethical issues, mainly when it is used to analyse users' data. Privacy control and the ethical use of data are key aspects in the development and application of NLP;

• Problems with grammar and structure: state-of-the-art NLP models may have problems understanding poorly worded or grammatically incorrect textual data. For example, emotion analysis can be complicated if the textual data contains errors or inaccurate constructions.

• Data scarcity: effective machine learning models for NLP often require large amounts of data to train, so collecting and training large and representative datasets can be significant challenges.

• Ambiguous interpretation of text data: several different interpretations are possible for one word or phrase, which makes it difficult for a computer to understand text data; the meaning used in each case is determined by context and semantics.

Recognising fake news using NLP is a challenging task due to the complexity of textual data and the ever-changing techniques used to create disinformation. However, continued research and improvement of NLP techniques can help improve the detection of fake news. However, several challenges are encountered at the current stage of IT development [110]. The limitations of NLP for solving the given task of recognising fake news are described below:

- ethical issues: consideration of ethical aspects, in particular data privacy, when using NLP to detect fake news, is an essential factor;
- The evolution of methods of creating fakes: with the constant development of technology, methods of producing fake news and disinformation are also evolving. Continuous improvement of NLP models may be required to detect new forms of fakes.
- speed of reaction: time and speed of response to the fake news detection are also important. The speed of analysis and determination of the content's credibility can be critical in preventing the spread.
- context issues: recognising fake news requires taking into account not only the textual data but also the context and the source. It is vital to take into account the authority of the source and the ability of NLP models to adequately take into account the context in the analysis.
- data limitations: building effective fake news detection models requires large and representative datasets. However, collecting reliable datasets for training can be challenging, as fake news can be rare or difficult to identify.
- ambiguity of textual data: fake news is often created to look like real news. It can lead to difficulties in identifying false information, as it can look like real data.

3.3. Material and methods

The growing rate of disinformation spread in the media, particularly on the Internet, during the information war, has long been a matter of public concern. As such, the spread of disinformation hurts the population. Disinformation source identification is based on the accurate and prompt detection results of stylistically similar text in propaganda and fake news publications. The system for recognising propaganda, fake news and disinformation S in textual content based on NLP and ML methods is presented as follows (Fig. 3.1):

$$S = < I, O, R, U, C_{AU}, C_{CU}, C_{UL}, C_{US}, L_R, \alpha, \beta, \gamma >, \quad (3.1)$$

where $R = \{r_1, r_2, r_3, r_4\}$ is the basic rules for processing input data; $O = \{o_1, o_2, o_3\}$ is the output dataset; $I = \{i_1, i_2, i_3, i_4\}$ is the input data set; $U = \{u_1, u_2, u_3, u_4, u_5\}$ is parameters for processing input data; L_R is an ML method; α is the operator for downloading input data; β is the operator for processing input data; γ is the operator for analysing articles based on ML.

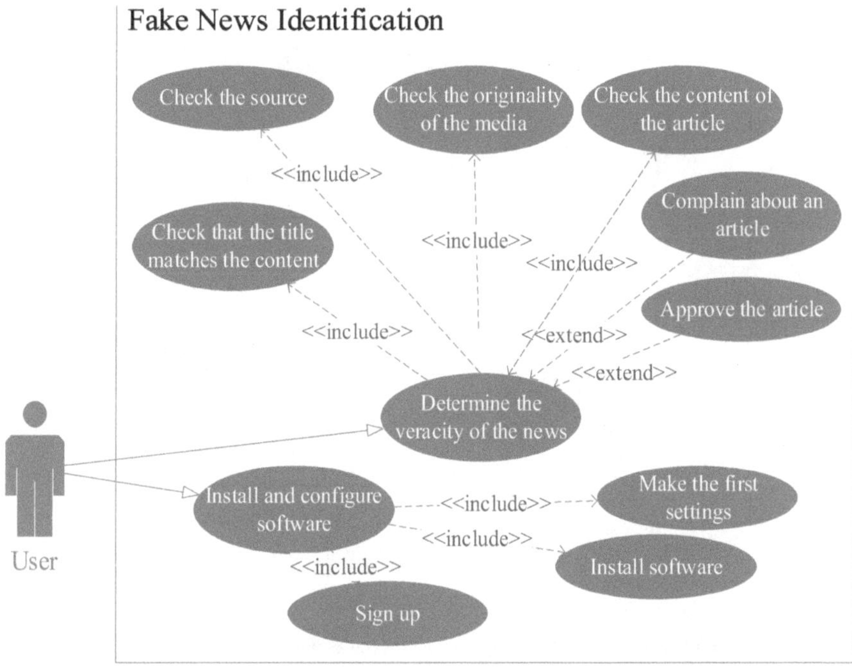

Fig. 3.1. The use case diagram for the system of recognising propaganda, fake news and disinformation in textual content based on ML and NLP methods

The main model processes for analysing the textual content of messages from Internet sources (Fig. 3.2) to recognise propaganda, fakes, and disinformation are "Collecting messages to form a dataset" C_{AU}, "NLP of textual content of messages to extract linguistic features" C_{CU}, "Machine learning for propaganda recognition"

C_{UL} and "Forming conclusions about the presence of propaganda" C_{US} (Fig. 3.3-3.5).

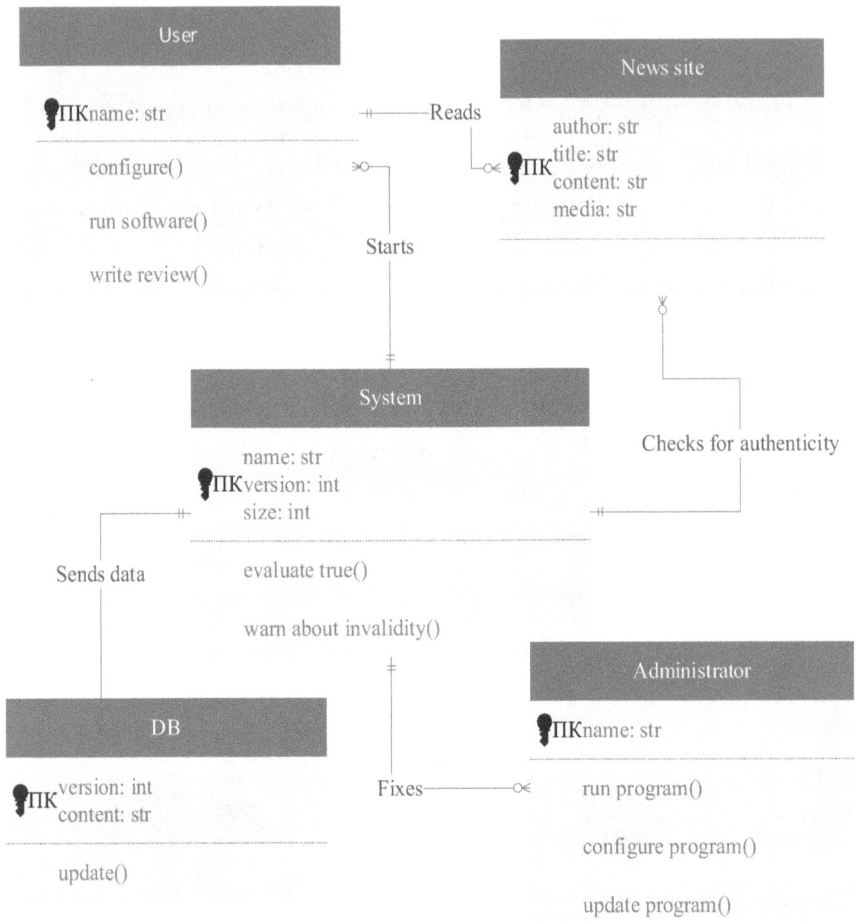

Fig. 3.2. The class diagram for the system of recognising propaganda, fake news and disinformation in textual content based on NLP and ML methods

"Collecting messages to form a dataset" process C_{AU} is described by superposition:

$$C_{AU} = \mu^\circ\beta^\circ\alpha, \tag{3.2}$$

$$C_{AU} = \mu(\beta(\alpha(i_1, i_2, i_3), r_1, u_1), u_2, o_1), \tag{3.3}$$

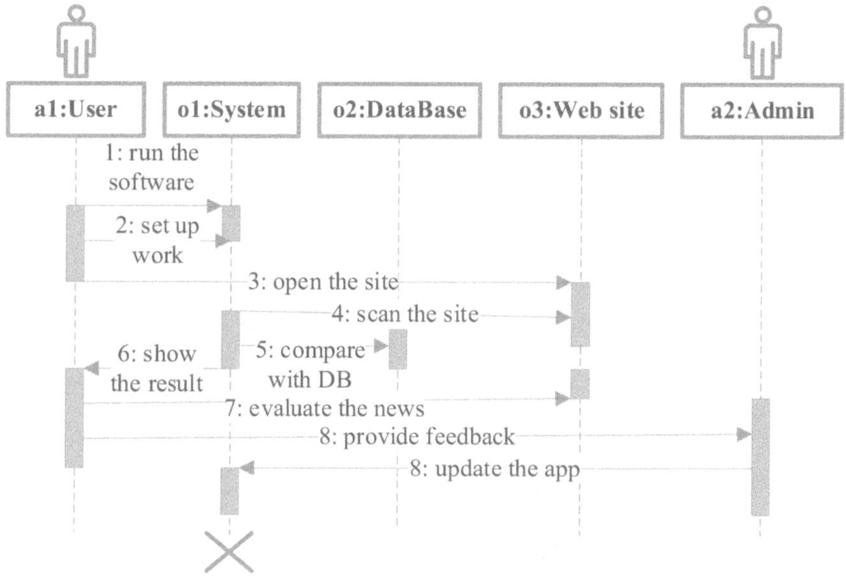

Fig. 3.3. The flow diagram for the system of recognising propaganda, fake news and disinformation in textual content based on NLP and ML methods

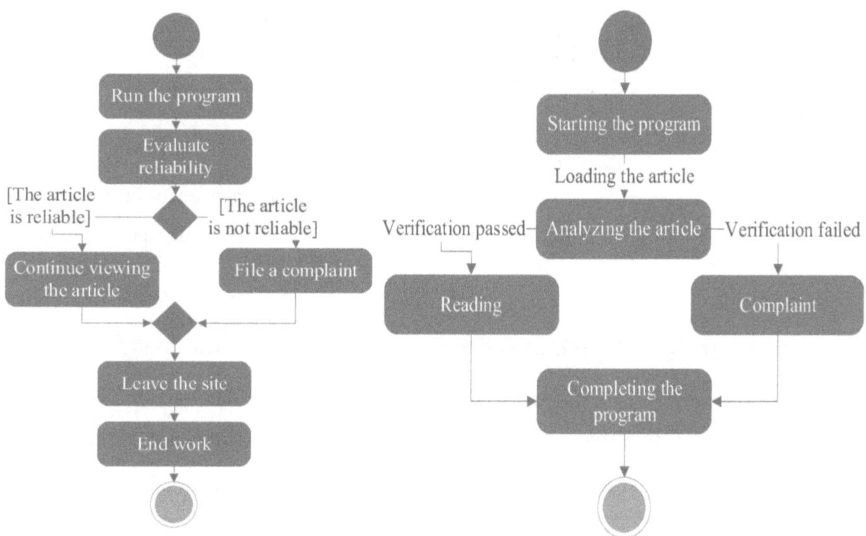

Fig. 3.4. Activity diagram and the state diagram for the system of recognising propaganda, fake news and disinformation in textual content based on NLP and ML methods

where μ is the operator for identifying thematic articles; i_1 is the data set from online sources; i_2 is the publication data repository; i_3 is the dictionary of propaganda markers; r_1 – is the rules for collecting data from online sources; o_1 are the periodic requests for collecting publications; u_1 is a condition set for collecting articles from online sources; u_2 is the set of requirements for filtering the dataset from noise.

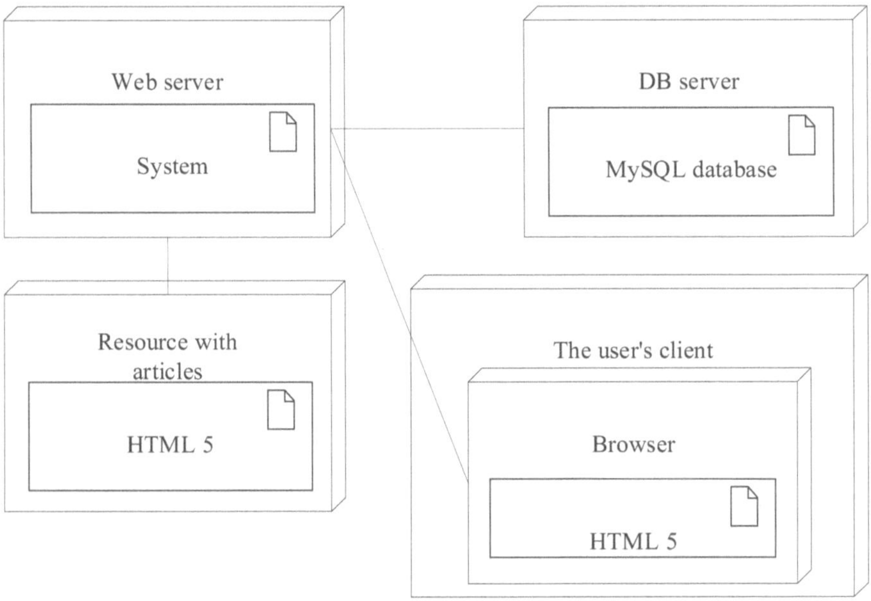

Fig. 3.5. The deployment diagram for the system of recognising propaganda, fake news and disinformation in textual content based on NLP and ML methods

Online disinformation features can be classified into two levels: peripheral (user behaviour features, sentiment features and linguistic features) and central (topic features). It is necessary to find behavioural features to reflect the user interaction characteristics: discussion initiation, engagement, relationship mediation, sphere of influence, and information independence. Therefore, we describe the "NLP of textual content of messages for linguistic feature extraction" process C_{CU} as a superposition:

$$C_{CU} = \chi^\circ\beta^\circ\alpha, \tag{3.4}$$

$$C_{CU} = \chi(\beta(\alpha(C_{AU}, i_2, i_3, i_4), r_1, u_3), r_2), \quad (3.5)$$

where χ – is the operator of the article dataset generation; i_4 – is a thematic keyword set in fakes; u_3 – is a condition set for processing the article dataset; r_2 – is the NLP rules for textual content.

Machine Learning for Propaganda Recognition Process C_{UL}– is described as:

$$C_{UL} = \omega^\circ\gamma^\circ\beta^\circ\alpha, \quad (3.6)$$

$$C_{UL} = \omega(\gamma(\beta(\alpha(C_{CU}, L_R, i_2, o_2), i_3), u_4), r_3), \quad (3.7)$$

where ω is the article labelling operator; o_2 – is the NLP application result; u_4 – is the ML conditions set for fake news recognition; r_3 – is the ML rules set for propaganda recognition.

We describe the C_{US} Propaganda Detection process:

$$C_{US} = \lambda^\circ\gamma^\circ\beta^\circ\alpha, \quad (3.8)$$

$$C_{US} = \lambda(\gamma(\beta(\alpha(C_{UL}, i_2, o_3), i_4), u_5), r_4), \quad (3.9)$$

where λ is the decision-making operator;o_3 is an application of ML result; r_4 – is the propaganda article marking rules; u_5 – is the requirements set for concluding. Logistic regression was chosen because of its simplicity and avoidance of overfitting.

Against the backdrop of information warfare, a lot of resources and time are spent on the rapid collection of content, its analysis and processing, and the generation of conclusions/decisions on its content [111-112]. It is also influenced by the language of publications, which significantly/partially distorts the content when translated. IS will not be able to completely replace the activities of cybersecurity and cyber warfare specialists. However, it will be an auxiliary tool for the rapid formation of relevant corpora/datasets of fake content and their sources, stylistic and linguistic analysis of disinformation text to form an information portrait of the authors, search for authors and distributors through the study of inauthentic behaviour and the content writing style analysis results, and responding to the dynamics of changes or local changes in the content flow by marking the relevant content as probably fake.

Within the framework of solving the text data analysis and recognition problem, in particular, fake news on the Internet, an essential component of NLP technology is the word classification in text data [113]. In this context, classification is the assignment of textual data to one or more predefined classes or categories. There are known studies where the classification of words is performed using statistical methods for assessing the importance of words [114-115]. For example, word classification can be done using ranking [38], but in this case, the textual data must be structured and formed by texts with the same topic, which is not characteristic of fake news texts. Another example is the application of intelligent language identification technology [116], which is based on speech recognition and the statistical method of spectrogram analysis. The research focuses on spoken language identification, taking into account several speech recognition solutions for binary classification and speech transformation. However, only defined languages and their dictionaries are taken into account, which is a limitation for solving the set goal.

A well-known way of assessing the importance of words in text data is to determine the statistical measure of word importance using the TF-IDF function, which determines the importance of a word in the text compared to other words. When words are weighted based on their contribution to understanding the text, they can be used for classification. This approach is the basis of the most widely used method of word classification of text data in NLP technology [117].

A common approach to improve the effectiveness of evaluating the importance of words in a text is to combine different word classification methods. Thus, work [118] describes the combination of the use of the TF-IDF statistical measure and the Naïve Bayes classifier. In this case, the Naive Bayes classifier is used to increase the accuracy of word classification. The researchers emphasise that the assumption of conditional independence, in which all the features used for classification are conditionally independent, that is, knowledge about one feature does not provide information about others, in the discussed algorithm, does not correspond to objective reality, which, to some extent, affects its effectiveness in classification. To improve the effectiveness of the Naive Bayes text data categorisation algorithm, the authors of the paper propose a Naive Bayes text data categorisation algorithm based on TF-IDF attribute weighting. The $\chi2$ statistic is used to extract the features of textual data before running the algorithm, then different weights are assigned to other sets of feature words according to the TF-IDF method.

In the article [119], the authors try to relax the attribute independence assumption when the attributes as input data are statistically independent of each other under the classification condition. This fundamental assumption makes the algorithm "naive" because in real data, there may be interdependence between features. To relax the assumption, a naive Bayes tree was proposed. It is a hybrid algorithm that deploys a simple Bayesian classifier at each terminal node of the constructed decision tree and thus exhibits excellent classification performance on textual data. To further improve the classification efficiency of MNBTree, researchers propose its multi-class training version called Multi-Class Multinomial Naive Bayes Tree by applying a multi-class technique to MNBTree.

Research [120] describes the use of a classifier using the Naive Bayes method. The purpose of this study was to compare the performance of the Naive Bayes method with TF-IDF weighting and without TF-IDF weighting for abstract-based thesis topic classification. Based on the results of the conducted tests, Naïve Bayes without TF-IDF weighting has better performance than TF-IDF weighting for the classification of these topics. Based on the authors' experiments, the use of such a classification method requires additional data processing and re-evaluation of the results of the trained model.

One of the proposed options for improving the efficiency of text data classification is described in the paper by Huilong Fan and Yongbin Qin, "Research on Text Classification Based on the Improved TF-IDF Algorithm". They improve the method of calculating the word frequency coefficient in textual data by introducing constants into the formula for calculating the IDF value. Thanks to this, it always becomes greater than zero, and the improved calculation method eliminates the problem of poor discrimination of the initial category of the calculation method [122]. The study presents an advanced feature weighting technique called FDCD-TF-IDF, which uses information from word frequency distributions and category distributions. This progression introduces the concept of word frequency distribution and class distribution to provide a more accurate representation of the importance of feature elements. The frequency distribution of words is mainly concerned with the relation between features and categories, while the category distribution offers a better understanding of the categorical characteristics of features. Therefore, this updated algorithm effectively takes into account the differences between different categories of textual data. However, this approach involves extensive calculations, which can critically increase the computational load in the case of real-time analysis of textual news data.

Another classification implementation is proposed by a vector representation of function words based on the Word2vec deep learning tool, and the weight of function words is calculated using an improved TF-IDF algorithm. Next, the multiplication of the weight of the word and the vector of the word, which implements the vector representation of the word, is performed. Finally, each text data element is represented by accumulating all word vectors [123].

In light of the traditional TF-IDF feature weighting algorithm presented in the article [124], which emphasises the problem of inefficient extraction of eigenvalues when working with heterogeneous text data for classification, the authors present a promising solution. They introduce an extended TF-IDF algorithm that takes into account the irregular distribution of textual content. Experimental results show that the performance of the classification algorithm using the proposed enhancement outperforms the original algorithm in terms of accuracy and recall. This innovation serves to eliminate the shortcomings inherent in the traditional TF-IDF algorithm, thus demonstrating its potential to significantly improve text data classification tasks in real-world scenarios. On the other hand, researchers [125] propose a term weighting scheme with a modified association concept. Another article [126] also elaborates on one of the shortcomings of the TF-IDF method – misunderstanding the essence of the entire sentence, only its division into words. The authors managed to modify this method so that it can classify speech features. This study [127] also carefully analysed the effect of using different term frequency ratios on seven controlled term weighting schemes. The results showed that the modification of the term frequency factor in the controlled term weighting schemes increased the efficiency of almost all weighting schemes.

In the field of textual content recognition, researchers involve all possible options for automatic verification of textual data. The classifier is a widespread classification algorithm that is widely used in ML algorithms. The research also describes mathematical solutions based on Naive Bayes and the BM25 ranking function [128-132].

Vectorisation of textual content is used to transform text data into a numerical vector, which is necessary for further application of ML methods in NLP. This process allows the computer to understand and process textual information, which is usually required for ML algorithms. Various methods are used for vectorisation, such as Bag of Words [133]. The works [134-135] describe the Word embedding methods used (for example, Word2Vec or GloVe).

Another approach to vectorisation is the special TF-IDF vectorizer used, which is described in [136] and is designed to convert text data into numerical data. This vectorizer already has a built-in TF-IDF word significance function, which is used to classify text data words as a statistical analysis strategy implementation. Thus, the presented tool combines the stages of vectorisation and word classification of text data. Vectorisation is based on the use of the sklearn.feature_extraction.text library module, which integrates the TfidfVectorizer function. It is a ready-made solution for widespread use in the field of solving vectorisation tasks for text data recognition, so this solution is also used in the method of recognising fake news on the Internet. Next, a typical example of the vectorisation implementation using the TF-IDF vectorizer is considered in detail.

The main stages of vectorisation consist of:

1. Loading the input data for the vectorizer, which is a set of tokens.

2. Performing a vectorisation where a set of tokens is converted to a numeric representation. As a result of vectorisation, a vectorised representation of text data is obtained, which is shown in Table 3.3.

Table 3.3. Vector representation of numerical data

Token	Vector value	Vector value	Vector value	Vector value	Vector value
Word 1	0.301	0.000	...	0.358	0.000
Word 2	0.261	0.000	...	0.000	0.000
Word 3	0.000	0.000	...	0.000	0.000
Word 4	0.174	0.000	...	0.368	0.000
Word 5	0.137	0.000	...	0.000	0.000

The resulting data vectors are input data for NLP models that implement the following stages.

- Syntactic analysis [137] in NLP determines structural relationships between words in a sentence and determines their grammatical structure. The primary purpose of the study is to understand syntactic relations and build a parsing tree. For syntactic analysis in NLP technology, specific concepts and methods are used [138], such as the Parse Tree, the use of grammatical rules of the language, POS-tagging (Part-of-Speech Tagging) to determine a part of speech, the dependence between words in a sentence, and grouping words into fragments. Syntax analysis is used to understand the grammatical structure of text data, as well as to improve the NLP model for further stages of NLP. This stage is necessary for the method of recognising fake news on the Internet to group nouns and adjectives based on their grammatical functions to expand the vocabulary of credibility markers, that is, to highlight those linguistic features that are inherent in the syntax of fake news.
- Semantic comprehension [139] refers to understanding what is expressed in textual data, including concepts, ideas, and meanings. The detection of semantic connections is based on semantic analysis and includes the detection of

connections between words and concepts. It may consist of identifying similar words, antonyms, associations, and other relationships between terms. Such an approach is necessary to increase the vocabulary of words inherent in fake news, which in turn expands the possibilities for computer training of the NLP model. Since semantic analysis takes into account the textual data context, words can have different meanings in different contexts, and semantic analysis takes this variation into account. During the semantic analysis, the evaluation of the emotional colouring of the text data is calculated. It is vital to take into account the emotionally charged words used in fake news texts and their use in the implementation of the attention mechanism.

- Semantic analysis [140] in the NLP context is the understanding of the words, sentences, and the meaning of textual data. The main goal of semantic analysis is to identify context, meaning and semantic relationships in textual data.

The TF-IDF word importance statistical measure is used in NLP technology [141] to calculate the importance of words in textual data compared to the entire set of documents. According to the well-known formula [142], the TF-IDF value is calculated for word *t* of document *d* in the set of text data documents. To do this, it is necessary to calculate the *TF* according to (10). It is the ratio of the number of mentions of a word to the total number of words in the document:

$$TF(t,d) = \frac{n}{N}, \tag{3.10}$$

where *n* is the number of times word *t* appears in document *d*, and *N* is the total number of words in document *d*.

IDF is the inverse of the frequency with which a particular word occurs in the documents of the collection. It is calculated according to the formula:

$$IDF(t) = log\left(\frac{D}{d(t)}\right), \tag{3.11}$$

where *D* is the number of all documents, *d*(*t*) is the number of documents with the word *t*.

TF-IDF for word *t* can be calculated using the general formula:

$$TF - IDF(t,d) = TF(t,d) \times IDF(t), \tag{3.12}$$

where $TF(t, d)$ is the frequency of t in d, and $IDF(t)$ is the number of documents that contain the variable t. To increase the effectiveness of frequency analysis of text data using the BM25 (Best Match 25) ranking function to solve the operational recognition of fake news, the problem arises of adaptive selection of the ranking function parameters based on experimental data obtained as a result of frequency analysis of news from reliable sources. Adaptive selection of parameters provides a balance between accuracy and speed when processing text data sets. To ensure this balance, adaptive selection of the optimal parameters of the ranking function [121], such as word frequency and length of text data, which affect the accuracy and speed of text data processing, is proposed. To select the optimal parameters of the frequency of words k_1 and the length of text data b of the BM25 ranking function, the following optimisation criteria were defined:

- Processing of textual data should be performed with a high accuracy rate, more than 90% classification accuracy.
- Textual data should be processed as quickly as possible.
- The set of textual data has specific themes that are characteristic of fake news.
- The input data set is not balanced.
- Text data can be of various unfixed lengths.

It is necessary to improve the method of selecting the optimal parameters of the ranking function that satisfy the specified criteria.

This approach is necessary to take into account all the specified input data criteria and optimally selected parameters. Verification of the obtained results is performed experimentally. It is essential to develop a way to optimise the parameters for adjusting the influence of word frequency and the length of text data of the BM25 ranking function. The selection and adjustment of the optimisation parameters must be adapted to the input text data, namely the structure, size, topics, and linguistic features, and they must form the basis of the BM25 ranking function implementation [143-147].

3.4. Analysing the system's results

Since propaganda detection in textual data [148-151] will be performed at two levels - at the document/phrase level, two separate datasets were selected for each task:

– Propaganda recognition at the document level. The propaganda detection dataset for this task consists of 35993 Messages (including headlines) in English, each labelled as "propaganda" or "non-propaganda". The dataset also contains a unique identifier for each message. The data is presented as a text file, with the message text separated from the identifier and category by tabs. After downloading the file, remove the identifier attribute and convert the data to pandas.DataFrame format (Fig. 3.6a).

– Recognising propaganda at the phrase level. The dataset for this task type contains about 450 English-language messages (including headlines), divided into separate phrases. Each phrase is labelled as "propaganda" or "non-propaganda". The dataset also contains a unique identifier for each message and a unique identifier for the phrase within the message to which it belongs. The data is presented as a set of text files, one for each message. Data attributes are also stored separately. In total, the dataset contains 15168 phrases (Figure 3.6b). After downloading each collection of files, we concatenate them to form a single pandas.DataFrame, removing the unique message/phrase identifiers from the dataset. Since both datasets are labelled into two classes, the project will solve the problem of binary classification. There are many well-known algorithms for solving this problem, including neural network algorithms, but to save computational resources, we will focus on classical ML methods with a teacher. Some of the most well-known and effective models are SVM, naive Bayes classifier, and logistic regression. Let us consider each of them:

	article	label
0	Et tu, Rhody? A recent editorial in the Provi...	non-propaganda
1	A recent post in The Farmington Mirror — our t...	non-propaganda
2	President Donald Trump, as he often does while...	non-propaganda
3	February is Black History Month, and nothing l...	non-propaganda
4	The snow was so heavy, whipped up by gusting w...	non-propaganda
5	Four months after the Sandy Hook School shooti...	non-propaganda
6	The first major newspaper article about Donald...	non-propaganda
7	For three years, starting in 2008, New York ar...	non-propaganda
8	President Donald Trump's tumultuous administra...	non-propaganda
9	With Hartford on edge about the future of Aetn...	non-propaganda

	sentence	label
0	US bloggers banned from entering UK	non-propaganda
2	Two prominent US bloggers have been banned fro...	non-propaganda
4	Pamela Geller and Robert Spencer co-founded an...	propaganda
6	They were due to speak at an English Defence L...	non-propaganda
8	A government spokesman said individuals whose ...	non-propaganda
...	...	...
15164	This is a Moon of Alabama fundraiser week.	non-propaganda
15165	No one pays me to write these blog posts.	non-propaganda
15166	If you appreciated this one, or any of the 7,0...	non-propaganda
15167	Posted by b on November 29, 2018 at 10:23 AM |...	non-propaganda
15168	Comments	non-propaganda

14263 rows × 2 columns

Fig. 3.6. Dataset for recognition at the a) message and b) phrase level

- The SVM method is a model designed for binary classification, in particular, for classifying text data (Fig. 3.7) using a non-probabilistic linear binary classifier. The SVM model is a sample's representation as points in space, where the optimal hyperplane separates samples from separate categories. The model can have several types of kernels, but it is most often used with a linear kernel. For a classical SVM model with a linear kernel to perform well, the data must be linearly separated. It works effectively when there is a clear separation between data of different classes, when the data is multidimensional, and when the number is greater than the total data instances. However, it is not designed to work with large data sets and is not effective when there is a lot of "noise" in the data set. When the data instances of one class exceed the number of data instances of another class, i.e. the data must be balanced. As we can see in Fig. 3.7, since our datasets are not balanced, the linear SVM model did not do a good job - many samples of propaganda texts were classified as non-propaganda.

– Naive Bayes classifier to determine the instance belonging probability to one of the classes, assuming the hypothesis of independence of variables (Fig. 3.8). The naive Bayes classifier is not too sensitive to the absence of specific attribute values in the set; instead, it works better when the training sample size is relatively large. However, it accepts the hypothesis of data independence, so it can be ineffective if the data are related, and it is also susceptible to the shape of the input data. As we can see in Fig. 3.9, since the text data has a lot of noise, the naive Bayes classifier also did poorly.

– Logistic regression is based on linear regression. Still, unlike linear regression, logistic regression is designed for the task of classification (Fig. 3.9). Predicting the variable's belonging probability to a particular class is determined by the value compared with the logistic curve. The logistic regression model is not sensitive to overfitting when the data set is not multidimensional, but even in this case, a regularisation algorithm can be used.

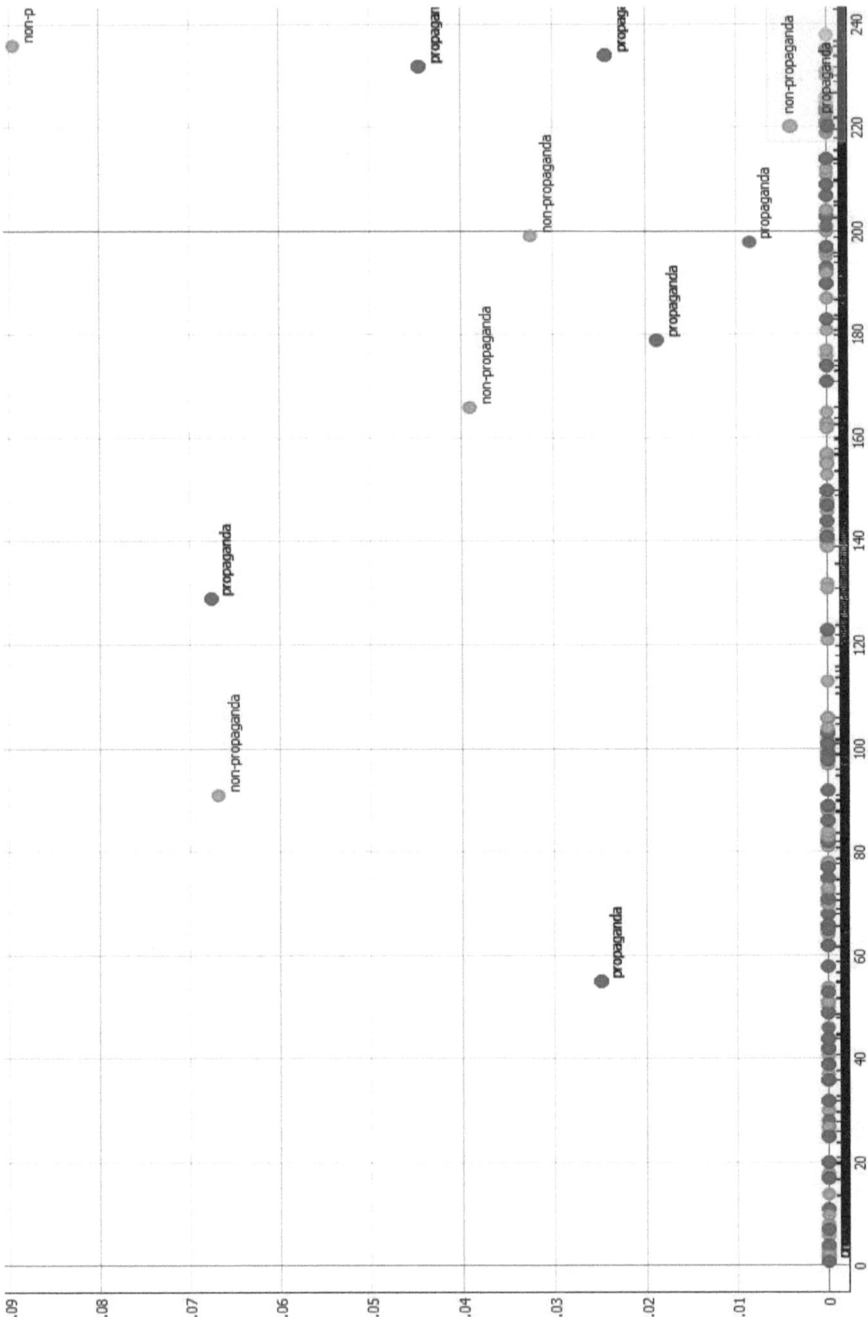

Fig. 3.7. Visualisation of the SVM algorithm

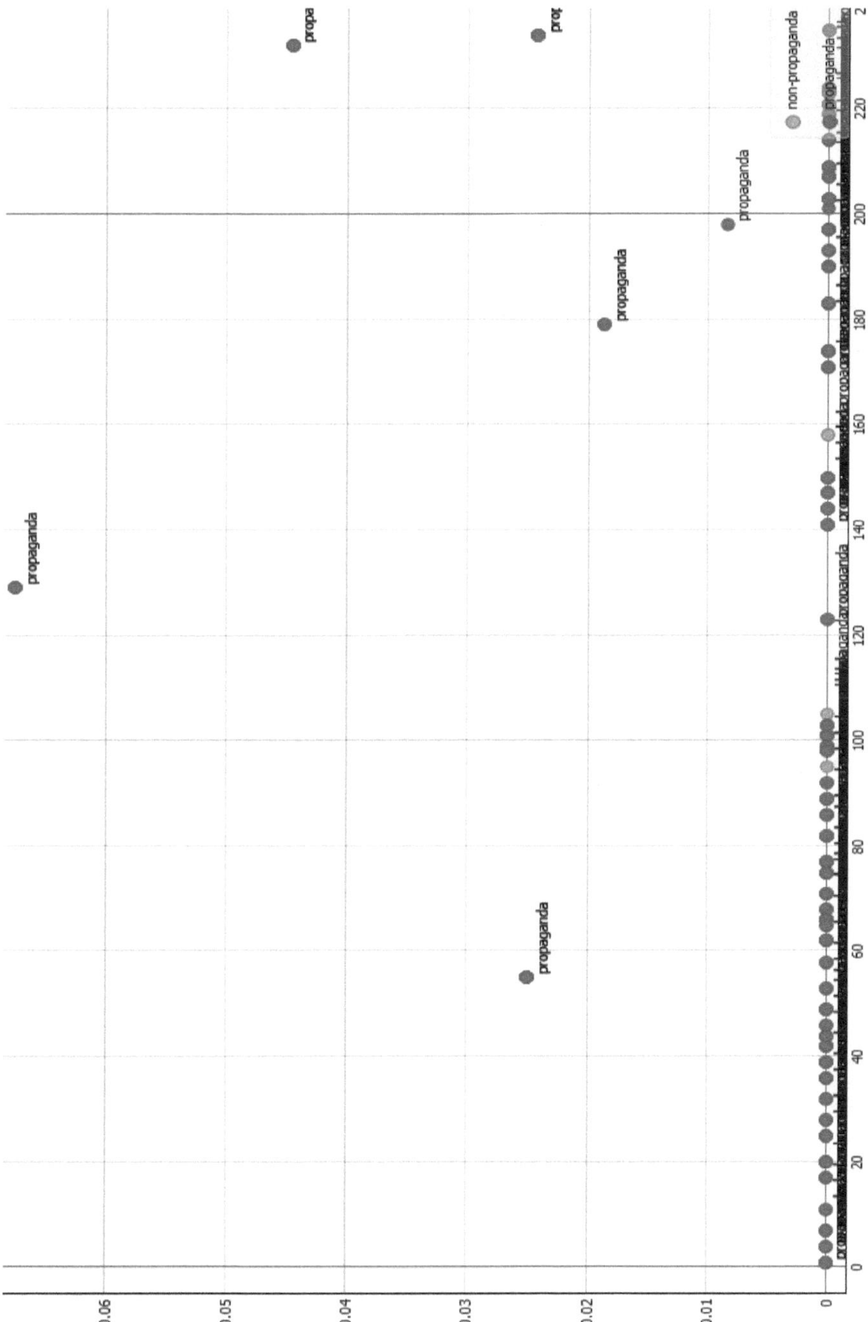

Fig. 3.8. Visualisation of the naive Bayes algorithm.

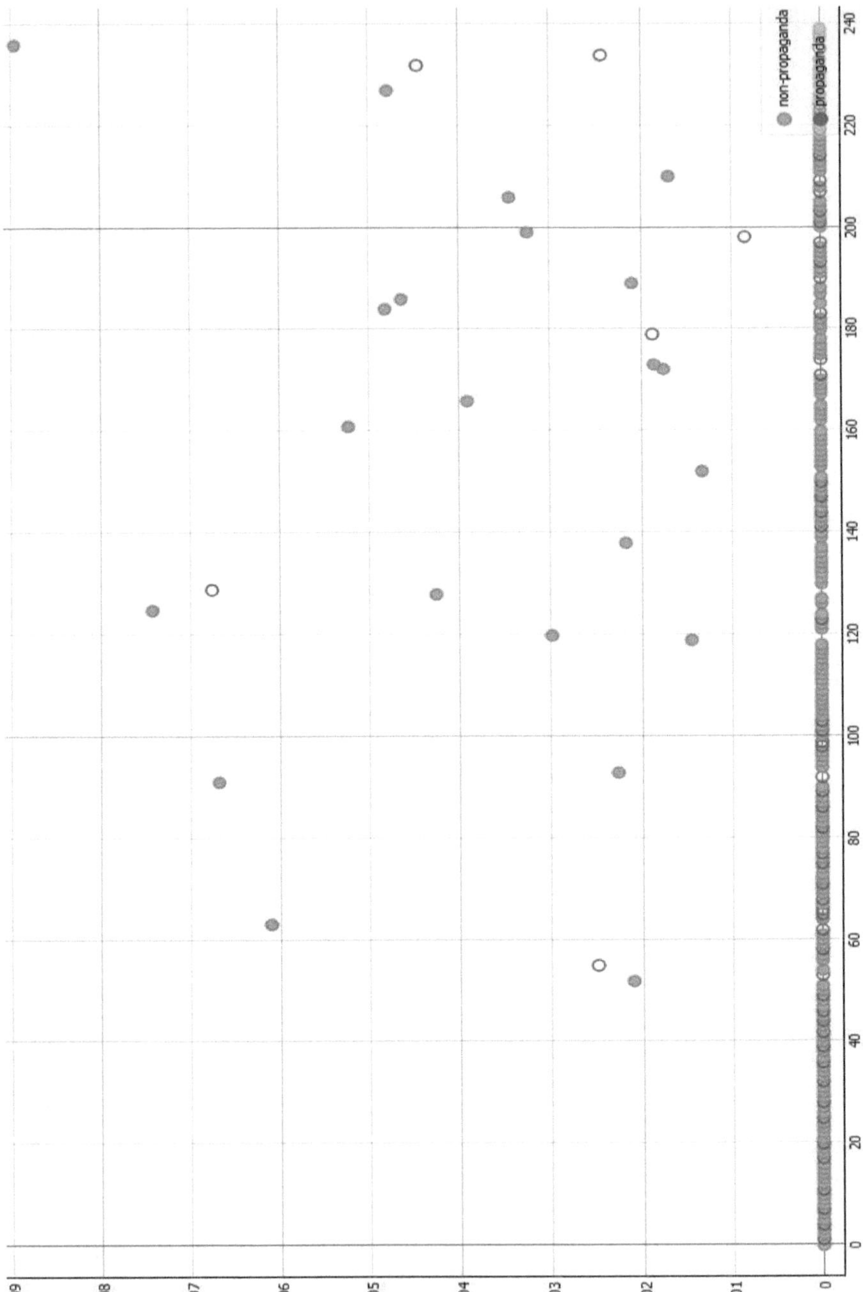

Fig. 3.9. Visualisation of the logistic regression model.

We chose the logistic regression model because we cannot guarantee the independence of the variables from each other for text data (a requirement of the naive Bayes classifier), and the absence of noise (which can cause inefficiency in the SVM). In addition, our data is not balanced in terms of class distribution. Since the raw text itself does not have any features and attributes and is not suitable for use in an ML model, it is also necessary to identify methods for feature extraction.

The list of methods is as follows:

– Vectorisation of text data using the Bag-of-Words model. Each word (term) in the corpus is assigned a specific number, and the text is transformed into a vector of dimension N, where N is the total number in the corpus, in which each element value is equal to the term frequency.

– TF-IDF is a transformation based on the words' importance evaluation in the phrase/message context, that is, the collection part of messages/phrases.

– Marking parts of speech. Formatting of text data in "%word%_%part of speech to which the word%_%lemma of the word% belongs" form.

– Using the Word2Vec model for word embedding. Use of a shallow two-layer neural network for word vectorisation while reducing the number of dimensions.

The basis of the research methodology is a synthesised technology based on the AI methods, computational linguistics, statistical data processing, data mining, machine learning, simulation/computer modelling, systems theory/analysis, etc. The problem consists of 2 main components: the data set identifying as false information (fake or propaganda), and sources finding and analysing inauthentic participants' behaviour.

The NLP process scheme of content topic identification:

Pipeline 1. Pre-labelled data → NLP → ML → Models/templates/metrics

Pipeline 2. New incoming data → Labelling of data (blocked/unblocked) → NLP → ML → Labelling of content or a potential reason for stopping. Fig. 3.10 shows a general diagram of the propaganda detection system. Fig. 3.6a shows the propaganda detection process at the message level, and Fig. 6b shows it at the phrase level.

Identification of propaganda at the message level (Fig. 3.11a):

– Data preparation - cleaning the data, removing unnecessary words and attributes (noise words and punctuation), converting the data to lowercase, splitting the data into training and test samples;

– Feature extraction - extracting attributes from text data - initialising the vectorizer and TF-IDF transformer, training them and performing the appropriate transformations for the training and test samples;

- Model building - initialising the model, training it, making predictions based on the test sample, and evaluating the model's performance.

Recognition of propaganda at the phrase level (Fig. 3.11b):

– Data preparation - removing noisy words and converting to lowercase (we will need punctuation to identify certain propaganda features), and splitting the data into test and training samples;

- Feature extraction - marking parts of speech, marking quotation marks, identifying so-called "shiny" words, reinforcing words and absolute pronouns, and vectorisation using the Word2Vec neural network;

- Building the model - initialising the model, performing Grid Search cross-validation, training the model, and making predictions using a test set.

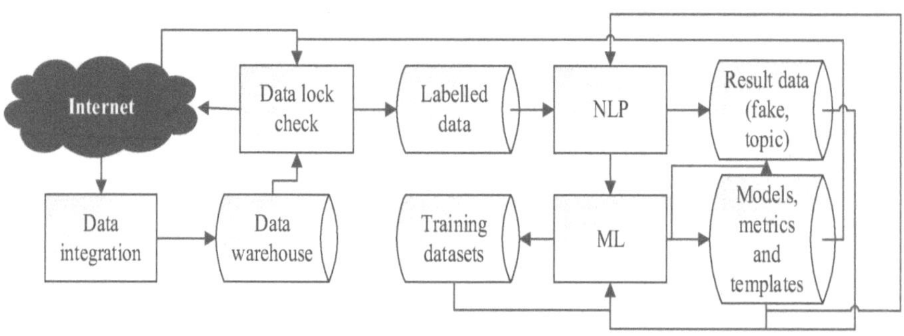

Fig. 3.10. General diagram of the propaganda detection system

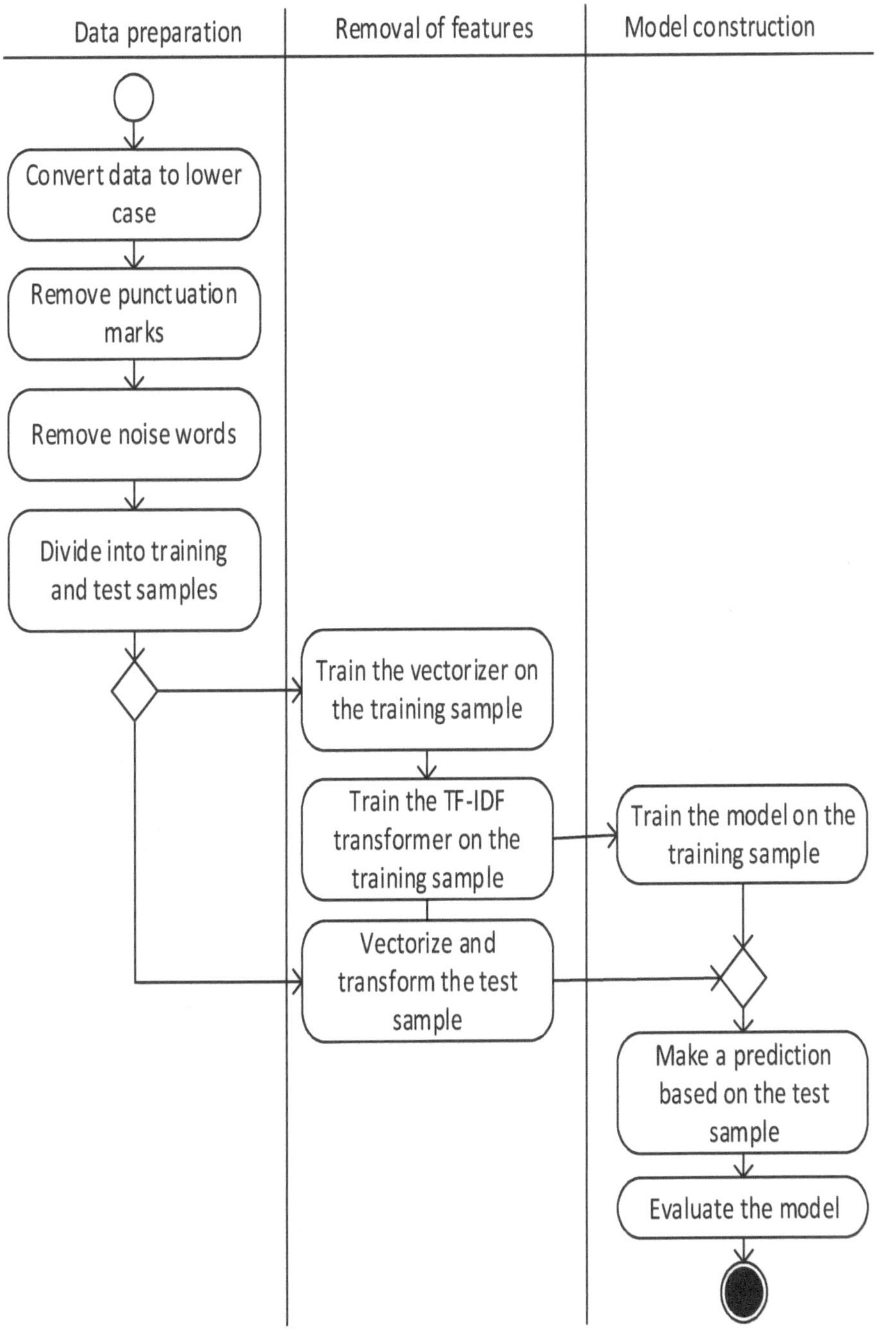
Data preparation
Removal of features
Model construction
Convert data to lower case
Remove punctuation marks
Remove noise words
Divide into training and test samples
Train the vectorizer on the training sample
Train the TF-IDF transformer on the training sample
Vectorize and transform the test sample
Train the model on the training sample
Make a prediction based on the test sample
Evaluate the model

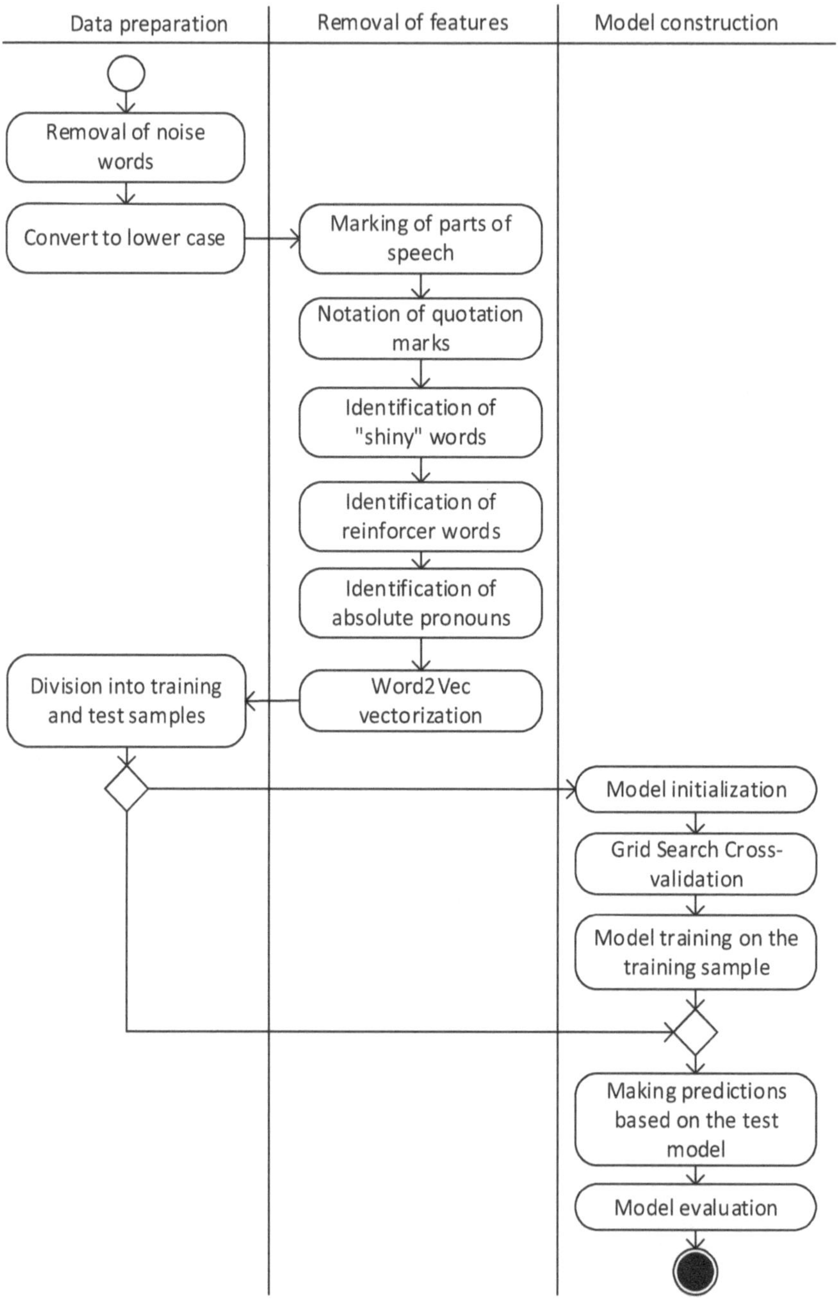

Fig. 3.11. Recognition of propaganda at the level of a) message and b) phrase

We chose Python due to its more straightforward future integration and computational capabilities. Specifically, we will use the following Python libraries: scikit-learn (for model building, feature extraction, and metrics application); pandas, NumPy (for data storage and manipulation); spacy (for part-of-speech markup); NLTK (for noise word removal); genism (for using the Word2Vec model); seaborn, matplotlib (for visualisation).

- Recognition of propaganda at the message level (Fig. 3.12a). Let's look at the distribution of data by their classes to understand the level of their balance. As we can see, the data is not balanced, and the set is significantly dominated by non-propaganda messages. Namely, the dataset contains about 32 thousand messages labelled as "non-propaganda" and about 4 thousand messages labelled as "propaganda". Before starting the feature extraction process, it is necessary to perform some operations to clean and prepare the data. We need to convert each word in the dataset to lowercase so that two identical words that start with different letter cases are not counted as separate tokens during the vectorisation process. We perform the following conversion:

```
data['article'] = data['article'].apply(lambda x: "
    ".join(x.lower() for x in x.split()))
```

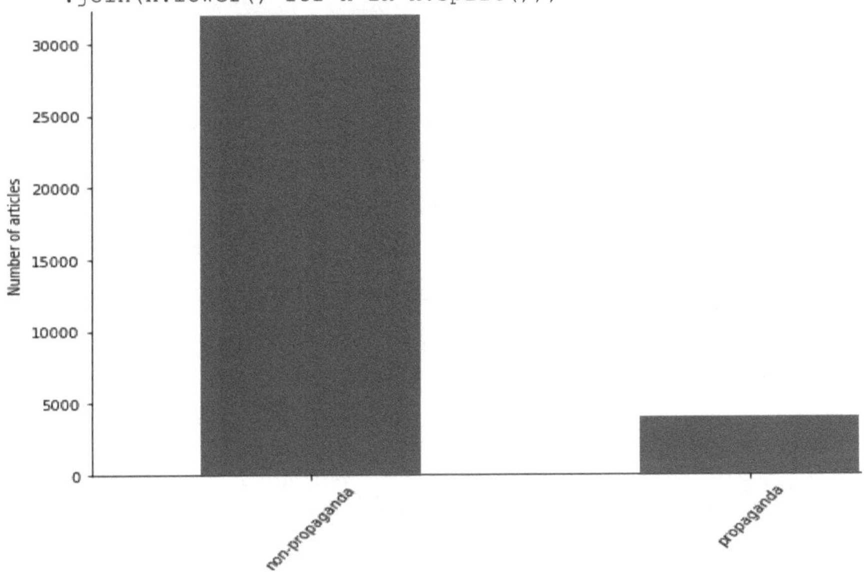

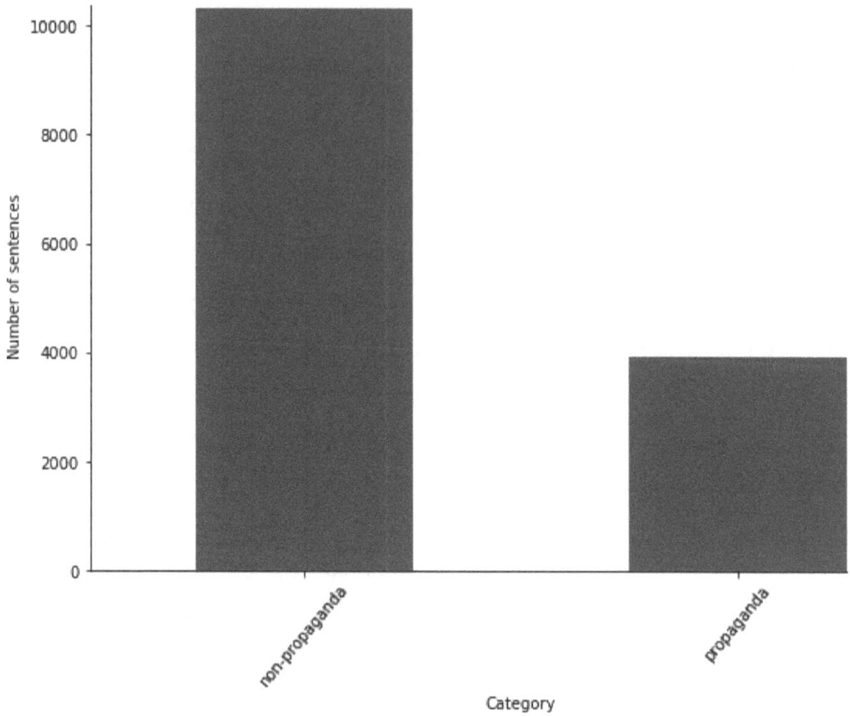

Fig. 12. Graph of data distribution for propaganda recognition by class at the level of a) message and b) phrase

Next, we remove punctuation marks from the dataset, since at this level of the problem, punctuation is not an informative feature, but it will be counted as a separate token during the vectorisation process, which can lead to the formation of excessive noise in the data. Perform the transformation:

```
data['article'] = data['article'].str.replace('[^\w\s]','')
```

Remove noise words (those that do not carry any meaning). Use the built-in noise word corpus of the NLTK library and remove them from the message in a loop.

```
stop = nltk.stopwords.words('English)
data['article'] = data['article'].apply(lambda x: " ".join(x
    for x in x.split() if x not in stop))
```

After that, we can divide the data into training and testing samples.

```
X = data['article']
y = data['label']
```

Feature extraction. Perform text vectorisation. Let's use the CountVectorizer class from scikit-learn.

```
vectorizer = CountVectorizer(analyzer='word',
    token_pattern=r'\w{1,}', ngram_range=(1,2),
    strip_accents='unicode', min_df=3, max_df=0.5)
X_train = vectorizer.fit_transform(X_train)
X_test = vectorizer.transform(X_test)
```

As an output result, the fit and transform methods of an instance of the CountVectorizer class produce a sparse matrix whose dimension is equal to the unique words in the text. Let's make sure that after the transformation, the number of attributes of the training and testing samples is the same (Fig. 3.13).

```
X_train.shape

(28794, 605048)

X_test.shape

(7199, 605048)
```

Fig. 3.13. Verification of training and testing dataset dimensions at the document level

Next, let's perform the TF-IDF transformation. We use the TfidfTransformer class from scikit-learn.

```
transformer = TfidfTransformer(use_idf=True, smooth_idf =
    True)
X_train = transformer.fit_transform(X_train)
X_test = transformer.transform(X_test)
```

The transformation is performed for a pre-formed sparse matrix of vectorised text data. Building a model.

```
LogisticRegression(C=1.0, class_weight='balanced', dual=False,
    fit_intercept=True, intercept_scaling=1, l1_ratio=None,
    max_iter=100, multi_class='auto', n_jobs=None,
```

```
    penalty='l2', random_state=None, solver='lbfgs',
    tol=0.0001, verbose=0, warm_stert=False)
```

For the simulation, we will use the LogisticRegression class from the scikit-learn library.

```
model = LogisticRegression(penalty='l2',
    class_weight='balanced', solver='lbfgs')
model.fit(X_train, y_train)
```

Among the parameters, we specify penalty='l2', which tells the model to use the method of ridge regression for regularisation, and solver='lbfgs', which tells the model to use the Broyden-Fletcher-Goldfarb-Shanno algorithm with limited memory usage for optimisation. Data preparation. Let's plot the distribution of data by category to assess the data imbalance level (Fig. 3.12b). The dataset is not balanced and is again dominated by non-propaganda phrases. Next, we repeat the process of removing noisy words from the dataset. After that, we again convert the text data to lowercase.

```
stop = stopwords.words('English)
data['sentence'] = data['sentence'].apply(lambda x: " ".join(x
    for x in x.split() if x not in stop))
data['sentence'] = data['sentence'].apply(lambda x: "
    ".join(x.lower() for x in x.split()))
```

At this level of the task, we do not remove punctuation marks from phrases, as they will be needed at the feature extraction stage. We mark the parts of speech. For this operation, we use the Spacy library.

```
nlp = spacy.load('en')
def tag(sentence):
        global nlp
        doc = nlp(sentence)
        return " ".join([f'{x.text}_{x.tag_}_{x.lemma_}' for
    x in doc])
sentences_pos = copy.deepcopy(data['sentence'])
tagged = pos_tagging(sentences_pos)
data['tagged'] = tagged
```

We mark each phrase in the dataset with the curly quotes. It allows us to track the propaganda technique as "Appeal to authority". Initialise the corresponding function.

```
def get_quotations(sentences):
    result = []
    for sentence in sentences:
        match = 1 if '"' in sentence else 0
        result.append(match)
    return np.array(result).reshape(-1, 1)
```

We check each phrase for the presence of the so-called "shiny words. Examples of such words are "patriotism", "freedom", "power", "idea", etc. We perform this operation to identify such propaganda techniques as "flag-waving" and "slogan". We calculate the match number between the words in the phrase and the words in the "shiny words" lexicon and divide this value by the total word number in the phrase to normalise the coefficient. We create the corresponding lexicon as a text file with "brilliant words" and initialise the corresponding function.

```
def get_glitter(tagged):
    filename = 'glitter_words.txt'
    glitters = []
    append = glitters.append
    with open(os.path.join(LEXICONS_PATH, filename),
    encoding='utf-8') as f:
        for line in f.readlines():
            append(line.replace('\n', ''))
    result = []
    for sentence in tagged:
        words = 0
        matches = 0
        for wline in sentence.split():
            try:
                w, t, l = wline.split("_")
            except:
                continue
```

```
            w = w.lower()
            l = l.lower()
            words+=1
            if l in glitters or w in glitters:
                matches+=1
        if words == 0:
            result.append(0)
        else:
            result.append(matches/words)
    return np.array(result).reshape(-1, 1)
```

We use a similar approach to search for word amplifiers ("incredibly", "very", "absolutely", etc.) and absolute pronouns ("all", "no one", etc.) in phrases. We try to identify the propaganda techniques as "Common Platform" and "Loaded Language" accordingly. We form similar vocabularies and categorise the corresponding functions. As the last step, we vectorise the text data using the Word2Vec model. We use a model trained in advance on a dataset from the social network Twitter, which has 200 dimensions. We use the gensim library.

```
w2v_file = os.path.join(WORD2VEC_PATH, 'twitter.27B.200d.txt')
w2v_model = KeyedVectors.load_word2vec_format(w2v_file,
    binary=False)
def w2v_vectorize(tagged):
    global w2v_model
    X = []
    ndims = 200
    for sentence in tagged:
        words = []
        for wline in sentence.split():
            try:
                w, t, l = wline.split("_")
            except:
                continue
            words.append(w)
        row_data = np.mean([w2v_model[w] for w in words if w
    in w2v_model] or
```

```
                                        [np.zeros(ndims)], axis=0).tolist()
            X.append(row_data)
        X = np.array(X)
        X_std = (X - X.min(axis=0)) / (X.max(axis=0) -
        X.min(axis=0))
        X_scaled = X_std * (1 - 0) + 0
        return X_scaled
```

Create a new DataFrame described above.

```
word2vec_features = w2v_vectorize(data['tagged'])
word2vec_columns = [f'dim{x}' for x in range(200)]
glitter_words = get_glitter(data['tagged'])
quotations = get_quotations(data['sentence'])
intensifiers = get_intensifiers(data['tagged'])
absolutes = get_absolutes(data['tagged'])
X = pd.DataFrame(word2vec_features,
    columns=[word2vec_columns])
X['quotations'] = quotations
X['glitter_words'] = glitter_words
X['intensifiers'] = intensifiers
X['absolutes'] = absolutes
y = data['label']
```

Divide the dataset into training/test samples. We use the Grid Search cross-validation algorithm to find the best parameters and initialise and train the model (Fig. 3.14).

```
lr_model = LogisticRegression()
penalty = ['l1', 'l2']
C = np.logspace(0, 4, 10)
hyperparameters = dict(C=C, penalty=penalty)
clf = GridSearchCV(lr_model, hyperparameters, refit='f1',
    cv=5)
best_model = clf.fit(X_train, y_train)
```

The best model parameters obtained are as follows: penalty='l2', C=7.74.

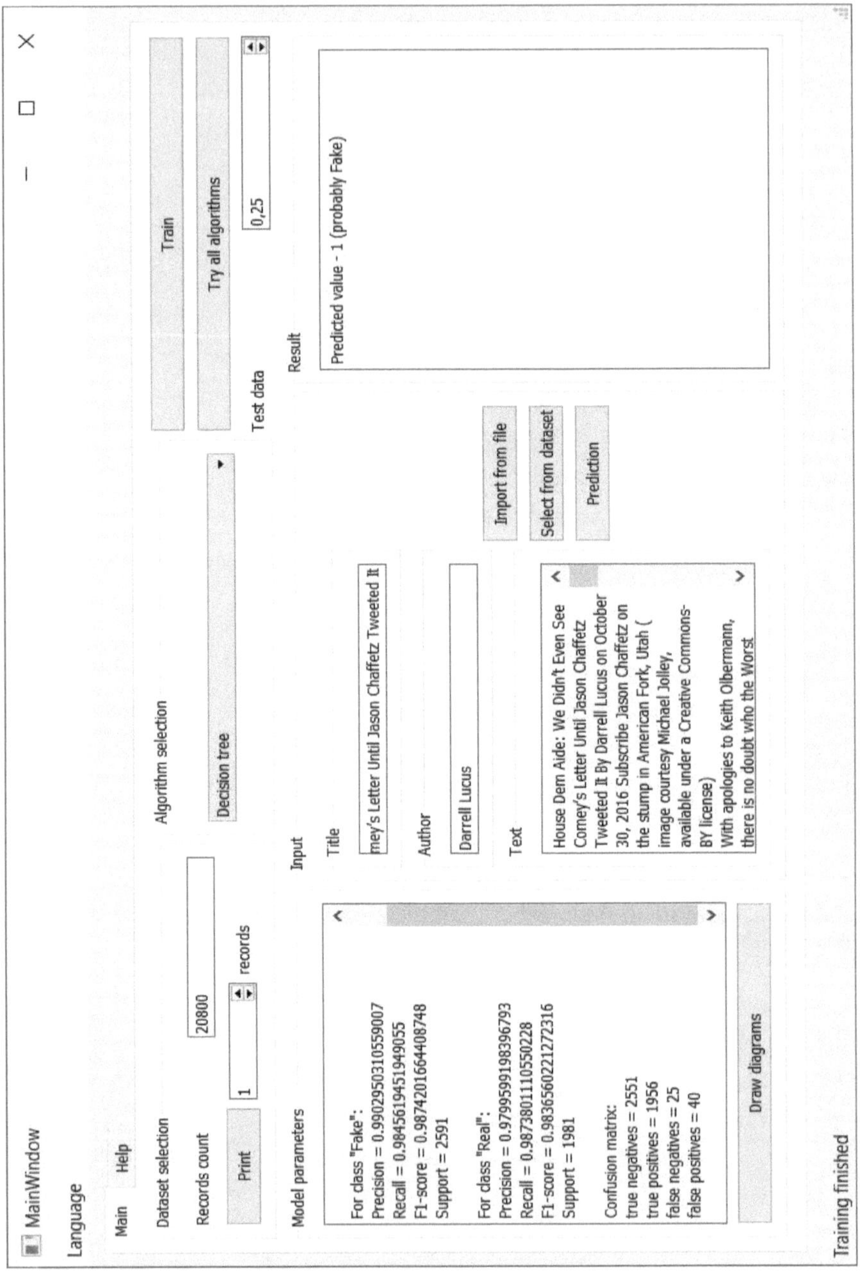

Fig. 3.14. Functionality of the system of recognising fake news, propaganda and disinformation in textual content based on NLP and ML methods

The model worked correctly, although it gave a relatively high probability of a fake identification. This code performs fakes/non-fakes recognition using a logistic regression, a decision tree, KNN, a random forest, a Bayes classifier, and a multilayer perceptron. It calculates recall, precision, and accuracy, as well as sensitivity for each algorithm. Accuracy is the ratio of the correct predictions to the total number of observations. It measures the overall accuracy of the fakes/non-fakes recognition model and is expressed as a percentage. A higher precision indicates a more accurate model of fakes/non-fakes recognition.

Accuracy = (TP + TN) / (TP + TN + FP + FN), where: TN (True Negative) is a correctly predicted negative classes' number; TP (True Positive) is a correctly predicted positive classes' number; FN (False Negative) is an incorrectly predicted negative classes' number; FP (False Positive) is an incorrectly predicted positive classes' number. Support is the number of examples in every class (non-fake identification or fake identification). F1-score is a harmonic mean between recall and precision. It provides a balanced measure of model performance that takes into account both recall and precision. Recall = TP / (TP + FN) is the ratio of the correctly predicted positive class's number to the total number of valid positive classes. It measures how well the model detects positive predictions. Precision = TP / (TP + FP) is the ratio of a correctly predicted positive class number to the total number of positive predictions. It measures how accurate the predictions of the positive class are. We will analyse and evaluate the propaganda detection model's performance at the message level. We make predictions based on the test sample. Let's build an error matrix (Fig. 3.15a). The error matrix can be interpreted as follows: the model managed to correctly classify 6097 non-propaganda messages and 694 propaganda messages. One hundred twenty-three propaganda messages and 285 non-propaganda messages were classified incorrectly. The resulting model score is 0.9988433254618697041.

```
predictions = model.predict(X_test)
n = len(conf_matrix)
plt.figure(figsize = (n, n))
```

```
sns.heatmap(conf_matrix, annot=True)
plt.title("Confusion Matrix")
plt.ylabel("Actual Value")
plt.xlabel("Predicted Value")
plt.show()
```

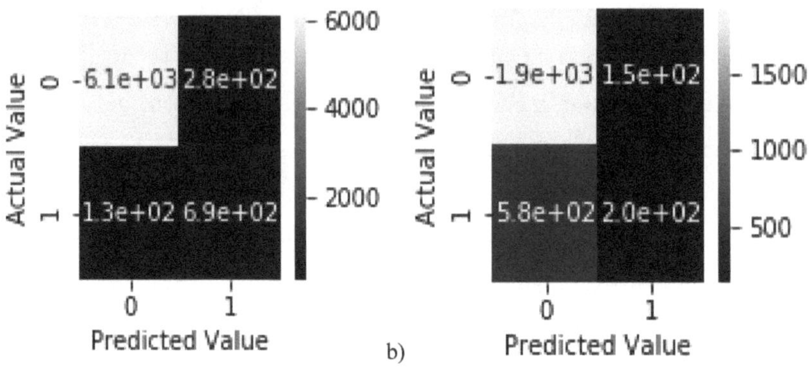

b)

Fig. 3.15. The error matrix for the propaganda recognition model at the level of a) message and b) phrase

After that, we perform similar steps for the model of propaganda recognition at the phrase level. So, again, we perform the prediction based on the test sample. We build a similar error matrix (Fig. 3.15b). The error matrix can be interpreted as follows: the model successfully classified 1917 non-propaganda messages and 205 propaganda messages, but 585 propaganda messages and 146 non-propaganda messages were misclassified. The model's score is 0.7437784787942516. Both scores are satisfactory, but the model for propaganda identification at the document level performed better. In addition, given the imbalance of both datasets, we can see that the 2nd model (for phrase-level propaganda detection) misclassified more instances of data that were labelled as propaganda. It may indicate that the model is not specific enough, meaning that the following tool developments (Fig. 3.16-3.21) should use a more complex algorithm and extract more particular features to be able to identify other propaganda techniques more accurately.

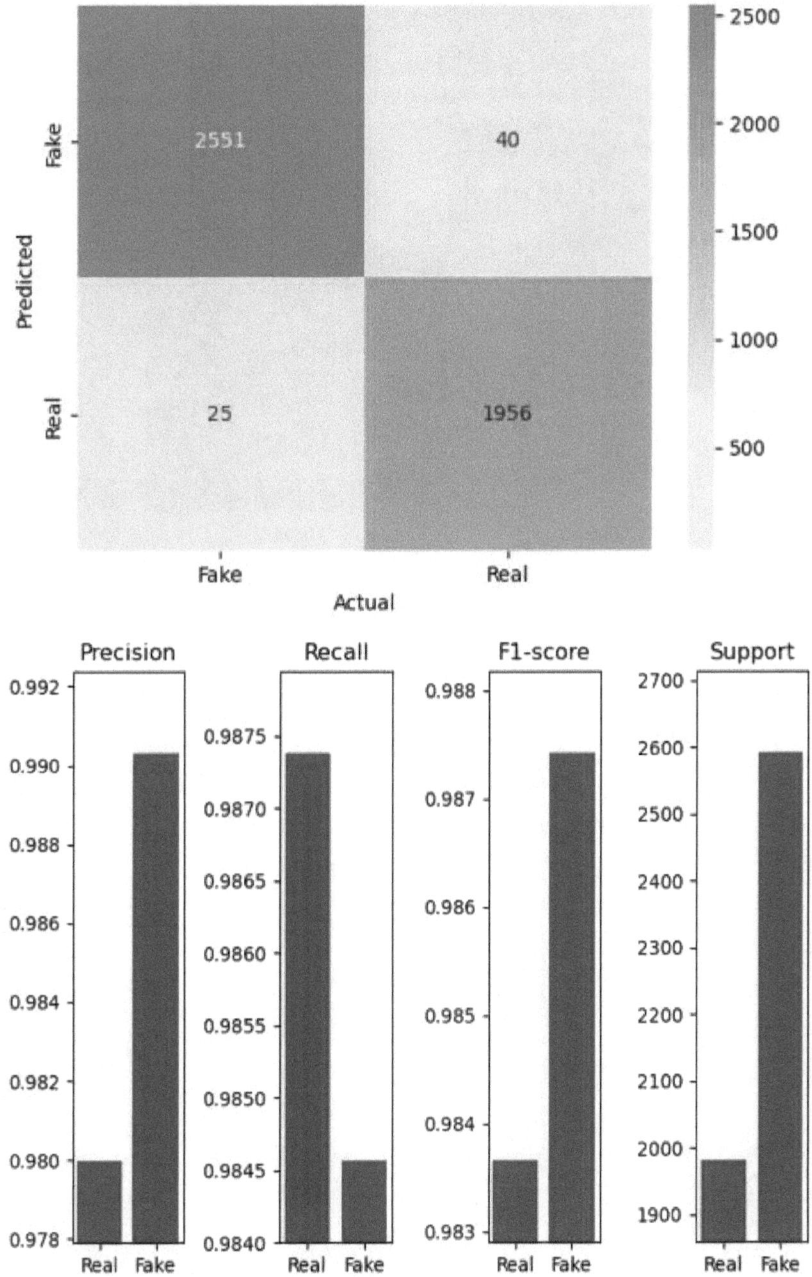

Fig. 3.16. The confusion matrix and graph for the decision tree model in the system of recognising fake news, propaganda and disinformation in content based on MLd NLP

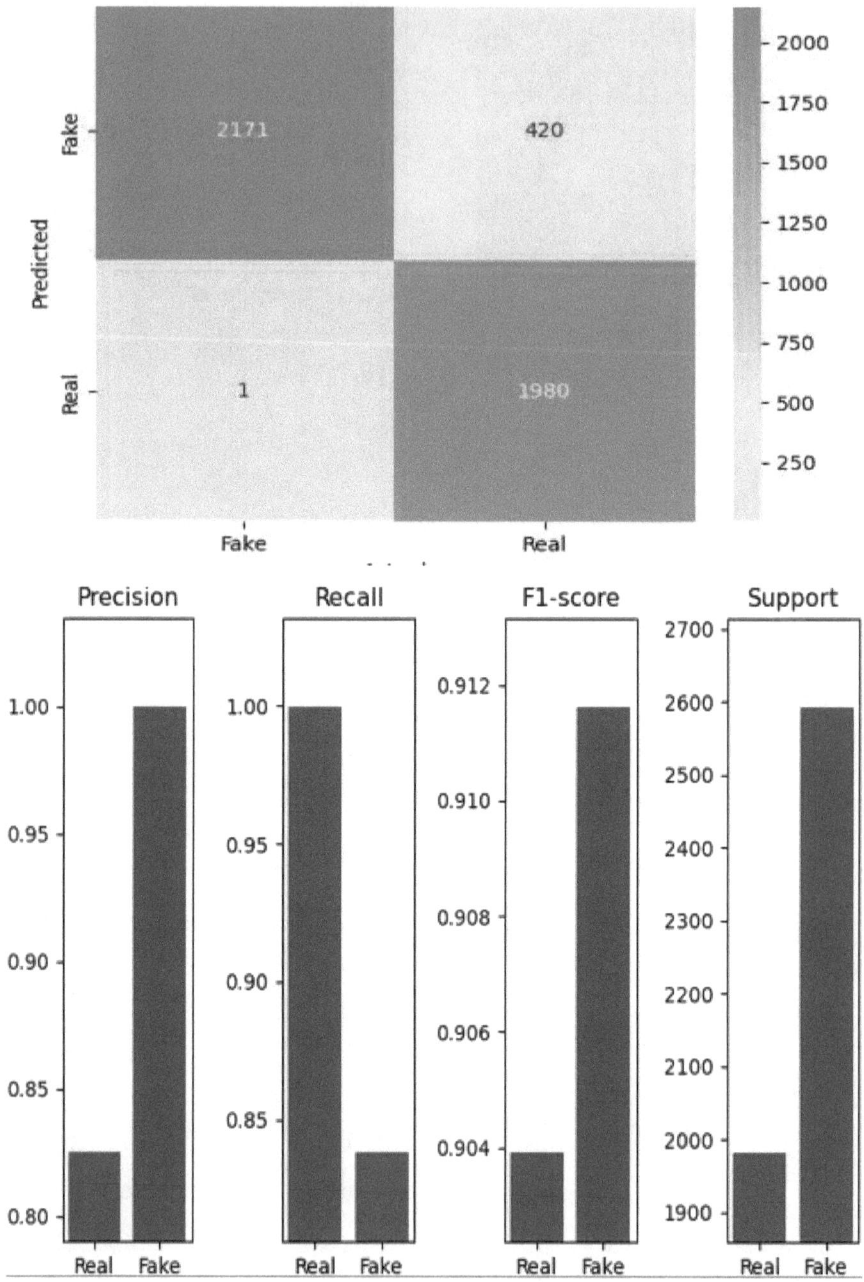

Fig. 3.17. The matrix confusion and graph for the KNN model in the system of recognising fake news, propaganda and disinformation in content based on ML and NLP

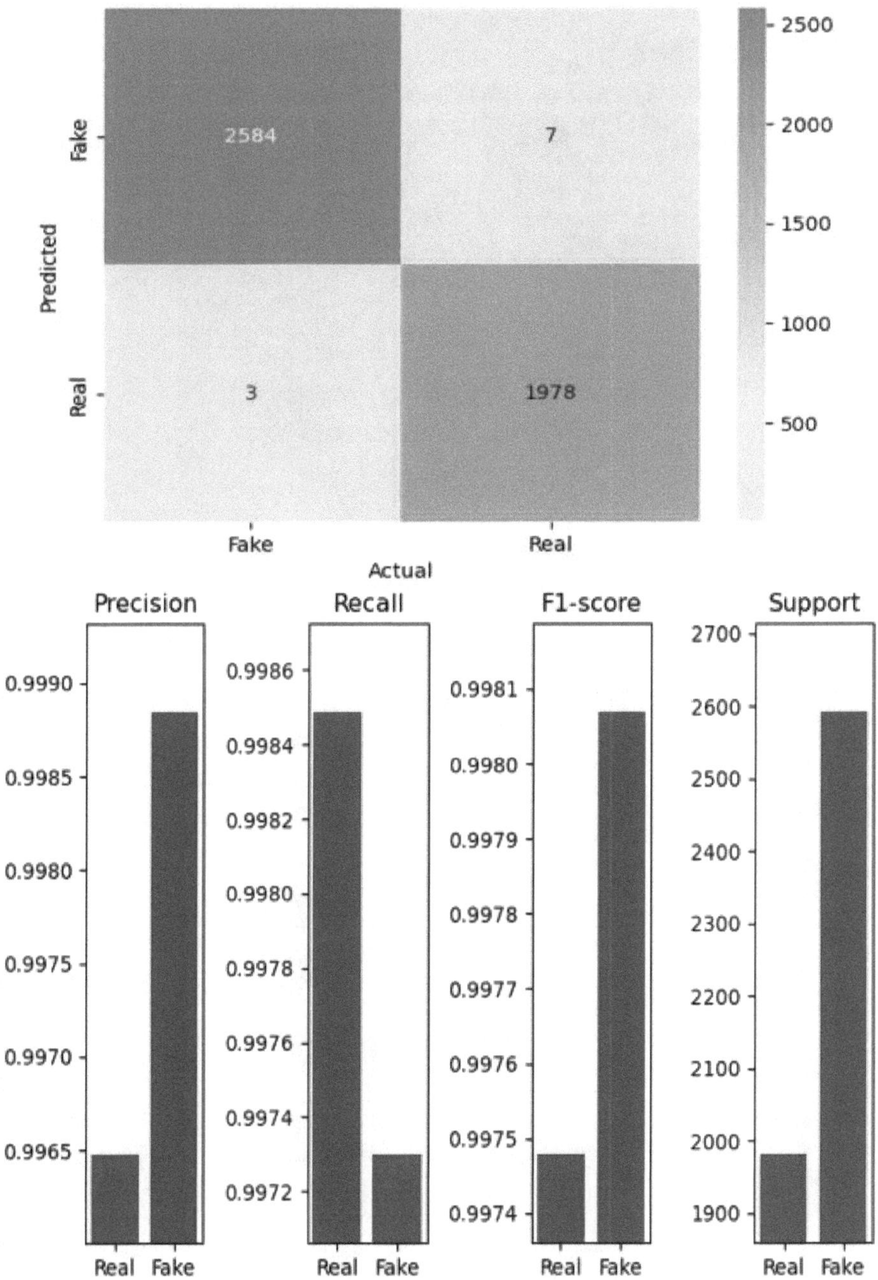

Fig. 3.18. The confusion matrix and graph for the logistic regression model in the system of recognising fake news, propaganda and disinformation in content based on ML and NLP

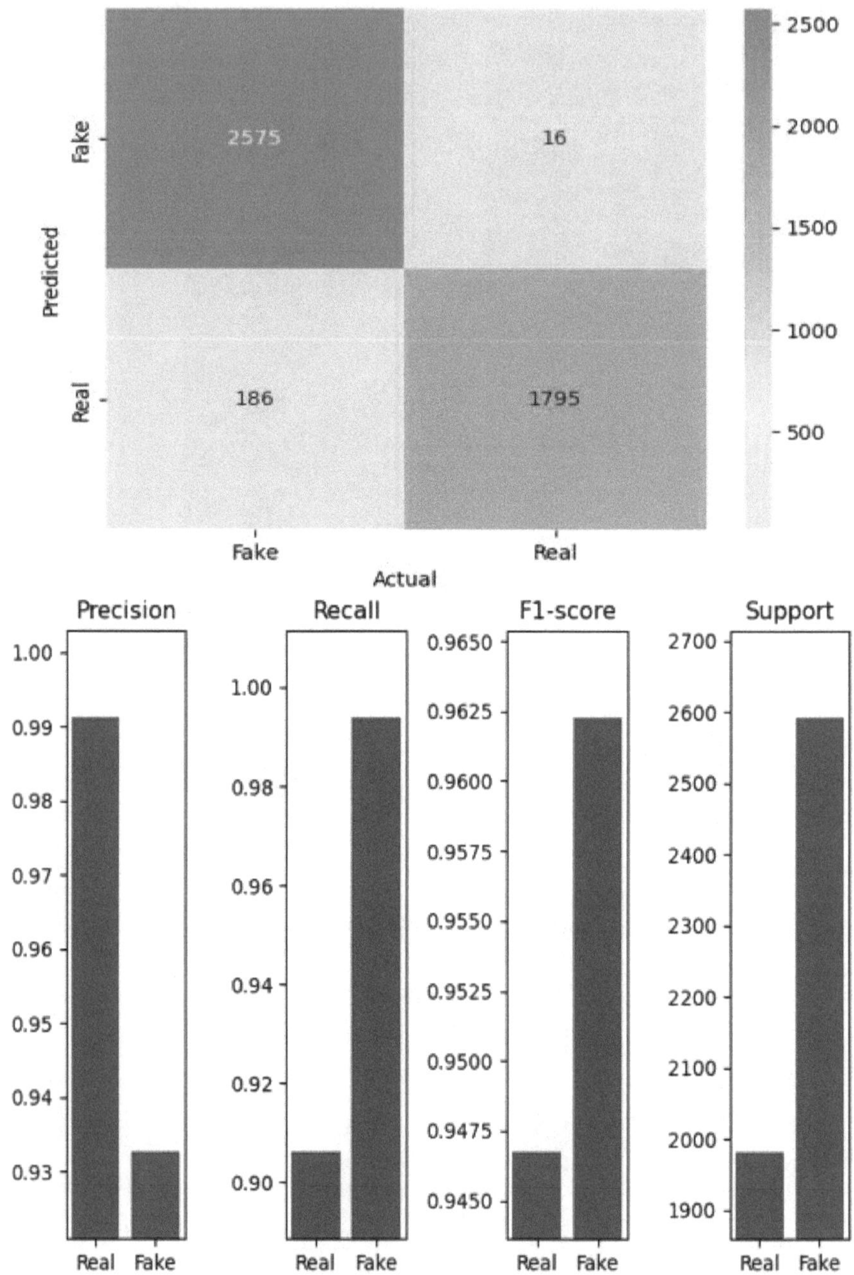

Fig. 3.19. The confusion matrix and graph for the random forest model in the system of recognising fake news, propaganda and disinformation in content based on ML and NLP

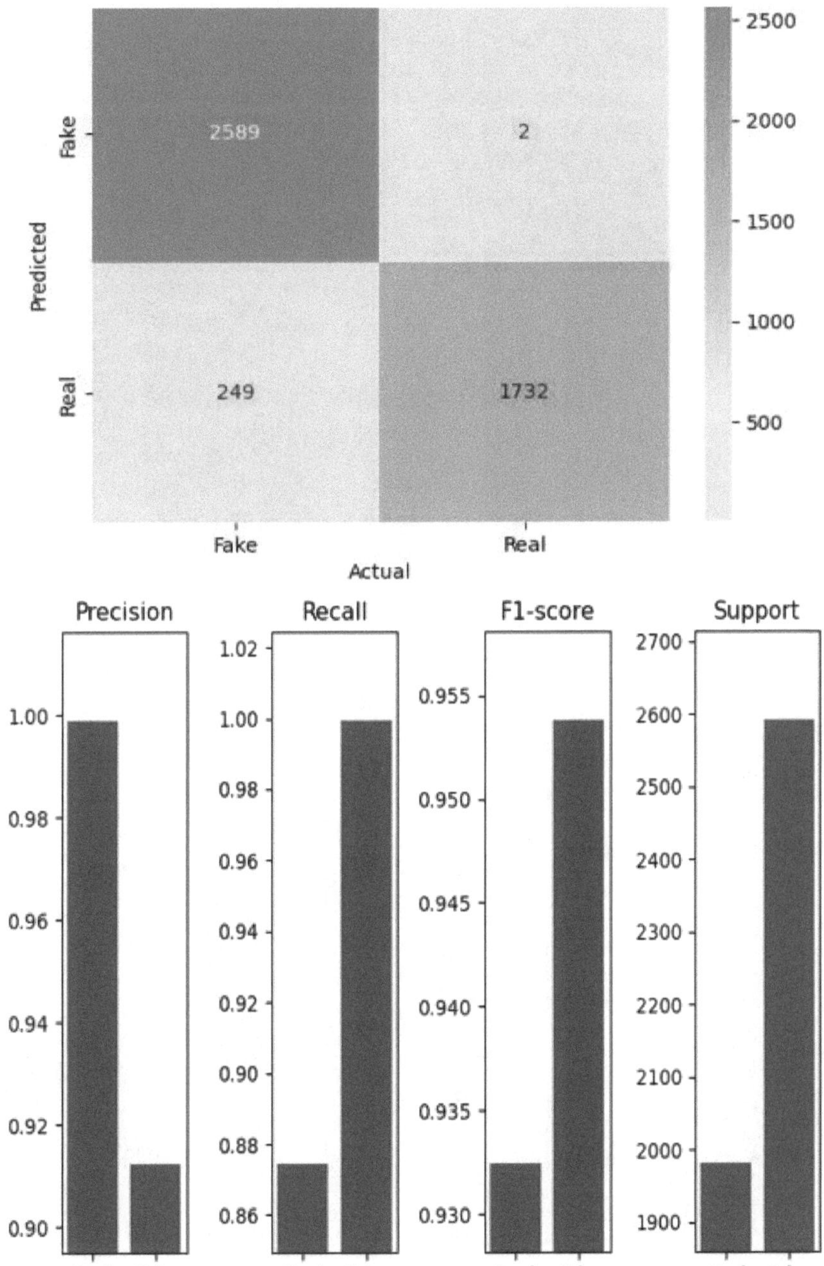

Fig. 3.20. The confusion matrix and graph for the Bayes classifier model in the system of recognising fake news, propaganda and disinformation in content based on ML and NLP

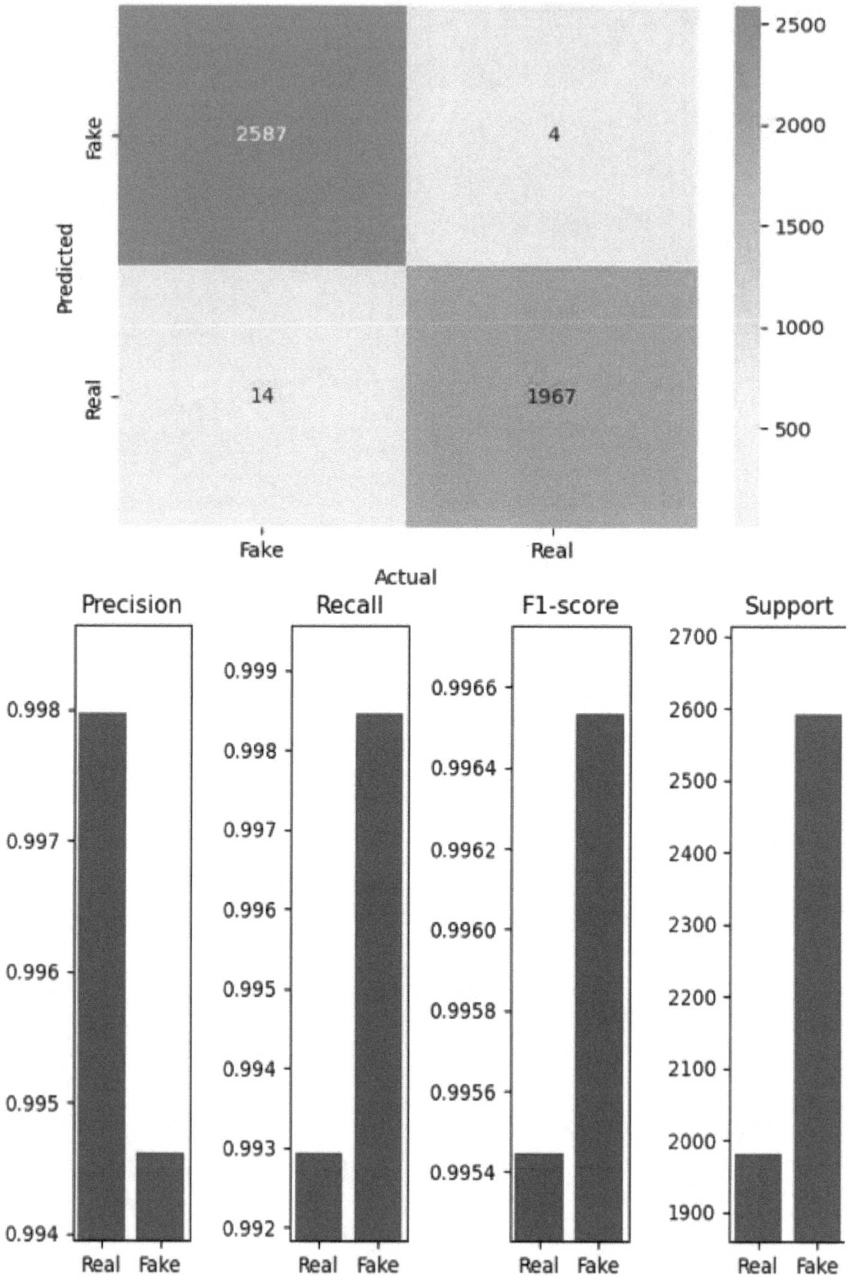

Fig. 3.21. The **confusion** matrix and graph for a multilayer perceptron model in a system of recognising fake news, propaganda and disinformation in content based on ML and NLP

Different ML algorithms have been analysed to give >91% accuracy for fake identification and >83% accuracy for non-fake identification. Some of them are better at non-fake identification, and some at fake identification. Different ML algorithms should be combined to improve the results (Table 3.4).

Table 3.4. Analysis of accuracy results for different ML algorithms

#	Name	non-fakes	fakes	difference
1	The multilayer perceptron	0.9979	0.9945	0.0034
2	The Bayes classifier	0.998	0.913	0.085
3	The random forest	0.991	0.933	0.058
4	The logistic regression	0.9965	0.9988	0.0023
5	The KNN	0.83	0.999	0.169
6	The decision tree	0.98	0.993	0.013

Today, it is essential to realise that disinformation remains one of the critical challenges facing states, civil society, and the population of countries (both less developed and highly developed). Disinformation hurts human consciousness, affects public opinion, elections, state security, and people's health, life, career, etc. In this regard, the world community is trying to develop new policies and recommendations for countering disinformation, while trying not to violate the right to free expression. At the same time, international practices cannot stand still, as the technologies for disinformation use are constantly changing. Ideally, new policies should be anticipatory and preventive, but now they are more of a reaction. Further research on the problem can be seen in highlighting the mechanisms of using AI in detecting and countering disinformation in its modern, distorted form.

3.5. Conclusions for Chapter 3

Today, it is essential to realise that disinformation remains one of the critical challenges facing states, civil society, and the population of countries (both less developed and highly developed). Disinformation hurts human consciousness, affects public opinion, elections, state security, and people's health, life, career, etc. In this regard, the world community is trying to develop new policies and recommendations for countering disinformation, while trying not to violate the right to free expression. At the same time, international practices cannot stand still, as the technologies for disinformation use are constantly changing. Ideally, new policies should be anticipatory and preventive, but now they are more of a reaction. Further research on the problem can be seen in highlighting the mechanisms of using AI in detecting and countering disinformation in its modern, distorted form.

Chapter 4. Methods of identifying fake news in social networks

The chapter is written based on scientific publications [152-157].

4.1. Dataset formation

Social networks are not only a communication tool and a source of information, but also a space for spreading various information threats. On the other hand, informational threats negatively impact the opinion of ordinary citizens, who are unprotected from the actions of intruders. The most relevant are disinformation, fakes, manipulation of public opinion, and publications by bots and trolls. Let's look at these threats and analyse their impact on domestic cyberspace. Misinformation is deliberately distorted or false information [152-153] disseminated to confuse people or influence their actions, emotions, or attitudes. Disinformation can manipulate public sentiment, discredit individuals or organisations, and weaken state structures. It is most often distributed through social networks, news portals or messengers. The potential of media literacy to respond to misinformation was analysed by R. Hobbs [154], who conducted an applied study on the right to teach responses to conspiracy theories. Subsequently, research in the international field of media literacy appeared to assess its ability to resist fake news [155]. The spread of fake news or distorted information is one of the biggest threats on social media. For example, much misinformation manipulates public opinion during war or political crises. Fakes are used to demoralise society and to increase panic. Most often, fakes are created through news, images or even videos. The primary purpose of a fake is to deceive or provoke an emotional response. Fakes can reach a vast audience in a short time. One thousand four hundred news stories that were distributed in Ukrainian content from September to October 2024 were analysed (Fig. 4.1). The dataset was built in such a way that it recorded information that was published on the Internet on sites that distribute news, on social networks Telegram, Facebook, and Instagram.

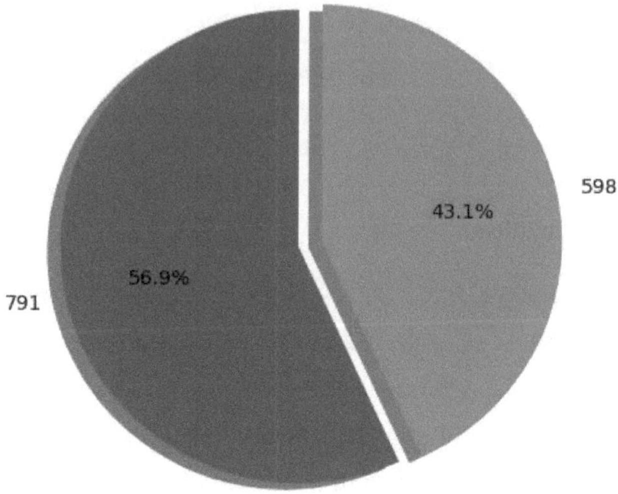

Fig. 4.1. The distribution of real news and fake news in the dataset

Distribution in the dataset of news Telegram, Facebook, news on sites, Instagram, Twitter, Vkontakte, and Yandex is shown in Fig. 4.2, Fig. 4.3, Fig. 4.4, and Fig. 4.5.

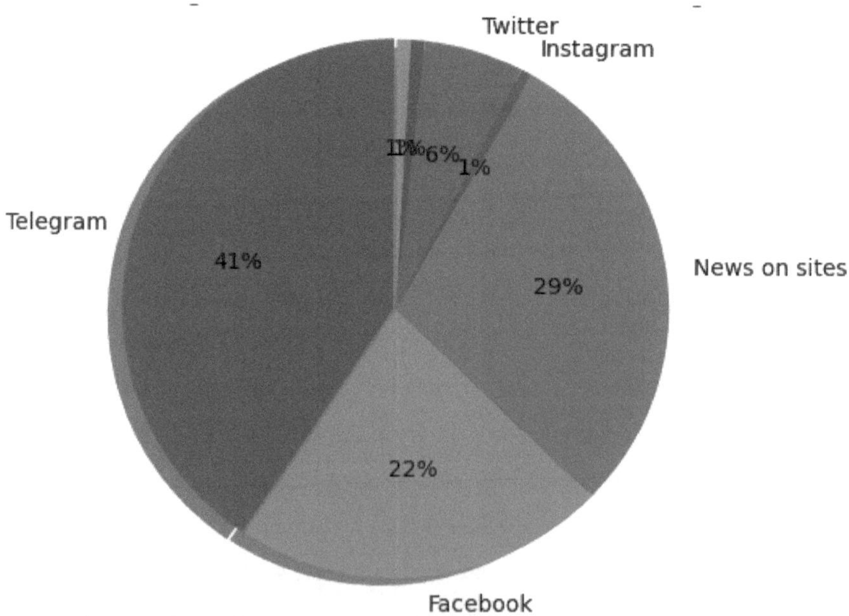

Fig. 4.2. Distribution of messages and fake messages in Telegram, Facebook, news on the sites, Instagram, Twitter, Vkontakte, Yandex

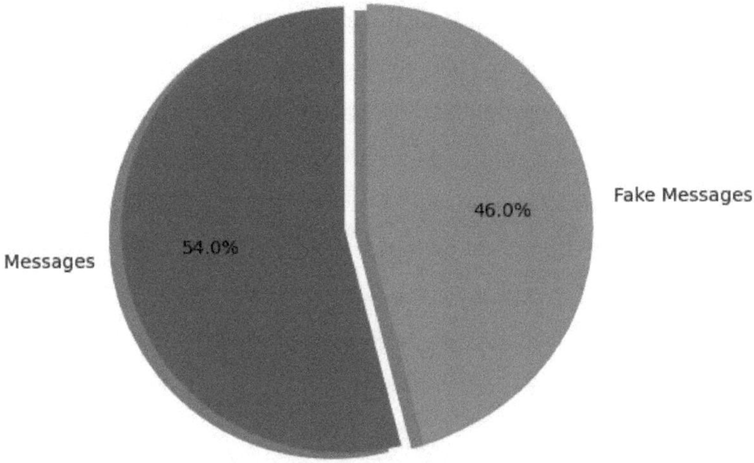

Fig. 4.3. Distribution of messages and fake messages on Facebook

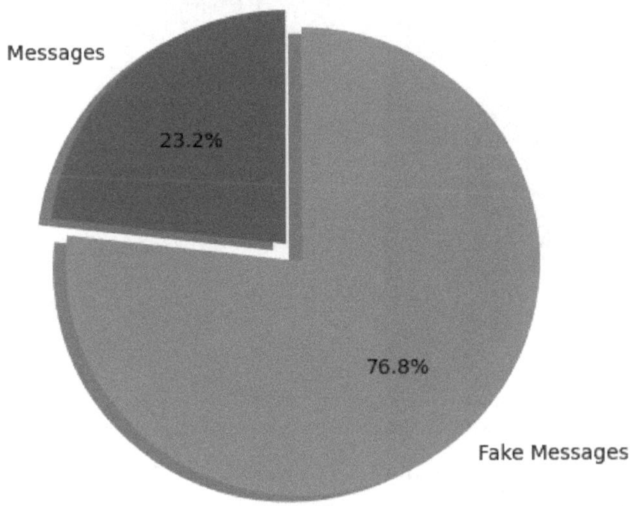

Fig. 4.4. Distribution of messages and fake messages in news on the sites

In this way, the dataset was formed because there were equal numbers of "true" and fake messages. Seven thousand likes were received by a fake Telegram message with the following content: "The Russian army destroyed the point of temporary deployment of Ukrainian fighters in Sumy – explosions can still be heard in the city. Today, the Air Force of the Russian Federation did not stop at what was achieved in Poltava and continued in the same spirit - yes, the Russian army struck the point of temporary deployment of the Armed Forces in Sumy. As is customary with the enemy, the location was in the building of the local university. According to preliminary information, the reserves were located there, which were probably supposed to go to the slaughter for Russian weapons in the Kursk border area. A little less, 6.7 thousand. Likes were received by a fake message on Twitter with the following content: "NEWSFLASH: 'If I wanted to see a drug addict, I'd just take a walk around Tijuana,' Mexico's elected president explained why she declined Zelensky's invitation to visit Kyiv." Third place, with 5 thousand likes, is taken by a fake message on Twitter with the following content.

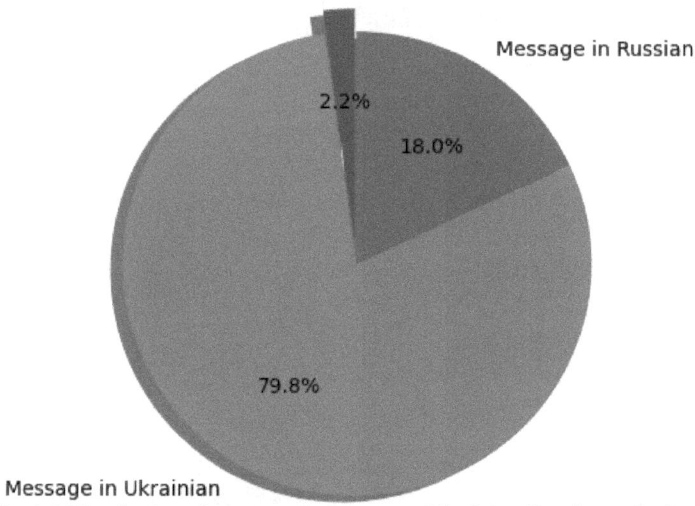

Fig. 4.5. Distribution of messages in languages Ukrainian, Russian and other

"AZOV committed atrocities. They cut off the heads of older people and tortured children. But the biggest horror is the mercenaries. They hung the flag of France in the neighbouring village" - Rashistka from Korenevo"

Among the actual messages, about 39,000 people liked the message with the following content: "15 Azov servicemen have been returned from captivity!" published in Telegram. Average readers also like the news: "The national futsal team of Ukraine defeated the Netherlands and reached the quarterfinals of the 2024 World Cup. In the 1/4 finals, 'blue and yellow' will play against the winner of the Spain-Venezuela match." More than 3,500 readers liked it.

People also like the news "Kyiv. Okhmatdyt Hospital. The largest children's hospital in Ukraine. Children and adults are pulled out from under the rubble – ruined resuscitation. The new hospital building and half of the old one have been destroyed. The situation is tough." 3.8 thousand people liked her on Facebook. Among the fake news, the words "warrior", "satisfied", "horror", "shock", "unbelievable", and "rashishtka" were most often found.

4.2. Model training using SVM

In the first stage, training data is formed. To train the model, we need samples of goods with already known HS codes and their descriptions. If you don't have codes for all products, some products will only be used for prediction (classification) when the model is ready. We divide the data into training and test sets - 70-80% for training and 20-30% for testing. We use the training set to train the SVM model. In the next step, the data is cleaned and standardised for further use in the algorithms. The product description undergoes linguistic processing to highlight critical characteristics. By tokenisation, we divide the text into separate words or phrases. Text conversion into numerical vectors occurs using the TF-IDF or Word2Vec methods.

Next, we train the model on the data where there are appropriate HS codes, and it will be able to use this information to predict the codes for new goods.

HS or HTS codes for new products are assigned after model training. Use a model to predict HS codes for goods for which a description is available, but the code is unknown. To assign HS codes, goods already described with known codes are used to train the classification model.

A program for detecting fakes in a dataset can use machine learning and natural language processing methods [156-157]. The basic idea is to train a model on a dataset where authentic and fake news (or other types of information) are already marked. The model can then be used to classify new data.

Machines are great at processing structured data. When it comes to processing free-form text, machines have a hard time. Natural Language Processing NLP aims to develop algorithms that allow computers to recognise free text. The sheer number of possible variations is one of the biggest challenges in natural language processing. Context is vital for understanding the meaning of specific sentences.

```
# 1. #Download dataset Fafes. xlsx
file_path = './Fakes-29.xlsx'
df = pd.read_excel(file_path)
```

1. Python programming was selected to implement the task. All new items were collected from the dataset, and the column under the name “mark” is equal to zero for further analysis. At the end of the analysis, the following will be identified:

- Suspicious words. These are the words that are most often used when writing fake news.
- The language in which fake news is most often written.
- The source of literature is the one who publishes such news most often.
- Confidence that the novelty is fake when guessing words, phrases, and sentences.

We analyse hundreds of data relations based on which dataset compositions:

```
# 2. Statistics by language
valid_languages = ['ukrainian', 'urk',
'russian','rus','english', 'french', 'rus', 'ros',
'ukrainian', 'ukr'] # Valid values of languages
df['Language'] = df['Language'].str.lower() # Lower the value
for correct counting
language_counts = df['Language'].value_counts(normalize=True)
* 100 # Percentage ratio
language_counts =
language_counts[language_counts.index.isin(valid_languages)] #
Leave only valid languages
print("Percentage of news by language:")
```

```
print(language_counts)
```

The Ukrainian language is implemented in the data set - 51%, Russian - 30%, English - 4%, other languages - 15%.

We analyse the number of new products at the right time.

```
# 3. Convert all data to a datetime format
# Let's try to convert string values to time format
df['time'] = pd.to_datetime(df['time'], errors='coerce',
format='%H:%M:%S')
# Let's check which lines could not be converted
invalid_times = df[df['times'].isna()]
if not invalid_times.empty:
 print(f"Number of invalid time data:
{invalid_times.shape[0]}")
# We extract an hour for further statistics
df['Hour'] = df['time'].dt.hour
# We determine the time of day based on the hour
def get_time_of_day(hour):
 if 6 <= hour < 12:
 return 'Morning'
 elif 12 <= hour < 18:
 return 'Day'
 elif 18 <= hour < 24:
 return 'Evening'
 otherwise:
 return 'Night'
# We use the function to determine the time of day
df['Time of day'] = df['Hour'].apply(get_time_of_day)
# We count the number of news by time of day
time_of_day_counts = df['Time of day'].value_counts()
print("Distribution of news by time of day:")
print(time_of_day_counts)
```

The results of this code are:

```
Day 353
Evening 305
```

```
Morning 222
Night 177
```

We filter the entries, and new ones are marked with a 0, which means they are fake. A new DataFrame, fake_news, has been created to replace the fake news. Three columns of fake news are collected – texts and movies.

```
# 4. # Filter records where "label" == 0 (fake news)
fake_news = data[data['label'] == 0]
# We receive texts, languages and sources of fake news
texts = fake_news['message text'].fillna("").astype(str) #
Replace missing values
languages = fake_news['Language']
sources = fake_news['Source']
```

It is possible to predict the frequencies of words that appear to be suspicious (those that move more often beyond the middle). The script combines all the texts of fake news in one row, breaks them down into words, and converts them to lowercase. For additional help, the frequency of the skin word is monitored. Then, the average frequency of words is calculated, and words that occur more often than the average are added to the list of suspicious words.

```
#5. Analysis of words: combine texts into one line and count
the frequency of words
combined_text = " ".join(texts) # All texts in one line
words = re.findall(r'\b\w+\b', combined_text.lower()) #
Tokenization of words (break into words)
word_counts = Counter(words) # Count the frequency of words
# Selection of words that occur frequently (above average
level)
average_word_frequency = sum(word_counts.values()) /
len(word_counts)
suspicious_words = {word: count for word, count in
word_counts.items() if count > average_word_frequency}
```

After selecting the data, the fake_probability_and_statistics function calculates the likelihood of a novelty being fake by analysing text, language and news. Vaughn calculates suspicious words in the text and phrases for language, then combines these factors with words: words (50%), language (25%), and language (25%). The result is a counterfeit virality of the fakeness of the new product.

```
#6. Function for calculating the probability of fakeness and
statistics
def fake_probability_and_statistics(text, language, source):
 # Text analysis: tokenisation and counting of "suspicious"
words
 words_in_text = re.findall(r'\b\w+\b', text.lower())
 total_word_count = len(words_in_text)
 # Probability by word: the ratio of the number of "fake"
words to the total number of words
 fake_words_in_text = [word for word in words_in_text if word
in suspicious_words]
 fake_word_count = len(fake_words_in_text)
 # We determine the probability based on suspicious words
 word_based_probability = (fake_word_count / total_word_count)
if total_word_count > 0 else 0
 # Probability based on language: frequency of fake news for
that language
 language_risk = language_distribution.get(language, 0) /
len(languages) if len(languages) > 0 else 0
 # Probability based on source: frequency of fake news for
this source
 source_risk = source_distribution.get(source, 0) /
len(sources) if len(sources) > 0 else 0
 # Total probability of fakeness (weights: words – 50%,
language – 25%, source – 25%)
 total_probability = word_based_probability * 0.5 +
language_risk * 0.25 + source_risk * 0.25
 return {
 "total_probability": total_probability,
 "words_stats": {
 "fake_word_count": fake_word_count,
 "fake_words_in_text": fake_words_in_text # Suspicious words
```

```
in the text },
 "language_stats": {
 "language": language,
 "language_risk": language_risk },
 "source_stats": {
 "source": source,
 "source_risk": source_risk } }
```

When working with the text, you must break it into smaller parts for analysis. Tokenisation breaks the input text into more minor elements, such as words or sentences. These elements are called tokens.

Let's move on to the analysis. The loop goes through all the fake news, extracts its text and language, calls the fake_probability_and_statistics function to expand the probability of fakeness, and saves the results in the statistics list.

```
#7. Analysis for each message
statistics = []
for i in range(len(fake_news)):
 text = texts.iloc[i]
 language = languages.iloc[i]
 source = sources.iloc[i]
 # We get probability and statistics
 stat = fake_probability_and_statistics(text, language,
source)
 statistics.append(stat)
```

Finally, the max() function is used to assign the index of the new product with the highest probability of fakeness, equal to the value of the total probability of all new products, after which data about this new product is saved.

```
#8. Finding the maximum probability of fakeness
max_probability_index = max(range(len(statistics)), key=lambda
i: statistics[i]['total_probability'])
max_stat = statistics[max_probability_index]
# Extraction of unique suspicious words from news text with
maximum probability
unique_suspicious_words =
```

```
set(max_stat['words_stats']['fake_words_in_text'])
# Output results for the most likely fake news
print(f"\ This news has the highest probability of being fake
with the following characteristics:"):")
print(f" Suspicious words: {',
'.join(unique_suspicious_words)}")
print(f" Language: {max_stat['language_stats']['language']}")
print(f" Source: {max_stat['source_stats']['source']}")
# Calculation of the probability of fakeness for the mentioned
words, languages and sources
combined_probability = max_stat['total_probability']
# Derivation of general probability with formulation
print(f"\ With the mentioned words, languages and sources, the
total probability of fakeness is {combined_probability:.2f}")
```

We finish everything by demonstrating the results of the robot script.

In this way, the most suspicious words in fake news were obtained: children, bribes, refugees, steel, classes, directors, Ukrainians, Poles, and a large number. The total probability of words being fake is 0.68.

4.3. Conclusions for Chapter 4

A dataset analysis on "Fake news" was conducted based on language, source, and news text criteria. After that, the maximum probability that the news is fake based on specific words, languages, and sources was determined. Python was also used to write the script.

A software product was obtained that allows you to identify words that appear in fake messages with a probability of 0.68 in current news.

Chapter 5. Relationships knowledge graphs construction between evidence based on crime reports

The chapter is written based on publications and research [158-189].

5.1. Concepts of relationships in knowledge graphs construction

Increasing the level of social crime and a lot of text data requires the use of intellectual analysis of the text to develop optimal prevention methods and tools [158-161]. We explore the extent to which thematic text analysis of crime investigation chronicle reports will lead to higher crime concentration and identification levels. The knowledge graph at work is based on a framework for the chronology of the investigation of murders. It can help investigators in analysing the data of the murder case. So, it allows for content analysis of identification keywords and whether the murder will eventually be solved. We use keyword extensions to identify different types of evidence and link these entities and evidence to build a knowledge graph about murder investigations. The effectiveness of the method lies in comparison with analogies for similar tasks in the application of semantic analysis to create a knowledge graph in the form of an ontology and further research of the relationships between the statistical data of the weighted graph for the subsequent disclosure of criminal offences, in particular, the disclosure of murders. Specialised, territorially distributed intelligent systems of preliminary investigation bodies are complex programs installed in automated workplaces of investigators and heads of preliminary investigation bodies, united in local computing networks and working with a dedicated database server or at autonomous workplaces. Structurally, the PSB consists of four levels of management: federal, regional, subscriber, and independent work. PSB at the national (federal), regional, and subscriber levels is a set of software and technical complexes consisting of AWP investigators, AWP heads of investigative units, and database servers combined into local computing networks. The functional purpose of the federal-level PSB is to automate procedural activities in investigating the most complex, interregional and international nature of organised crimes and control their investigation [162-165]. Interpol's Global Closed Information and Telecommunication System is designed to solve the following tasks:

- Improving the efficiency of exchanging official and confidential (operational-search) information on combating international crime;
- The access system organisation of law enforcement agencies to the information stored in international banks of criminal information data;
- Implementing the information strategy of the General Secretariat of Interpol based on new information technologies;
- Improving reliability and ensuring the continuity of international information exchange.

A centralised interdepartmental data bank of electronic copies of materials of criminal cases is designed for prompt submission of information of the following form: about the investigating body; about persons who have been brought to criminal responsibility; the nature and qualification of the crime committed; about the objects of criminal encroachments; about witnesses who have been held in criminal cases. The structure of the central library consists of the following subsystems:

- An information input subsystem is designed to ensure the functioning of the mechanisms for replenishing the central bank, delivering new ones and changes to existing storage facilities. The result of the work of this subsystem is the accumulation on the disk subsystem of the Centre for storing electronic copies of materials of criminal cases received in the form of original files containing them.
- A subsystem of primary information processing, designed for processing electronic copies of materials of criminal cases.

So, at present, the following promising directions for the use of computer technologies in the activities of the investigator are distinguished:

1. Registration of materials of criminal cases and official

documentation with the help of standard programs;

2. Obtaining consulting legal assistance, legal and regulatory documents, as well as the generation of forms of procedural documents using automated reference and legal systems and Internet resources;

3. Automation and improvement of the efficiency of detection, fixation, seizure, and preliminary study of evidence in criminal cases.

5.2. Methods and materials

The project begins with selecting text documents to be used as input for the Natural Language Processing System [166-170]. These documents are in English and can be found on the websites referenced by this report. The information that will be seized includes people, places, dates, events, relationships, weapons, crimes committed and others [171]. Users can choose the text data they want to use as input for the system. The system must extract information from the selected document. We also present a methodology for expanding keywords to extract evidence from chronology records [172-173]. The system architecture provides detailed information on how components or modules are integrated as Tokeniser, Sentence Crusher (this component divides the input text into sentences), POS Tagger, Named Entity Recognition and also [174-175]:

- Annotations. The annotation template language is used to map patterns and add annotations to the corresponding templates.
- Coreference Resolution. The Deterministic Coreference Graph (dCoref) is integrated into the Stanford NLP Toolkit. dCoref is added to the end of the list of text annotations.

Based on the research [176-189] and requirements by the system (Table 5.1), the following features of software solutions that work in the field of NLP are highlighted:

- Use of private datasets. Considered analogues most likely use machine learning to implement sentiment analysis, namely the methods of "learning with a teacher" and deep learning. These methods require a training sample on which the accuracy of the analysis depends. There is a limited number of public datasets for sentiment analysis of text, and their use in different software solutions can lead to similar text analysis results. However, using private datasets gives the product uniqueness, and such a dataset will have a larger sample. Thus, Google has access to much personal data in many world languages, which makes it possible to constantly train a machine learning model, directly affecting its accuracy. Confirmation of these words is the popularity of the Google NLP API.

- Running the service in the cloud. The ability to run a software solution in the cloud has many advantages, among which are the following: use on different devices, reduction of hardware costs, secure data storage, and ease of installation and service. The following analogues use cloud technology: Google NLP API, Lexalytics, MeaningCloud, and Microsoft Azure text analytics API.
- Several methods of working with the text are provided. The main problem described in this work is sentiment analysis, or extracting emotions from the text. Analogous software solutions and direct sentiment analysis enable the user to perform Summarisation, Intention Analysis, Categorisation, Theme Extraction, Named Entity Extraction, etc. Additional modules provide a larger volume of service users.
- Working with text involves additional functionality. These software solutions perform direct sentiment analysis of arbitrary entered text and other types of text analysis. They may also have different capabilities for working with various data sources, such as user searches, Twitter, etc. For example, for a user to perform a sentiment analysis of his product on Twitter, he does not need to collect data manually - the software solution will do it for him and show the result.
- It is possible to use it for users who do not know the NLP area. The essence of this point is that users of the service do not need knowledge of NLP to use the software solution. So, the user can enter only arbitrary text, press the analysis button, and visualise the required results.
- Ability to use as an API. Some analogues have the possibility of

integration into other systems. That is, the owners of software solutions provide their API to developers who seek to integrate them into systems.

Table 5.1. Fulfilment of requirements by the system developed in the innovative DS-Startup for the linguistic system for fake/propaganda identification or criminal report analysis

Class	Business	User	Functional	Non-functional
Requirements content example	Product based on the semantic analysis of texts, websites of newspapers, or criminal reports. Relevant to businesses that conduct field marketing surveys. Works with typed text, text from text files, and specified newspaper websites. Provided an API for working with neural networks for external systems. Effects: time, economic, and technological.	1. Visitor/user with subscription, marketer. 2. Semantic analysis of the text. Automated analysis of a sample of newspapers/reports. 3. Effects: time 4. To use all functions, the user must register and subscribe to the service. 5. API access must be confirmed for developers.	1. Executes processes of user authorisation; analyses the entered text, text from files, and text from websites of natural language newspapers/reports. 2. Textual content downloading, text input, and parsing of websites according to selected markup elements. 3. A single flow carries out all actions.	Users are divided into roles to which part of the functionality is attached. System quality attributes: efficiency, reliability, and convenience. Requirement for interfaces: users without specialised knowledge must be able to use them.
Fulfilment of requirements in the developed information technology	Reduce the time needed to analyse arbitrary text/reports. Provide the user with truthful information about emotions/keywords in the text/reports. Provide developers with quick access to ready-made models designed for content analysis.	- System authorisation. - Text interface. - Interface for working with files. - Results display interface.	- Semantic analysis of any textual content/reports. - Semantic analysis of content from text files.	The functionality does not require the user to have specialised skills. The accuracy of the neural network should be greater than 92%.

– Along with using NLP methods, we will also use the solution tree method to classify crime types (Fig. 5.1) [174].

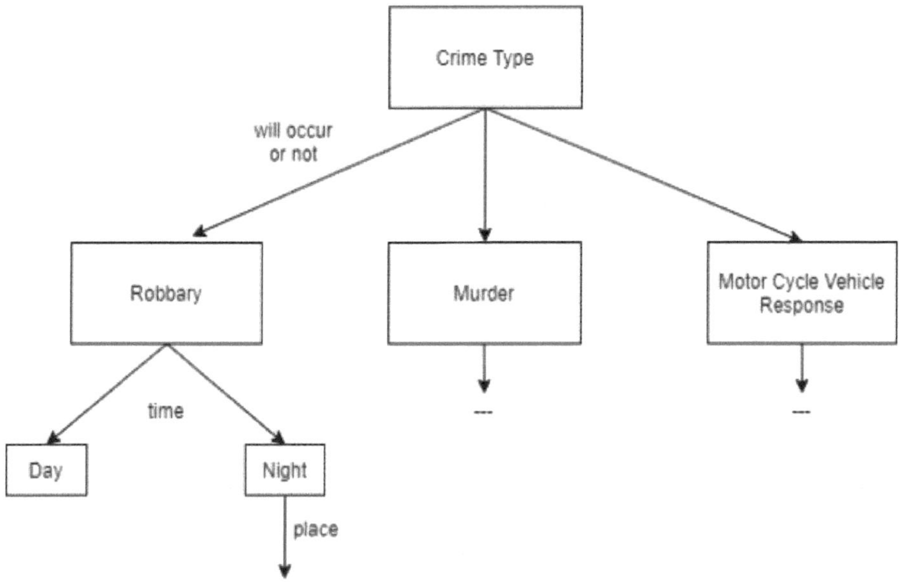

Fig. 5.1. Using the solution tree

For this project, the following methods were chosen (Fig. 5.2) [174]: semantic analysis, semantic role labelling, frame semantics, pre-processing, data clean-up method, missing data, filling missing values, and level encoding [175].

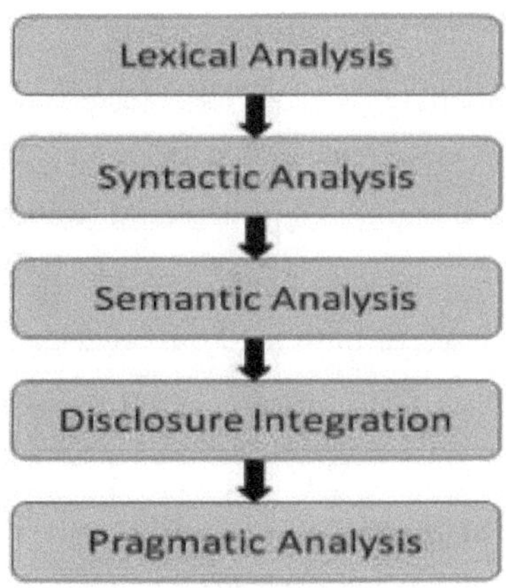

Fig. 5.2. The sequence of application of NLP techniques

5.3. Experiments and results of the system

A. Description of design requirements for the product. Stakeholders of the precedent and their requirements:

- The Ministry of Internal Affairs: should monitor the entire investigation process and, if necessary, adjust its progress;
- Investigator: must correctly enter all known data into the system, which will model the crime based on it;
- Police officers and/or detectives: must investigate the crime scene, interview witnesses, and provide the investigator with all other necessary information;
- Commissioner of Police: strives to keep the investigation under control, to have quick access to the progress of the research;
- Criminal: commits a crime, wants to avoid punishment;
- Victims and victims of crime: they want the perpetrator to be punished.

The leading actor of the precedent: the investigator simulates the circumstances of the crime using a computer. Preconditions of the precedent:

- The perpetrator commits a crime;
- Detectives and/or police officers or others must discover the crime;
- Eyewitnesses must testify;
- Police officers and/or detectives must find all possible leads to pass on to the investigator;
- The investigator must pass identification before they can work with the computer.
- The investigator must analyse the evidence obtained from the crime scene and select the most significant features suitable for processing in the computer;
- The investigator should write down these signs as conditions that should be taken into account when putting forward possible versions;

- The system should form versions composed of features that create the criminal portrait/profile;
- The system conducts a comprehensive assessment of the version, which allows weighing enough known data to decide the features of the criminal's portrait/profile.

Basic successful scenario:

- The investigator enters the necessary data into the system;
- The investigator analyses the obtained results (posterior probabilities of versions);
- The investigator decides on the reliability of the results and further actions.

Expansion of the main script or alternative flows: (inaccuracy or insufficient data):

- The system informs the investigator about the error, who, in turn, initiates the cancellation of data entry;
- System of some data, or the possibility of analysing with existing data, or the possibility of filling in the "gaps" with data from other similar crimes;
- The investigator chooses one of the proposed options, and then starts the procedure again (step one in the "successful scenario").

Post-conditions: all data (evidence) known to the investigation have been processed and stored in the system; a knowledge-based graph and an assessment of possible connections between evidence of a crime; the relevant results are transferred to the database and/or to the appropriate authorities for further investigative actions (arrest, filing of suspicion, etc.). Special requirements: it is necessary to provide a multilingual user interface; it is essential to ensure the reliability of preservation of investigative evidence; it is required to conduct the primary analysis; it is necessary to verify the evidence authenticity from the crime scene; it is required to update the system protocols and principles in parallel with the development and complication of crimes. List of necessary technologies and additional devices:

- The system must be synchronised with the database of other services of the Ministry of Internal Affairs;
- The system must use data encryption technologies;
- The user (investigator) enters data using a keyboard, touch screen or voice input or imports it from another source.

Actors of the proposed product:

- Ministry of Internal Affairs: an actor who controls the entire investigation process and, if necessary, adjusts its progress; it is also responsible for the further fate of the criminal after capture.
- Investigator: an actor who enters all known data into the system, which models the crime based on it;
- Police and detectives: actors who investigate a crime scene, question witnesses and provide the investigator with all other necessary information; police officers also report to criminal investigation officers.
- Police commissioner: the actor who keeps the investigation under control, has quick access to the course of the inquiry, carries out various procedural and investigative actions;
- Criminal investigation officer: the actor who is responsible for the transfer of the criminal to the Ministry of Internal Affairs;
- Criminal: an actor who is wanted for a crime;
- Injured (victim): provide testimony; they want the perpetrator to be punished.

We will describe the central stereotypes, attributes and operations of the system classes ():

- For the Access class, add operations: Add, Create, Delete, Edit and Find access. Each listed process has the identifier of the criminal investigation worker (Integer) and the visibility quantifier private, having previously checked his role (cio_role_id: String). As the type of the returned result, choose the Boolean type and set the employee ID in the system as an integer argument.
- For the Case class, add an operation: Add, Create, Delete, Edit, Close

and Find case and Attach crime. Attach the crime operation as an integer argument, and set the crime identifier in the system.

- For the Crime class, add operations: Add, Delete, Edit, Add evidence, Edit evidence, Search crime.
- For the Criminal Investigation Officer class, add the operation: Add, Delete, Edit, and Submit a report.
- For the Intruder class, add an operation: Addition, Removal, Editing, Accusation, Removal, Arrest, Search for an intruder.
- For the Criminal report class, add the following operations: Add, Delete, Search, and Print report.
- For the Investigator class, add the operation: Add, Edit, Delete, Search for an investigator, Conduct an analysis, Create a portrait of a criminal (posterior probabilities of versions: Float).
- For the Policeman (detective) class, add the operation: Add, Edit, Delete, Search for a police officer, Collect evidence, Identify a criminal.

Each of the operations has a public visibility quantifier. The type of the returned result should be chosen as the Boolean type. Table 5.2 shows a description of the main product classes and also describes the relationship between the primary classes. The component diagram shows service components, dependencies and connections between them. Fig. 5.3 shows a diagram of service components. The diagram has two main components: the service and the application. Interaction between them is carried out using the application interface. The service component provides everything related to the user account, such as registration, authorisation, subscription, etc. Through the service, the user connects to the application and can use the analysis of manually entered text or use the analysis of articles in English. With the help of the application name, the connection between text input and the sentiment analysis component is made. With the application method, there is a connection between the elements of working with websites and the sentiment analysis component.

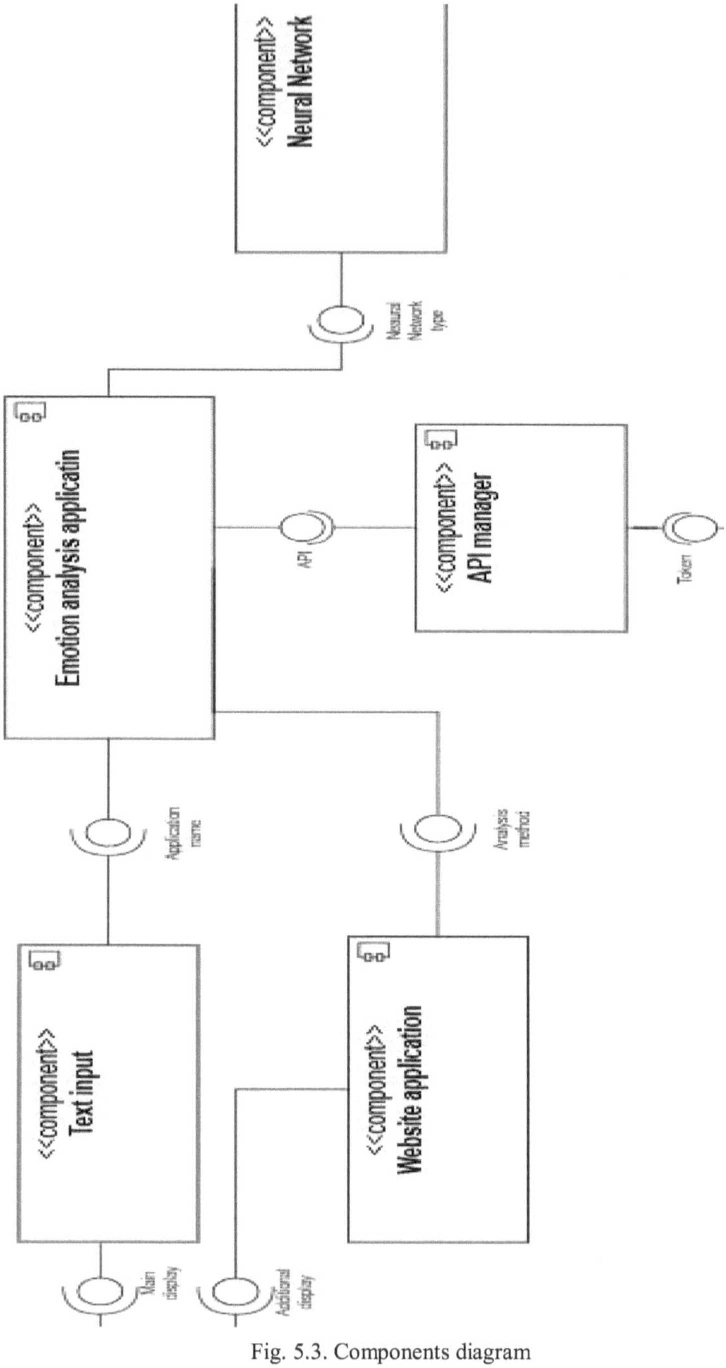

Fig. 5.3. Components diagram

Table 5.2. Description of main product classes

Classes		Attributes	Methods	
Intruder	Crime commitment	Intruder ID, Intruder Name, Phone number, Intruder Address, Etc.	addCriminal(), accuseCriminal(), arrestCriminal(), etc.	Adding an Intruder, Accusing an Intruder, Arresting an Intruder.
Police-man	Data collection	Police ID, Policeman's name, Phone number, E-mail, Login, Password, Etc.	addPolice(), searchCrimeScene(), collectEvidence(), findCriminal() etc.	Adding a police officer, collecting evidence, searching for an intruder, Etc.
Case	Display of processes and the order of execution of actions	Case ID, investigator ID, Attacker ID, Case Description, Case Name Etc.	addCase(),searchCase() , addEvidence(),deleteEvidence() etc.	Adding a case, searching for a case, and adding and removing evidence.
Inves-tigator	Develop a solution model	Investigator ID, Contact details of the investigator, Etc.	addInvest(), performAnalysis(), estimateVetsions(), createCriminalPortrait( )	Adding a crime, analysing versions, and creating a portrait of a criminal.
Crime	Everything related to the description and preservation of the crime	Crime ID, Crime Name, Type of Crime, Crime Description, Intruder ID	addCrime(), addEvidence(), editEvidence(), editCrime() etc.	Adding crime/evidence. Editing crime/evidence.

The sentiment analysis component is connected to the neural network by calling this neural network. The sentiment analysis component provides an API to the manager API connected to the external environment using a token. Additional objects, connections and methods:

- Objects of classes with the names: Commissioner, Criminal, Police / Detective, System interface, Database, Personal cabinet, Corresponding analysis algorithm;
- Links connecting objects of classes with names: Personal cabinet with the Database, Database with the Police / Detective and System Interface with

the Corresponding algorithm of analysis;

- Method: catch(), directed from the object of the Police / Detective class to the object of the Criminal class;
- Method: pass_identification(), sent from the object of the class-actor investigator to the Personal object cabinet;
- Method: provide_testimony (), directed from the object of the Police / Detective class to the object of the actor class Investigator;
- Method: add_access(), directed from the Personal account to the object of the class-actor investigator;
- Method: request_additional_evidence() sent from the object of the actor class Investigator to the object of the class Police / Detective;
- Method: enter_known_data(), directed from the object of the class-actor investigator to the object System Interface;
- Method: transfer_list_possible_versions (List) sent from the object Corresponding algorithm of analysis to the object of the class-actor investigator;
- Method: compare_portrait_intruder(), directed from the object of the actor class Investigator to the object database;
- Method: make_corrections(), sent from the object of the class-actor investigator to the object corresponding to the algorithm of analysis;
- Method: send_omens() directed from the object Database of days to the Police / Detective class object.

B. Create a network graph and add nodes. First, we initialise an empty network graph object. Graph() relies on code at the beginning of the notebook that says that networks are imported as nx (replace 'nx' with 'networkx' if preferred).

```
In [ ]:
social_network = nx.Graph()
social_network.add_nodes_from(unique_people)
social_network.nodes
```

C. Add borders to a network graphic. Assuming we don't want a directional or weighted graph, we can up-give edges quite simply with code almost identical to the code we used to add nodes. This time, another line of code calls for a different but obviously similar function to look at the edges.

```
In [ ]:
social_network.add_edges_from(co_occurring_pairs)
social_network.edges
```

We need to run more complex code that checks if there is an edge and then either creates it or adds weight to it if appropriate, social_network_weighted.

```
In [ ]:
social_network_weighted = nx.Graph()
social_network_weighted.add_nodes_from(unique_people)
for edge_pair in co_occurring_pairs_weighted:
    if social_network_weighted.has_edge(edge_pair[0],
           edge_pair[1]):
               w = int(edge_pair[2])
               social_network_weighted[edge_pair[0]]
                     [edge_pair[1]]['weight'] += edge_pair[2]
    else:
               social_network_weighted.add_edge(edge_pair[0],
                     edge_pair[1], weight = edge_pair[2])
social_network_weighted.edges
```

D. Introduction to graph information. First, some basic information about our two graphs using the nx.info function.

```
In [ ]:
print(nx.info(social_network))
print('...')
print(nx.info(social_network_weighted))
print("Network density:",
        nx.density(social_network)
print("Network density:",
        nx.density(social_network_weighted))
```

E. Drawing a graph. Now we need different visualisations for our other graphs. Fig. 4 presents an example of the sentence, “The cheerful and drunken men talked aggressively and very loudly”. The two blocks of code below show different ways to visualise graphics (layout, colour, node size, etc.) [14].

This sample code should emphasise that the proposed system extracts keywords related to crime. Crime-related activities can be performed to report crimes or news articles in any regional language.

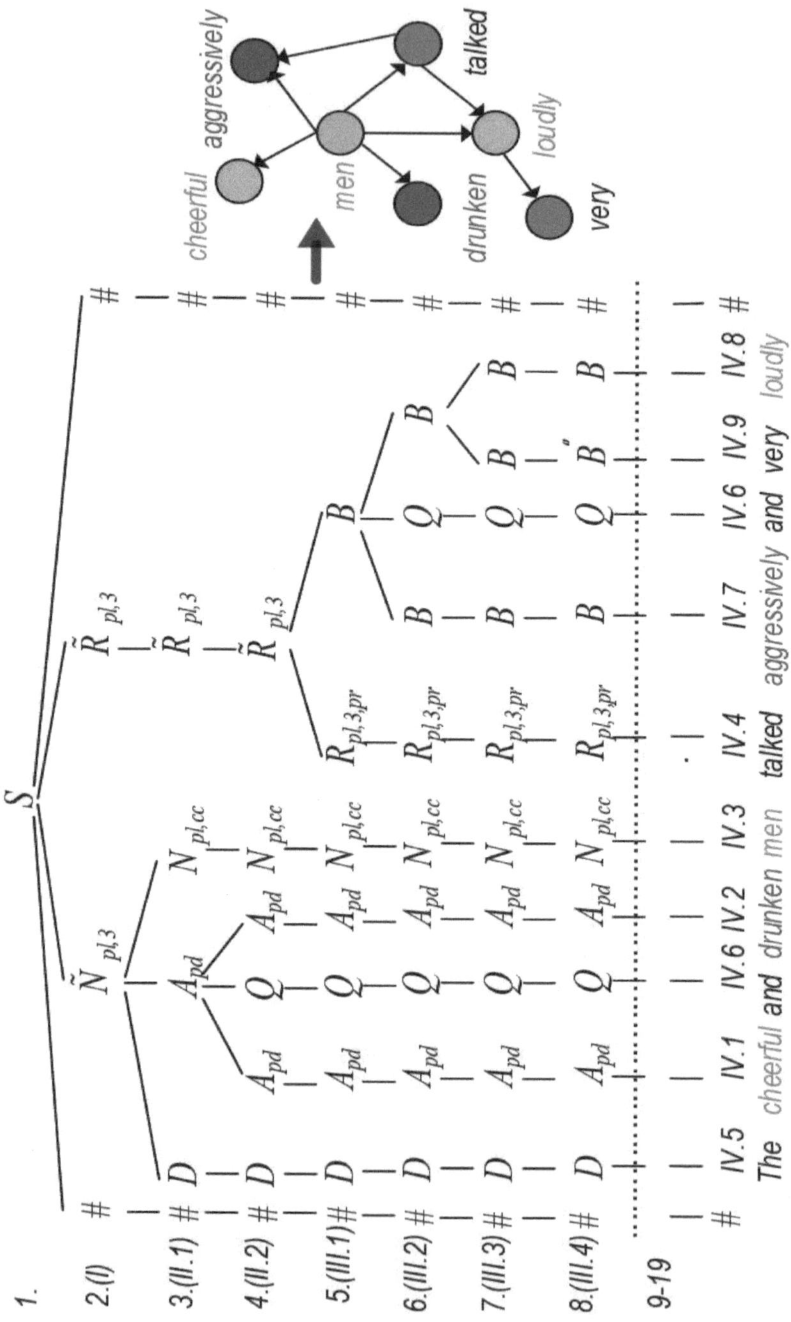

Fig. 5.4. Results of work on the test dataset

5.4. Conclusions for Chapter 5

The chapter describes the knowledge network construction based on knowledge base graphs to timeline the murder investigation. In the context of this project, it is worth thinking about another way to summarise the text with the help of previously built knowledge graphs. Because they are not far from how a typical sentence is constructed, these require contributing factors to be accounted for in artificial intelligence murder investigations. Wrongful convictions can sometimes be related to the false testimony of witnesses, forensic error or unlawful actions of the police. Ultimately, considerations of fairness, accountability, and transparency should be central to developing machine-learning techniques for investigating murders. When writing this work, we show that it is possible to build graphs of knowledge representing the investigation of murders from textual information about the case materials. Features that are important in classifying the solvability of murders (for example, nodes of evidence, suspicious nodes) are consistent with the analysis of the investigation process using other methods.

Chapter 6. Using bigrams with Laplace smoothing to identify disinformation in social media chats

The chapter is based on publications and research [190-194].

6.1. Analysis of smoothing techniques

Effective disinformation detection often requires a combined approach that combines several methods. For example, deep learning for context analysis and machine learning methods for classification can be used, combining them with network analysis or anomaly detection methods to increase the accuracy and efficiency of disinformation detection. The Laplace smoothing method is based on the use of probability correction to avoid zero values in statistical models.

In the case of disinformation identification, it is proposed to use Laplace smoothing to calculate the probabilities of words and bigrams in texts and determine the likelihood of whether the text is authentic or fake. It helps to take into account all possible word variants, even if some of them do not occur in the training data and, accordingly, improve the accuracy of identification.

Laplace smoothing is a powerful mathematical method that can be used to build more stable and efficient models for disinformation identification problems. It has the potential to be used in the context of data processing and analysis, in particular for detecting distorted or false information flows in large volumes of text or media content. In the processes of disinformation identification, Laplace smoothing is proposed to be used for:

- Improving anomaly identification to avoid situations where the model is unable to adequately identify new or unpredictable patterns, as is the case with disinformation using neural networks, respectively.
- Reducing the influence of data on the classification result.
- For tone analysis, thematic modelling or text vectorisation. In the process of generating probabilities for each of the classes (e.g., FAKE-TRUE),

especially when working with Naive Bayes methods or similar statistical models.

In [190], the theory and methods of applying Laplace smoothing to solve nonlinear approximation problems are presented.

In [191], a comparison of several smoothing techniques, including Laplace smoothing, is considered in the context of language modelling. The authors investigate the effect of training data size, corpus, and n-gram order on the effectiveness of the methods.

In [192], the basics of natural language processing are described, including bigram-based models and Laplace smoothing, and how these methods are used to improve probabilistic models.

The book [193] describes algorithms for building in Python and allows for the effective use of Laplace smoothing.

The open web resource [194] analyses the role of propaganda in the context of the war in Ukraine, in particular the use of social networks and traditional media for information dissemination and manipulation.

Various courses and webinars on open web resources allow you to study the features of disinformation processing in depth, for example:

- Stanford CS224N (2022): A course on natural language processing, which includes lectures on probabilistic language models, bigrams, and various smoothing methods, including Laplace, theoretical and practical materials explaining the application of these methods in modern NLP systems. Fig. 6.1 shows the main screen of the course.
- DeepLearning.AI – Natural Language Processing Specialisation (2021): A webinar and course from DeepLearning.AI that covers statistical models, such as bigrams, and smoothing techniques, including Laplace smoothing, as part of the broader concepts of probabilistic language models for NLP tasks. It allows the use of bigrams with Laplace smoothing in the context of recent trends in machine learning and natural language processing. Fig. 6.2 shows the main screen of the webinar.

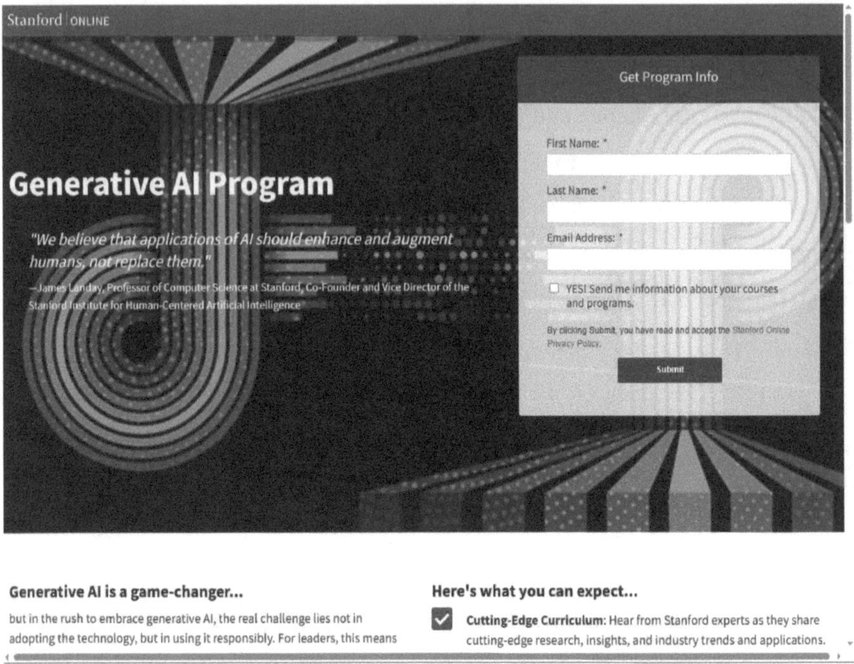

Fig. 6.1. Main screen of the Stanford CS224N course (2022)

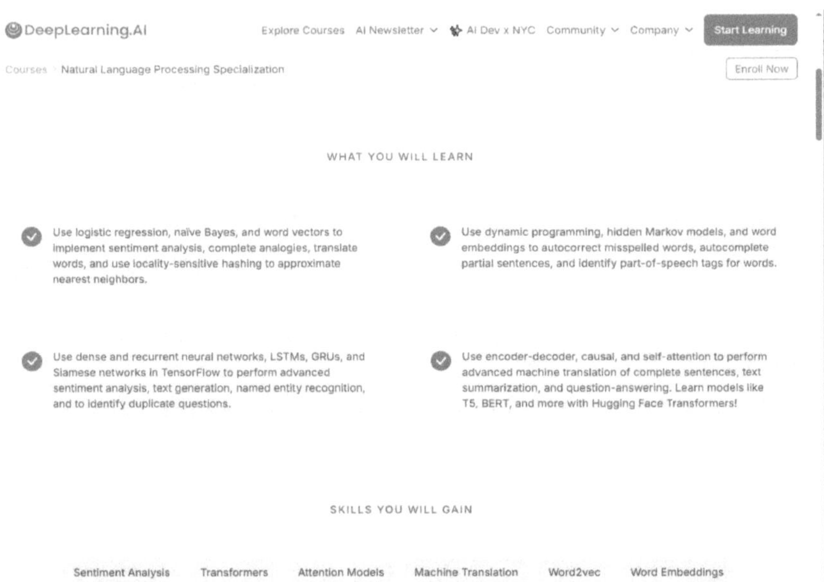

Fig. 6.2. DeepLearning.AI – Natural Language Processing Specialisation webinar

The purpose of the research is to analyse the features of using Laplace smoothing to detect fake news and reduce the likelihood of inappropriate results.

6.2. The main material and substitution of the research results

The features of Laplace smoothing when building a model for classifying news in the context of disinformation, based on individual words or word combinations, make it possible to develop a more accurate architecture for identifying disinformation. It is crucial to train the disinformation processing model on real data, taking into account the fact that some words or word combinations may not occur in the training data, which will lead to incorrect classification and erroneous conclusions. Laplace smoothing accordingly allows the model to make better predictions even with new or rare words that were not previously displayed in the model. Step-by-step algorithm for identifying disinformation using Laplace smoothing:

STEP 1. Data collection and processing. First, you need to collect a large corpus of texts that contain both reliable and unreliable information, for example, news articles, tweets or blog posts. This data should be labelled by type of information. Fig. 6.3 shows a fragment of the developed disinformation dataset for training the model using fake-truth classification.

STEP 2. Decompose the text into bigrams. For example, in the sentence Automatic identification of disinformation there are the following bigrams: Automatic identification, identification of disinformation. Fig. 6.4 shows a fragment of the dataset, demonstrating the presence of a field with expanded texts for further analysis.

STEP 3. Pre-smoothing, i.e., using the Laplace smoothing algorithm. Used in the study to avoid zero probabilities for bigrams that did not occur in the training data using Python tools:

- Example of adding demo data for training the model

```
data = [
    ("Видання Financial Times написало, що після початку
```

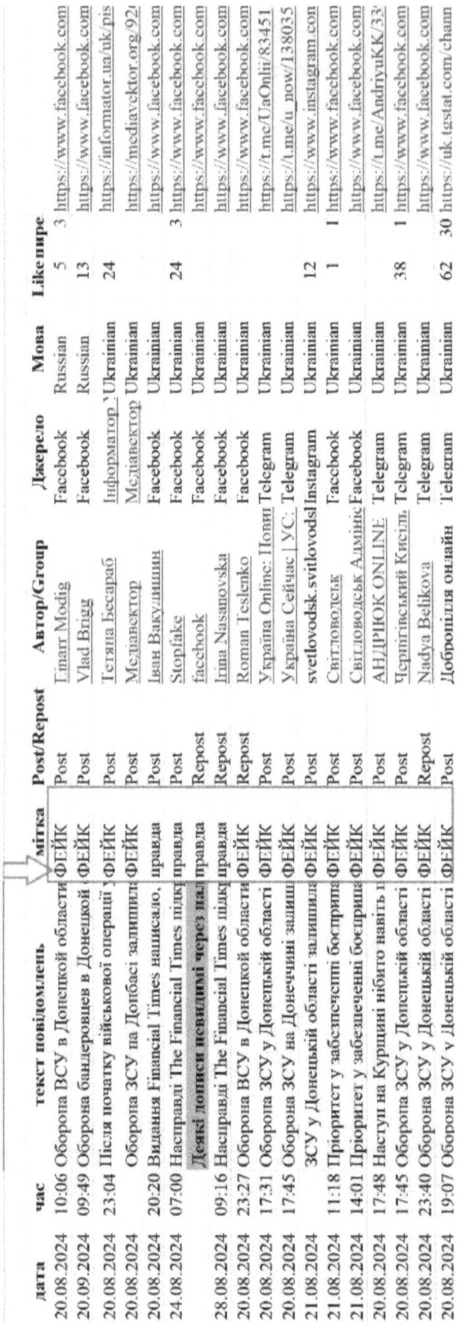

Fig. 6.3. Fragment of the developed dataset

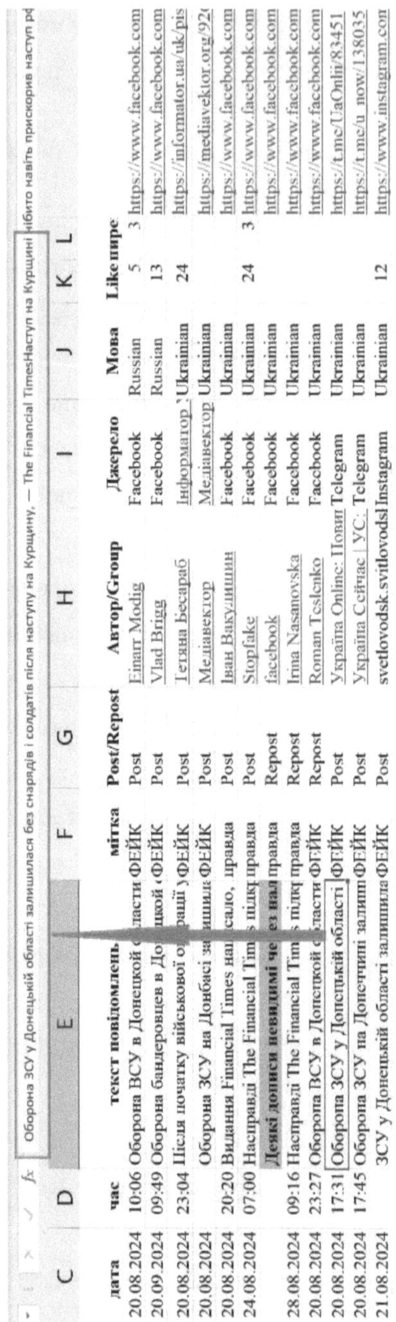

Fig. 6.4. Fragment of the disinformation dataset

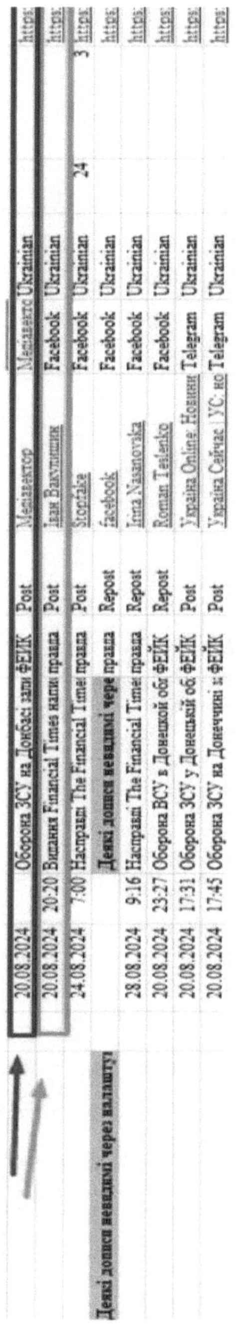

Fig. 6.5 Fragment of the developed dataset

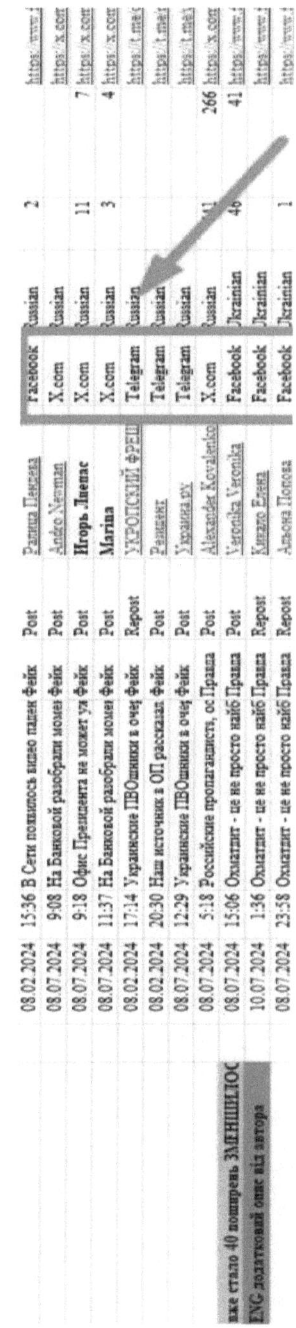

Fig. 6.6. Fragment of the disinformation dataset

```
військової операції у Курській області РФ Збройні сили, які стримують російські війська у Донецькій області, повернулися до нормування снарядів.", "real"),
    ("Оборона ЗСУ на Донбасі залишилася без снарядів і солдатів через Курську операцію", "fake"),
    # Додати інші приклади для більш чіткого навчання]
```

In particular, these texts are added from the developed dataset (Fig. 6.5).

- Example of using bigram frequencies

```
def build_bigram_model(texts, labels):
    bigram_counts = {'fake': defaultdict(int), 'real': defaultdict(int)}
    unigram_counts = {'fake': defaultdict(int), 'real': defaultdict(int)}
    vocab = set()
```

- Example of using Laplace smoothing to calculate probabilities

```
 for text, label in zip(texts, labels):
        words = text.lower().split()
        for i in range(len(words)-1):
            bigram = (words[i], words[i+1])
            bigram_counts[label][bigram] += 1
            unigram_counts[label][words[i]] += 1
            vocab.update([words[i], words[i+1]])
    return bigram_counts, unigram_counts, vocab
```

- An example of using Laplace smoothing

```
 prob = (bigram_count + 1) / (unigram_count + V)
        log_prob += math.log(prob)
    return log_prob
```

STEP 3. Model training and testing. Next, more complex machine learning methods or neural networks are used for classification, while smoothing will help reduce the probability of large errors.

```
bigram_counts, unigram_counts, vocab = build_bigram_model(train_texts, train_labels)
```

STEP 4. Disinformation identification. Based on the training model, it is proposed to create a system that analyses new information flows and determines the probability of whether a text is disinformation, using smoothed probabilities for different categories. It is proposed that Laplace smoothing be integrated into automatic reading of news from files, the web, or telegram channels for analysis, for example, in .txt format. In Fig. 6.6, a fragment of the developed disinformation dataset is shown, which demonstrates the availability of information about the source of the spread of fake or accurate texts.

The text processing algorithm is as follows:

STEP 1. Develop the structure of the texts. Group the texts into FAKE-TRUE folders based on the developed dataset. Each .txt file in these folders is a separate news item.

STEP 2. Read all .txt files:

```
import os
def load_news_from_folders(fake_folder, real_folder):
data = []
```

STEP 3. Read FAKE

```
for filename in os.listdir(fake_folder):
if filename.endswith(".txt"):
with open(os.path.join(fake_folder, filename), "r", encoding="utf-8") as f:
text = f.read().strip()
data.append((text, "fake"))
```

STEP 4. Read TRUE

```
for filename in os.listdir(real_folder):
if filename.endswith(".txt"):
with open(os.path.join(real_folder, filename), "r", encoding="utf-8") as f:
text = f.read().strip()
data.append((text, "real"))
return data
```

STEP 5. Integrate with code Laplace smoothing

Connect the previously described functions: tokenize(), build_bigram_model(), classify()

Therefore, Laplace smoothing adds stability and improves the results of the model, especially in tasks with large amounts of text data.

6.3. Conclusions for Chapter 6

Laplace smoothing allows the model to adapt to situations where certain words or bigrams do not occur in the training data, but may be necessary for identifying fake texts. It allows you to avoid inaccuracies in the processing results and improves the overall efficiency of classification. It is taken into account that bigrams will enable you to take into account the context, unlike individual words, which is especially important for text classification tasks, such as fake-truth (as in the developed disinformation dataset). The study takes into account that for each new text, it is necessary to calculate the logarithmic probability for each class, taking into account Laplace smoothing, which is planned to be shown in subsequent studies, as well as integrating Laplace smoothing with other methods necessary for automatic identification of disinformation.

Chapter 7. Features of identifying product placement misinformation using spaCy to form multiple criteria of inauthentic chat user behaviour

The chapter is written based on publications and research [195-199].

7.1. Basic principles for the formation of a set of criteria for identifying inauthentic behaviour of chat users

The formation of a set of criteria for identifying inauthentic behaviour of chat users allows for effective reduction of the risks of fraud and manipulation in the digital environment. In this context, the analysis of fake product placement is relevant, namely the use of fictional brands, products, or services in the media, which allows for manipulating the context and moods of users. Product placement related to war can be used to create the effect of reality or even strengthen propaganda narratives. Such products can change the perception of society regarding real military conflicts or even push for ideological or political positions.

That is why the identification of disinformation in product placement requires critical thinking. It is necessary to pay attention to the lack of realistic details and the presence of manipulations or similar political narratives that can encourage the creation of false ideas about reality.

To analyse text for product placement, different approaches, such as context analysis, emotional load detection, or pattern recognition models, are proposed to indicate marketing techniques.

In [195], a step-by-step introduction to NLP using spaCy is described with practical tips relevant to the research. Article [196] provides an overview of research on the aggressive behaviour of users on the Internet, in particular, content detection and behavioural analysis on social media. The definition of cyber-aggression, the processes of detecting aggressive content, and the study of the behaviour of aggressive users are considered.

Article [197] describes the prevalence of antisocial behaviour and emphasises that most antisocial behaviour remains unmoderated.

Article [198] examines the features of the use of social networks, in particular Telegram and Viber, as information channels during wartime. Their role in the spread of news and disinformation is considered.

The paper [199] examines the effectiveness of product placement as a tool for influencing consumer behaviour in Ukraine.

The purpose of the study is to analyse the features of product placement analysis regarding disinformation to form a set of criteria for the inauthentic behaviour of chat participants.

7.2. Using spaCy for the text analysis

Determining the criteria for inauthentic behaviour of chat participants is an essential task for analysing interaction in digital environments, such as social networks, forums, chats, or other online platforms. Such behaviour may include manipulation, deception, spam, aggressive interactions or artificially created narratives. The developed disinformation dataset uses the approach of identifying narratives for more accurate text content. Fig. 7.1 shows a fragment of the dataset with a list of manipulative topics.

The analysis of texts is proposed to be carried out using Python code that uses libraries for text analysis, in particular spaCy for natural language processing and TextBlob for simple sentiment analysis, for the following purposes:

- Brand detection using Named Entity Recognition

```
for ent in doc.ents:
print(f'{ent.text}: {ent.label_}')
```

- Use of spaCy for context analysis

For example, analysis using tokenisation using additional libraries or based on syntactic dependencies.

```
for token in doc:
if token.text.lower() == 'propaganda':
```

```
print(f"Found brand '{token.text}' at position {token.i}")
print(f"Previous token: {doc[token.i - 1].text if token.i - 1 >= 0 else 'None'}")
print(f"Next token: {doc[token.i + 1].text if token.i + 1 < len(doc) else 'None'}")
```

НАТО, ЄС
КИЇВСЬКИМ РЕЖИМ-нацистський і терорестичний
МАРОДЕРСТВО на КУРЩИНІ
ПОРУШЕННЯ МІЖНАРОДНОГО ГУМАНІТАРНОГО ПРАВА
ОХМАТДИТ -воєнний госпіталь дитячу лікарню влучила укр ракета
МІНУВАННЯ КУРСЬКОЇ АЕС
УНІВЕРСИТЕТ В СУМАХ
ТОРГОВИЙ ЦЕНТР В ХАРКОВІ
ХІМІЧНА ЗБРОЯ
БІОЛОГІЧНА ЗБРОЯ
БРУДНА ЯДЕРНА БОМБА
ТІЛА НА БЕРЕЗІ ДНІПРА
ЗДАЧА ТЕРИТОРІЙ ПОЛЬЩІ
ВИПЛАТИ ГРОШОВОЇ ДОПОМОГИ
ЦІНА НА СІЛЬ
ЗНИЩЕННЯ ОРЛІВ
ЕПІЦЕНТР В ХАРКОВІ -базування військових
ХАРКІВСЬКА ТИПОГРАФІЯ - безпілотники
ТЕРАКТ В КРОКУС СІТІ ХОЛ
ПОВТОРНЕ ХРЕЩЕННЯ

Fig. 7.1. Fragment of the developed disinformation dataset with propaganda narratives

- Detecting fictional brands. Fake product placement can be searched for using lists of fictional brands if they are already known (e.g. "FAKE Cola" or "TRUE Helmet"). It can be implemented by matching text with predefined lists of brands.

```
fake_brands = ["FAKE Cola ", " TRUE Helmet"]
# Текст з фейковим продакт-плейсментом
text = "He should buy FAKE Cola and TRUE Helmet "
```

- Finding context related to product placement. Syntactic analysis is suggested to understand how brands interact with other parts of the text.

```
# Syntactic dependency analysis
for token in doc:
if token.text == 'Coca-Cola':
print(f'Brand: {token.text}
```

- Search for brands in text

```
brands_found = []
for ent in doc.ents:
if ent.text in target_brands:
brands_found.append(ent.text)
```

- Emotional context analysis using TextBlob

```
blob = TextBlob(text)
sentiment = blob.sentiment.polarity # Values from -1 (negative)
to 1 (positive)
```

- Example of a condition

```
if brands_found and sentiment > 0:
print("This is probably product placement.")
elif brands_found and sentiment < 0:
print("This may be manipulation or negative product placement.")
else:
print("No product placement detected.")
```

Figure 7.2 shows a fragment of the developed disinformation dataset with text content used for analysis.

Product placement as a tool of disinformation in wars can be highly effective in shaping public opinion, increasing political loyalty or creating false images of reality. Using fictional products, brands, and technologies, it is possible to develop ideologically directed narratives that reinforce stereotypes, manipulate emotions, and shape perceptions of war. It is essential to be critical of media content, since such use of product placement can significantly affect the perception of war and politics in general. Identifying disinformation in product placement is a difficult task. To check product placement for disinformation, you need to do the following:

Step 1. Fact checking

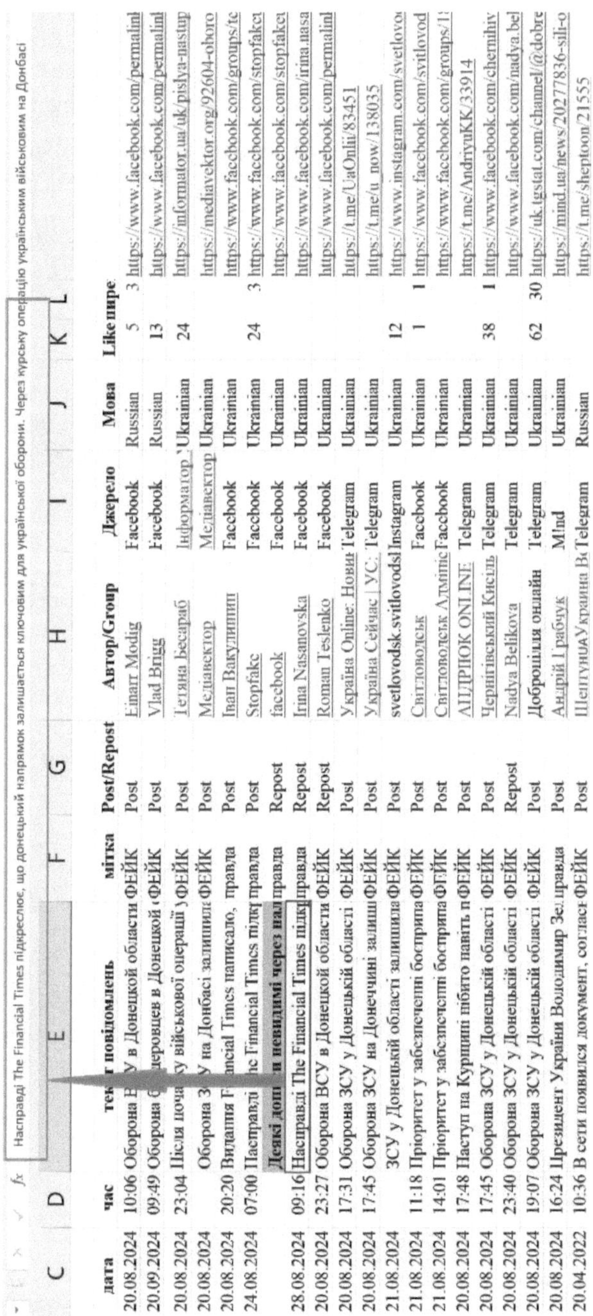

Направді The Financial Times підкреслює, що донецький напрямок залишається ключовим для української оборони. Через курську операцію українським військовим на Донбасі

дата	час	текст повідомлень	мітка	Post/Repost	Автор/Group	Джерело	Мова	Like	пере	
20.08.2024	10:06	Оборона ВСУ в Донецкой области	ФЕЙК	Post	Einarr Modig	Facebook	Russian	5	3	https://www.facebook.com/permalinl
20.09.2024	09:49	Оборона бандеровцев в Донецкой	ФЕЙК	Post	Vlad Brigg	Facebook	Russian	13		https://www.facebook.com/permalinl
20.08.2024	23:04	Після початку військової операції	ФЕЙК	Post	Тетяна Бесараб	Інформатор	Ukrainian	24		https://informator.ua/uk/pislya-nastup
20.08.2024		Оборона ЗСУ на Донбасі залишила	ФЕЙК	Post	Медіавектор	Медіавектор	Ukrainian			https://mediavektor.org/92604-oboro
20.08.2024	20:20	Видання Financial Times написало,	правда	Post	Іван Вакулишин	Facebook	Ukrainian			https://www.facebook.com/groups/te
24.08.2024	07:00	Наспраді The Financial Times підк	правда	Post	Stopfake	Facebook	Ukrainian	24	3	https://www.facebook.com/stopfakeu
		Деякі допи.. и невидимі через нал	правда	Repost	facebook	Facebook	Ukrainian			https://www.facebook.com/stopfakeu
28.08.2024	09:16	Насправді The Financial Times підк	правда	Repost	Irina Nasanovska	Facebook	Ukrainian			https://www.facebook.com/irina.nasa
20.08.2024	23:27	Оборона ВСУ в Донецкой области	ФЕЙК	Repost	Roman Teslenko	Facebook	Ukrainian			https://www.facebook.com/permalinl
20.08.2024	17:31	Оборона ЗСУ у Донецькій області	ФЕЙК	Post	Україна Online: Нови	Telegram	Ukrainian			https://t.me/UaOnlii/83451
20.08.2024	17:45	Оборона ЗСУ на Донеччині залиш	ФЕЙК	Post	Україна Сейчас | УС:	Telegram	Ukrainian			https://t.me/u_now/138035
21.08.2024		ЗСУ у Донецькій області залишила	ФЕЙК	Post	svetlovodsk.svitlovodsl	Instagram	Ukrainian	12		https://www.instagram.com/svetlovo
21.08.2024	11:18	Пріоритет у забезпеченні боєприпа	ФЕЙК	Post	Світловодськ	Facebook	Ukrainian	1	1	https://www.facebook.com/svitlovod
21.08.2024	14:01	Пріоритет у забезпеченні боєприпа	ФЕЙК	Post	Світловодськ Адмініс	Facebook	Ukrainian			https://www.facebook.com/groups/1
20.08.2024	17:48	Наступ на Курщині нібито навіть п	ФЕЙК	Post	АНДРІЮК ONLINE	Telegram	Ukrainian			https://t.me/AndriyuKK/33914
20.08.2024	17:45	Оборона ЗСУ у Донецькій області	ФЕЙК	Post	Чернігівський Кисіль	Telegram	Ukrainian	38	1	https://www.facebook.com/chernihiv
20.08.2024	23:40	Оборона ЗСУ у Донецькій області	ФЕЙК	Repost	Nadya Belikova	Telegram	Ukrainian			https://www.facebook.com/nadya.bel
20.08.2024	19:07	Оборона ЗСУ у Донецькій області	ФЕЙК	Post	Доброволля онлайн	Telegram	Ukrainian	62	30	https://uk.tgstat.com/channel/@dobre
20.08.2024	16:24	Президент України Володимир Зе.	правда	Post	Андрій Грабчук	M!nd	Ukrainian			https://mind.ua/news/20277836-sili-o
20.04.2022	10:36	В сети появился документ, соглас	ФЕЙК	Post	ШептунUAУкраина В	Telegram	Russian			https://t.me/sheptoon/21555

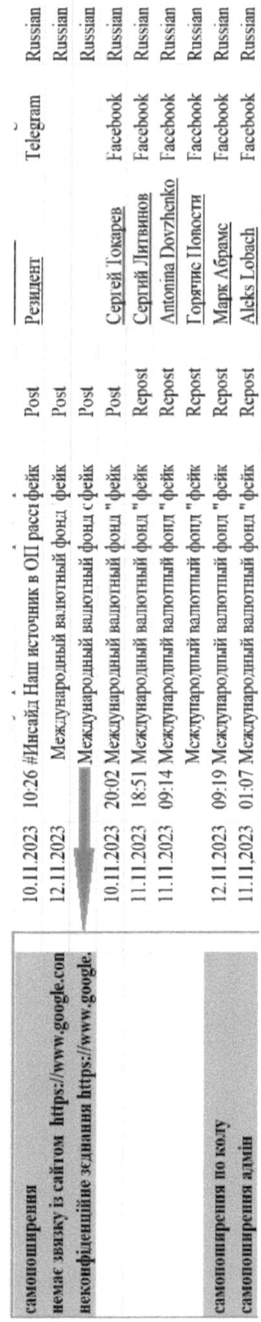

самопоширення	10.11.2023	10:26	#Инсайд Наш источник в ОП расс	фейк	Post	Резидент	Telegram	Russian
немає звязку із сайтом https://www.google.con	12.11.2023		Международный валютный фонд	фейк	Post			Russian
неконфіденційне зєднання https://www.google.			Международный валютный фонд с	фейк	Post			Russian
	10.11.2023	20:02	Международный валютный фонд "	фейк	Post	Сергей Токарев	Facebook	Russian
	11.11.2023	18:51	Международный валютный фонд "	фейк	Repost	Сергий Литвинов	Facebook	Russian
	11.11.2023	09:14	Международный валютный фонд "	фейк	Repost	Antonina Dovzhenko	Facebook	Russian
			Международный валютный фонд "	фейк	Repost	Горячие Новости	Facebook	Russian
самопоширення по колу	12.11.2023	09:19	Международный валютный фонд "	фейк	Repost	Марк Абрамс	Facebook	Russian
самопоширення адмін	11.11,2023	01:07	Международный валютный фонд "	фейк	Repost	Aleks Lobach	Facebook	Russian

Fig. 7.2. Fragment of the dataset Fig. 7.3. Dataset with inauthentic behaviour elements

Step 2. Context analysis

Step 3. Critical approach to media content

It is important to examine product placement for fakeness, taking into account the criteria of inauthentic behaviour of social media chat users, namely

- Check message frequency

```
time_threshold = 5 # Number of messages per unit of time (for example, in 1 minute)
if len(messages) > time_threshold:
print("Abnormal activity: excessive number of messages.")
else:
print("Activity within normal limits.")
```

- Check manipulative language

```
def check_manipulative_language(text):
# Check for aggression or manipulation in language
negative_keywords = ["stupid", "idiot", "conspiracy", "hate", "fake"]
for keyword in negative_keywords:
if keyword in text.lower():
print(f"Suspicious language: word '{keyword}' found. May be manipulation.")
return True
return False
```

- Check profile

```
def check_fake_profile(user_info):
if "no profile picture" in user_info or len(user_info) < 10:
print("Suspicious profile: no avatar or little personal information.")
return True
return False
```

- Analyze the text

```
for message in messages:
if check_manipulative_language(message):
print("Manipulation found in message:", message)
```

After applying these manipulations, the activity of chat participants is analysed, and the profile is checked to detect bots, keywords of manipulative messages are identified, and the profile is checked. Fig. 7.3 shows a fragment of the dataset with inauthentic behaviour of chat participants.

Therefore, the features of inauthentic behaviour of chat participants on military topics for the formation of a set of generalised criteria are as follows:

- a significant number of messages in a short period of time;
- short phrases or templates without interaction with other participants;
- repetitive or identical messages that are published automatically;
- provocative statements to cause emotional reactions;
- spreading or commenting on misinformation without fact-checking, often with the aim of manipulating or disorienting other participants;
- using manipulative phrases that force people to adopt a particular point of view under pressure;
- inducing actions using intrusive or covert methods;
- illogical constructions, automatically generated phrases, or lack of natural flow of dialogue;
- spreading specific hashtags that appear to be part of a manipulative campaign.

7.3. Conclusions for Chapter 7

Thus, the study found that product placement as disinformation can influence consumer behaviour and political or social views and is part of information warfare strategies. In this context, the need to develop algorithms and methods for detecting disinformation, taking into account product placement, is justified, in particular, using spaCy, which allows you to effectively work with texts, identifying fake and manipulative statements. Identification of inauthentic behaviour of chat participants is an essential part of ensuring information security. The study analysed the features of such behaviour and took it into account in the processes of disinformation analysis. Further work is planned to improve the analysis by adding more complex strategies for detecting hidden manipulations, using more complicated models based on transformers, such as BERT, and tuning algorithms for recognising manipulative sentiments.

Chapter 8. Method for the detection of disinformation based on text data analysis using TF-IDF and transformer embeddings

The chapter is written based on scientific publications [200-215].

8.1. Analyses of known machine learning algorithms for identifying disinformation

Most modern tools for countering disinformation are primarily focused on English-language content. At the same time, the Ukrainian-language segment of the information space has a number of unique features – linguistic, cultural and historical. The creation of specialised tools explicitly adapted to the Ukrainian-language context will allow us to overcome this problem and ensure compliance with current requirements and challenges. In addition to tools, the formation of Ukrainian-language datasets is of great importance and relevance, as they are valuable for the international scientific community and will contribute to further research in this area [200]. Traditional approaches to detecting fakes or bots are increasingly losing their effectiveness due to the constant improvement of disinformation tools. Therefore, there is a need to create multifunctional tools capable of automatically processing large volumes of data, detecting fake content, analysing user behaviour and identifying coordinated bot networks.

The authors propose an approach that includes data collection from various digital sources, pre-processing and content cleaning, detection of disinformation messages, analysis of user behaviour to detect bots, and generation of analytical reports with appropriate recommendations. The implementation of such an approach has significant applied value for government agencies, journalists, experts in the field of information security, and all those interested in countering threats to the digital information space. Today's digital environment is characterised by the active spread of disinformation and the growth of the use of chatbots, which poses a serious challenge to information security. That is why machine learning and natural language processing methods are an essential component in identifying the sources of fake messages and detecting inauthentic behaviour of chatbots. The use of these methods makes it possible to identify not only the sources but also the ways in which disinformation narratives are spread. Thanks to machine learning algorithms, it is possible to automate the process of identifying fake messages, in particular by recognising repetitive language structures and patterns characteristic of disinformation. There are two key approaches to identifying sources of disinformation [201]:

• manual – involves fact-checking by experts through manual analysis;

• automated – involves the use of deep learning algorithms for automatic analysis of large information flows.

Chatbots, which are increasingly used in digital communications, can serve as a means of spreading fake messages. Identifying their behaviour and differences from human behaviour is an essential aspect of countering disinformation. Machine learning algorithms demonstrate high efficiency in detecting information manipulation. It is able to process data in real time, detect new ways of spreading fakes and adapt to changes. This approach allows you to quickly detect false information and respond to it. Machine learning systems and natural language processing make it possible to analyse large amounts of text data, detect patterns, automatically interpret content, and generate speech content. Their applications include: machine translation, chatbot creation, text sentiment analysis, automatic summarisation, disinformation detection.

Text classification, i.e., determining whether a text belongs to a specific category (fake/genuine, positive/negative, etc.), is performed using machine learning methods such as naive Bayesian classifier, logistic regression, decision tree method [202], support vector method [203], and deep neural networks [204].

In the study [205], classification models were developed for detecting fake news using machine learning algorithms. The models were tested on a dataset that includes examples of fake and real news and contains 42,000 examples. Preprocessing methods were applied to improve the quality, accuracy, and usability of the dataset. The models were created to detect fake news using singular and ensemble feature classification algorithms. The highest performance results were observed in the random forest classification algorithm with an accuracy rate of 76%. The authors [206] investigated the use of four well-known machine learning algorithms, namely random forest, naive Bayesian classifier, neural network, and decision trees, to separately test the classification efficiency in detecting fake news. The experiments were conducted on the public LIAR dataset [207]. The experimental results showed that the naive Bayesian classifier significantly outperforms other algorithms on this dataset.

The study [208] proposed a method that combines machine learning and deep learning algorithms to detect fake information compared to real information. The authors presented the results of applying the algorithms and comparing their performance. The results of this study show that algorithms that use the inverse frequency of documents by the frequency of terms, TF-IDF, achieved better results than algorithms that use Word2Vec. However, the long short-term memory algorithm, LSTM, achieved the best performance, with an accuracy of 99% when using TF-IDF and 94% when using Word2Vec.

Current research in the field of natural language processing and machine learning offers practical approaches to the automated detection of fake information. The paper reviews techniques for analysing text content, social media interactions, and user behavioural characteristics to detect disinformation [209]. The authors emphasise the key role of annotated datasets, which are necessary for the practical training of models. In the scientific paper [210], an approach for automated detection of disinformation using NLP is proposed. This approach includes a comprehensive overview of disinformation analysis, detection, and containment, presenting key methods, functions, models, and datasets. Thus, the use of NLP in the fight against disinformation includes:

- automatic recognition of fake messages,
- assessment of the reliability of sources,
- fact-checking by comparison with databases of reliable information.

In order for machine learning models to be able to process texts, they must be represented in the form of numbers (vectors). Among the stages of preparing the text for processing, tokenisation, lemmatisation, removal of stop words, and vectorisation can also be distinguished. The most common vectorisation algorithms are the “bag of words” algorithm [211], TF-IDF [212], the embedding algorithm (Word Embeddings) [208], BERT [204], RoBERTa [213], and transformers. Machine learning and natural language processing technologies are practical tools for automated analysis of text information, detection of disinformation, and identification of bots. Thanks to modern approaches, in particular neural networks and transformative models, the quality of speech content processing is significantly improved, which opens up new prospects in the field of cybersecurity and analytics.

8.2. Logistic regression with TF-IDF and transformer embeddings

Before starting the modelling, a preliminary analysis of the structure of the input dataset [214] was performed, which was supplemented with updated information, using the exploratory data analysis method EDA [215]. The main goal of this stage was to identify key patterns, possible anomalies, missing values, imbalance between classes, and other data features that may affect the further choice of processing and modelling approaches.

During the analysis, the following was performed:

- visualisation of the distribution of the language variable (“lang”) and the target variable “label”, which indicates whether the record belongs to the “true” or “fake” category;
- assessment of data types (text, categorical, numeric, dated);
- checking for missing or duplicate records;
- fundamental analysis of texts by length and word frequency, as well as preliminary text processing.

The results obtained allowed us to make informed decisions regarding:

• selection of relevant variables (for example: “text”, “label”, “source”, “lang”, “link”);

• removal of duplicate texts and irrelevant records;

• construction of histograms for such indicators as text length, number of words (based on separation by spaces), and number of tokens generated by the embedding model tokeniser.

At the first stage, the general structure of the dataset was derived (Fig. 8.1), as well as examples of the first four rows (Fig. 8.2). The analysis showed that the first two columns contained uninformative values. Still, the total number of meaningful records allowed us to continue processing. Some of the records contained messages about the unavailability of content, and some system messages. Empty values were recorded in the “text message” column (which was later renamed to “text”), and based on additional sources, it was possible to partially restore the content for individual records. The next step was to clean the dataset: only those variables that have practical value for the classification task were retained, in particular “text”, “label”, “source”, “lang” and “link” (Fig. 8.3). Records with empty text were also removed.

```
<class 'pandas.core.frame.DataFrame'>
RangeIndex: 965 entries, 0 to 964
Data columns (total 23 columns):
 #   Column        Non-Null Count  Dtype
---  ------        --------------  -----
 0   Unnamed: 0    185 non-null    object
 1   №             150 non-null    object
 2   дата          738 non-null    object
 3    час          691 non-null    object
 4   text          960 non-null    object
 5   label         958 non-null    object
 6   Post/Repost   963 non-null    object
 7   Автор/Group   942 non-null    object
 8   source        929 non-null    object
 9   lang          960 non-null    object
 10  Like          258 non-null    object
 11  Поширення     84 non-null     object
 12  link          954 non-null    object
 13  Unnamed: 13   0 non-null      float64
 14  Unnamed: 14   2 non-null      object
 15  Unnamed: 15   0 non-null      float64
 16  Unnamed: 16   0 non-null      float64
 17  Unnamed: 17   0 non-null      float64
 18  Unnamed: 18   0 non-null      float64
 19  Unnamed: 19   0 non-null      float64
 20  Unnamed: 20   0 non-null      float64
 21  Unnamed: 21   0 non-null      float64
 22  Unnamed: 22   1 non-null      float64
dtypes: float64(9), object(14)
memory usage: 173.5+ KB
```

Fig. 8.1. General information about the dataset

	0	1
Unnamed: 0	NaN	NaN
№	NaN	NaN
дата	20.08.2024	20.09.2024
час	10:06	9:49
текст повідомлень	Оборона ВСУ в Донецкой области осталась без сн...	Оборона бандеровцев в Донецкой области осталас...
мітка	ФЕЙК	ФЕЙК
Post/Repost	Post	Post
Автор/Group	Einarr Modig	Vlad Brigg
Джерело	Facebook	Facebook
Мова	Russian	Russian
Like	5	13
Поширення	3	NaN
веб-адреса	https://www.facebook.com/permalink.php?story_f...	https://www.facebook.com/permalink.php?story_f...
Unnamed: 13	NaN	NaN
Unnamed: 14	NaN	NaN
Unnamed: 15	NaN	NaN
Unnamed: 16	NaN	NaN

Fig. 8.2. General structure of the dataset

```
df.rename(columns={' мітка': 'label',
                   'текст повідомлень': 'text',
                   'Джерело': 'source',
                   'Мова': 'lang',
                   'веб-адреса': 'link'}, inplace=True)

df = df[['text', 'label', 'lang', 'source', 'link']]
```

Fig. 8.3. Renaming and selecting the necessary columns

Since some duplicates in the dataset differed only in minor details (case, spaces), duplicate cleaning occurs after the completion of text preprocessing. To ensure stable and efficient operation of the logistic regression model, processing of the text variable "text" and the target variable "label" is implemented. The main goal of this stage is to reduce variability in the data, eliminate redundant elements, and normalise class values. The main stages of text preprocessing:

1. Lower case conversion: all characters in the “text” and “label” fields are converted to lower case to avoid duplication of identical words with different spellings (for example, “Pravda”, “PRAVDA” and “pravda”).

2. Text cleaning: all URL addresses and HTML tags that do not carry an informative load are removed.

3. Removing unnecessary characters: all non-letter and non-numeric characters, including punctuation, emojis, and special characters, were removed from the text. Extra spaces were also removed.

4. Removing duplicates: unique records were saved, which allows you to avoid re-training the model on identical examples.

5. Label normalisation: the value of the “label” variable was unified to two valid options: “fake” and “true”. It ensures a clear separation of classes during the modelling process.

The results of text pre-processing showed that all duplicate values were successfully removed, and “label” now contains only two valid values (Fig. 8.4). Updated information about the dataset after cleaning is shown in Fig. 8.5. After these steps, the data is ready for the following stages – tokenization, division into training and test samples, vectorization, and building a model for classifying messages by reliability.

```
df['label'].unique()

array(['фейк', 'правда'], dtype=object)
```

Fig. 8.4. Unique values of the “label” column after processing

Vectorisation methods and classification model. The study applied a combined approach to text representation, combining frequency characteristics (TF-IDF) and contextual vector representations (Granite Embeddings). Such a hybrid strategy allows the model to take into account not only the number and uniqueness of words, but also their semantic context within the text.

```
df.info()

<class 'pandas.core.frame.DataFrame'>
Index: 483 entries, 0 to 962
Data columns (total 5 columns):
 #   Column  Non-Null Count  Dtype
---  ------  --------------  -----
 0   text    483 non-null    object
 1   label   483 non-null    object
 2   lang    483 non-null    object
 3   source  460 non-null    object
 4   link    473 non-null    object
dtypes: object(5)
memory usage: 22.6+ KB
```

Fig. 8.5. Updated information about the dataset

TF-IDF is a method that reflects how often certain words occur in the text, as well as how unique these words are for a particular document compared to the entire corpus. This method does not take into account word order or context, but provides a stable numerical representation, especially effective for short texts.

Combining frequency and contextual features for text classification. Two approaches were used to represent text data: TF-IDF and contextual embeddings, which provided a hybrid vectorisation model.

The following parameters were chosen for TF-IDF:

• max_features = 4000 – limiting the number of features to 4000 most significant terms, which is justified by the size of the dictionary (8816 words);

• tokeniser = lambda x: x.split(' ') – simple division of text into words by spaces.

Contextual embeddings (IBM Granite). The TF-IDF addition is implemented using the multilingual model ibm-granite/granite-embedding-107m-multilingual, which belongs to the transformer class of Granite models created by IBM. This model can process up to 512 tokens and form 384-dimensional vector representations of the text. Its advantage lies in the ability to take into account the context and semantic relationships between words, regardless of their order, which is especially important for detecting content disinformation. To combine the advantages of both approaches, a hybrid representation was created by concatenating TF-IDF and Granite vectors into an extended feature vector.

Logistic regression as a classification model. The logistic regression model was used as the classification model, which is a reliable method for binary classification problems, especially in conditions of a large number of input features. It demonstrates good performance, learning speed and ease of interpretation. Hyperparameters used for logistic regression:

• penalty = 'l2' – regularisation to avoid overfitting;

• solver = 'lbfgs' – an optimiser that scales well on problems with a large number of parameters;

• class_weight = 'balanced' – automatic adjustment of weights for classes with different representation;

• random_state = 42 – fixing randomness to ensure reproducibility of results.

Thanks to the combination of frequency and semantic features, the model was able to analyse the text content of news more deeply, identifying signs of disinformation. All stages from processing to training are combined into a single structure, which allows the model to be flexibly applied in different information environments. For practical use, the FakeNewsClassifier class has been built, which combines all the key stages of text data processing. The class includes functionality for pre-processing, vectorisation, hybrid feature construction, model training, and results visualisation. It ensures the integrity and stability of the classification process and allows for easy repetition of experiments on new data sets. Visualisation of class balance and text features, sample division and vectorisation. To analyze the distribution of the target variable, the target_balance() method was used, which plots the frequency of the "fake" and "true" classes (Fig. 8.6). The visualization indicates that there is no significant imbalance between the classes and the model is able to learn without a bias towards the advantage of one of the classes, ensuring balanced performance.

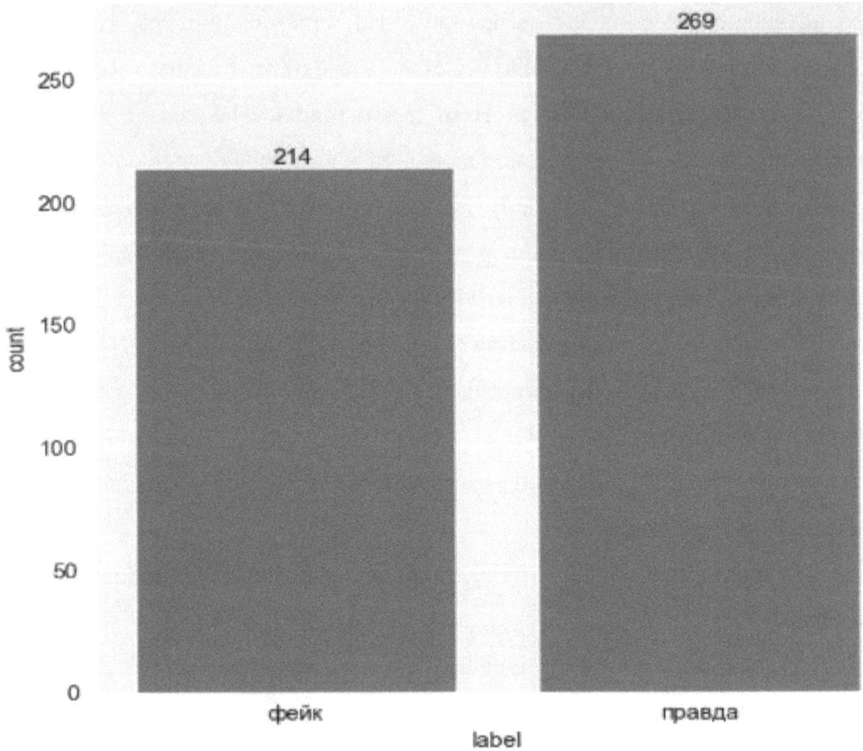

Fig. 8.6. Balance of the target variable

To study the structural properties of text data, the visualize_text_features() method was used, which creates histograms of text lengths in characters and the number of words, with subsequent saving of the image (Fig. 8.7). The results show that most texts have from 50 to 500 characters. The number of words mainly varies from 24 to 41. There is a right-side shift, that is, a significant part of the messages is short, although there are exceptions with excessive length. This information is vital for improving the quality of training and diagnosing the model. The training and test samples constitute 80% and 20% of all records, respectively. As a result, the training part consists of 386 records, and the test part consists of 97.

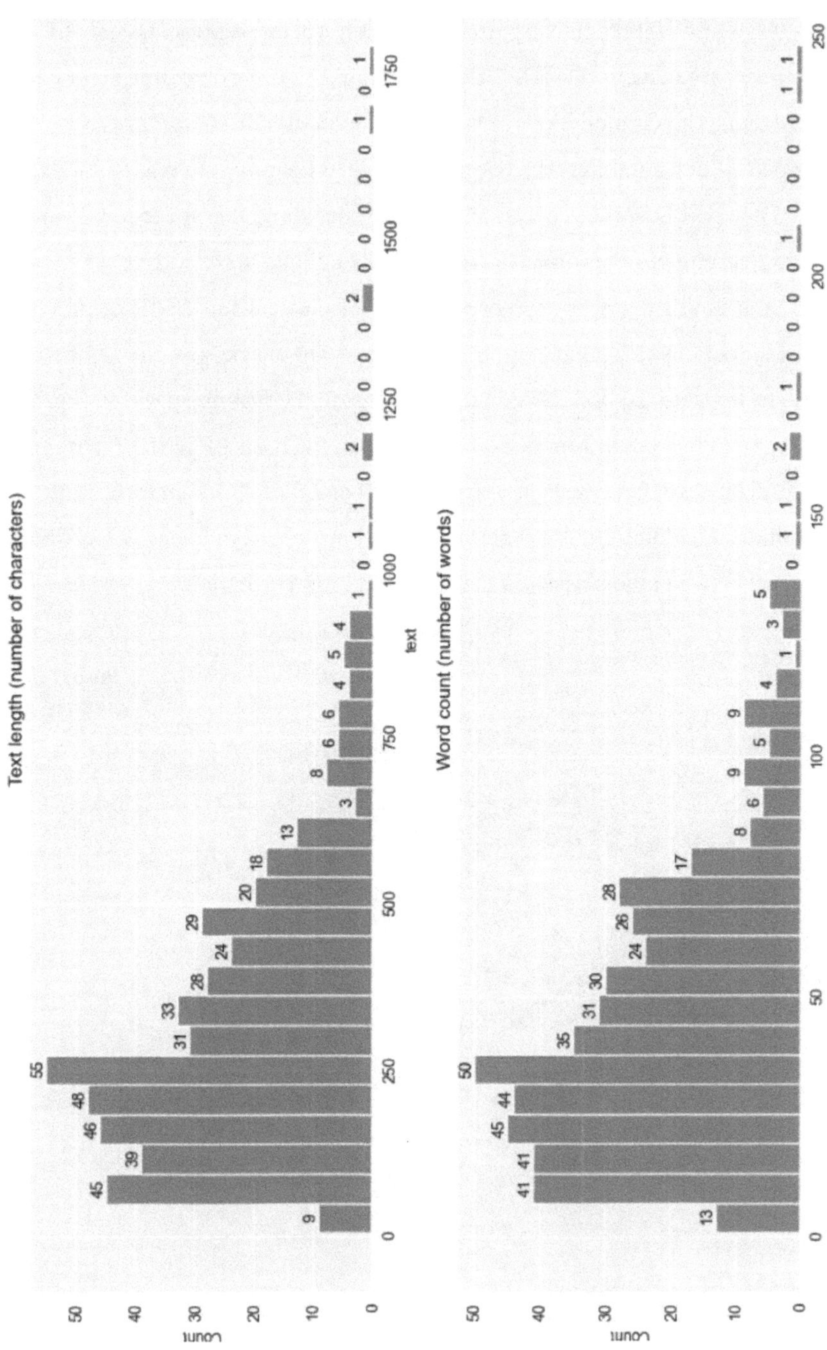

Fig. 8.7. Visualization of structural characteristics of the text

A hybrid approach was used to obtain vector representations of texts, combining frequency TF-IDF representations with contextual embeddings created using the Granite model. As a result, a feature matrix of size (386, 4384) is formed, which combines the two types of vectorisation into one feature space.

To assess how the separation of classes occurs in this space, a method was applied that reduces the dimensionality of embeddings to two components using t-SNE and builds a graphical representation of clusters for TF-IDF and Granite features. Such visualisation (Fig. 8.8) allows you to check how clearly the model is able to separate the “fake” and “true” classes in the feature space. In Fig. 8.8, it is shown that the vector representations built on the basis of TF-IDF demonstrate a clear distinction between the classes "fake" and "true". In contrast, in the case of Granite embeddings, there is partial overlap, which may indicate a more blurred boundary between the classes in the contextual representation.

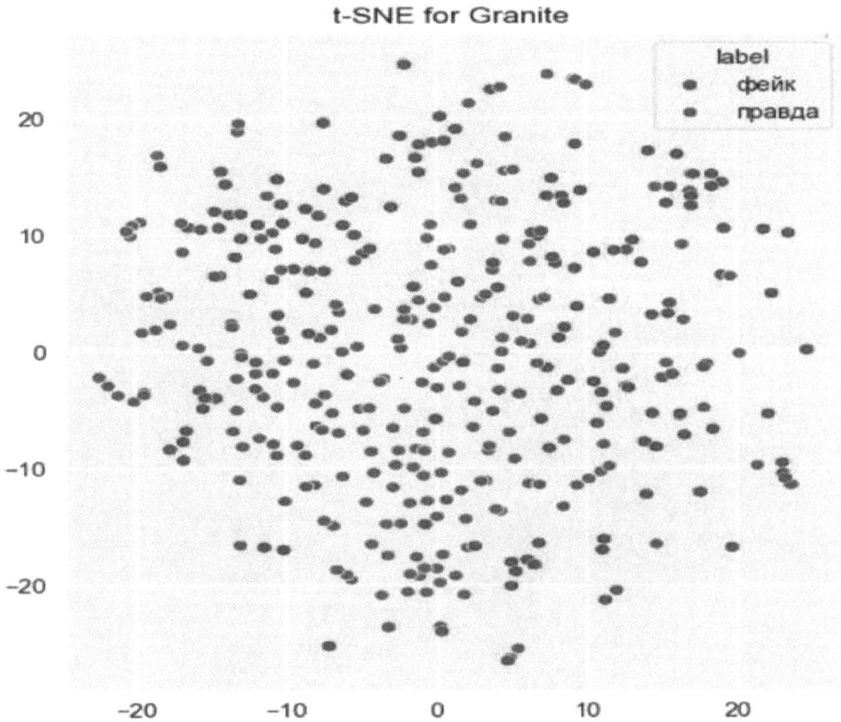

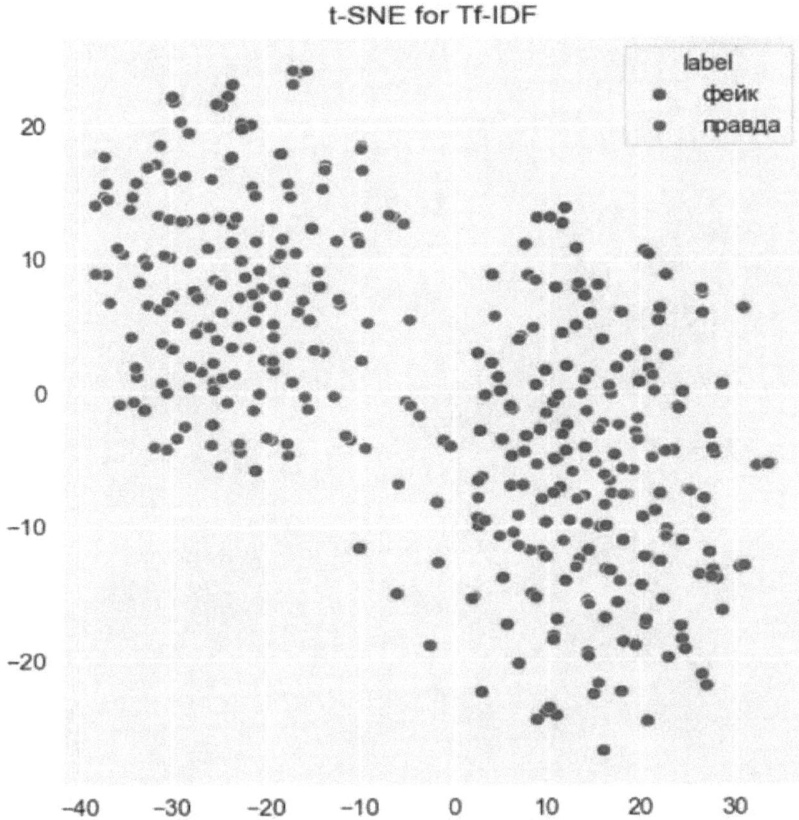

Fig. 8.8. Visualisation of results for both types of features

A histogram was constructed to analyse the features of tokenisation when using the Granite model and display the number of tokens in each text for the training and test samples. This allows us to assess how the model breaks texts into tokens before building embeddings (Fig. 8.9). From Fig. 8.9, it is clear that most texts in the training sample have a length of 18 to 42 tokens, with a peak in the range of 37-42 tokens. The test sample demonstrates a more scattered distribution with a less pronounced peak. It indicates a relatively stable length of texts after tokenisation and the correct operation of data preprocessing before using them in the Granite model. The classification model was trained using the logistic regression method based on previously constructed hybrid features.

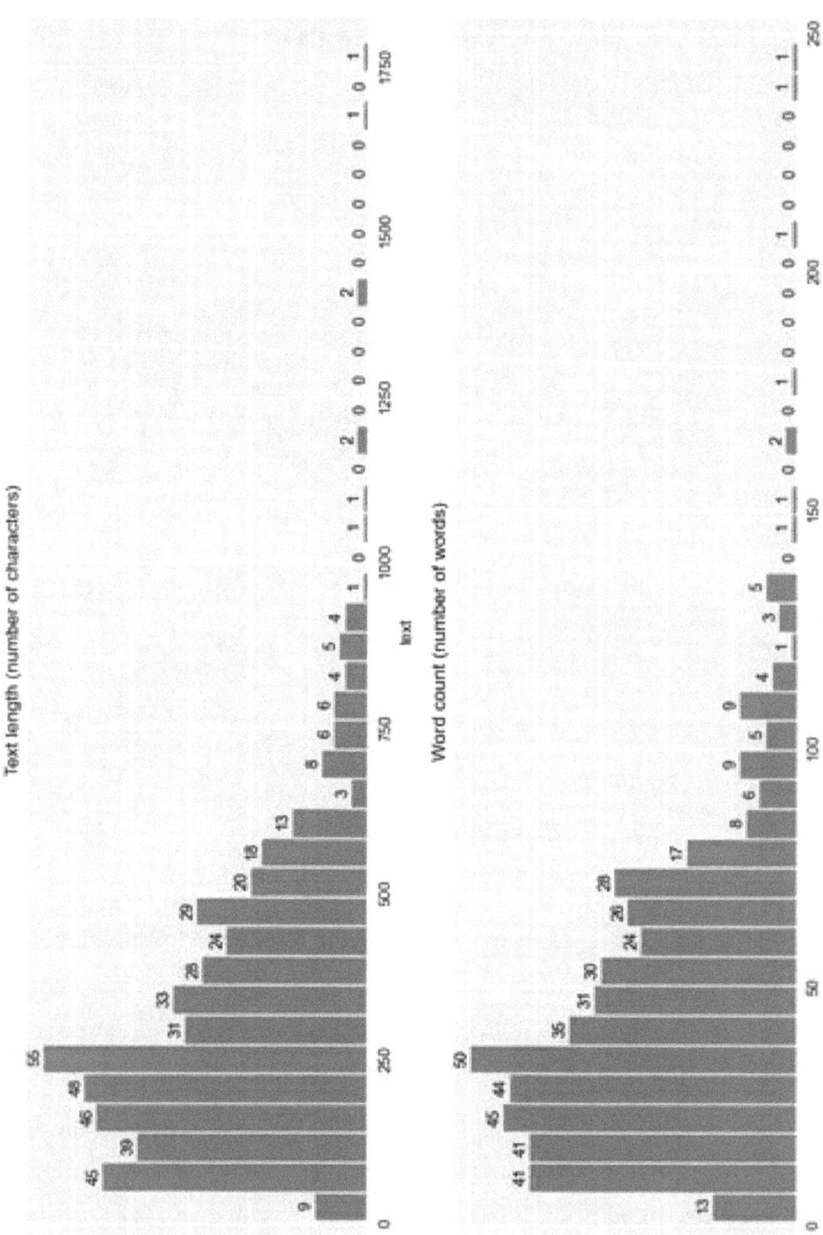

Fig. 8.9. Granite tokenization visualization

In classification tasks, it is advisable to evaluate the effectiveness of the model by its ability to correctly identify each class separately. For this, the recall, precision, accuracy, and F1-measure metrics were chosen. Recall reflects the proportion of objects of the positive class, which, in our case, is the "fake" class, that the model was able to correctly identify. In turn, precision reflects what proportion of all documents predicted as fakes are actually fake news.

According to the classification results (Table 8.1), the overall accuracy of the model (accuracy) is 0.82. The model demonstrates an F1-measure of 0.84 for the "true" class and 0.80 for the "fake" class, which indicates a relatively balanced performance across the two classes. The *macro avg* and *weighted avg* metrics are also at the level of 0.82, which means a stable quality of predictions regardless of the class distribution.

Table 8.1. Metrics indicators for the classification model

Metric	*Precision*	*Recall*	*F1-score*	*Support*
True	0,84	0,85	0,84	54
Fake	0,81	0,79	0,80	43
Accuracy			0,82	97
Macro avg	0,82	0,82	0,82	97
Weighted avg	0,82	0,82	0,82	97

To assess the quality of classification, three discrepancy matrices were constructed: without normalisation, normalised by precision, and normalised by recall (Fig. 8.10). This approach allows for a comprehensive assessment of how the model copes with the prediction of each class and how prone it is to errors in one form or another. In addition to visualisation, the method additionally calculates the value of the Fβ-measure with the default parameter $\beta = 1.3$, which shifts the emphasis on recall, in accordance with the focus on fake news detection chosen in the study. From the matrix without normalisation (Fig. 8.10, graph on the left), it is clear that the model correctly classified 46 examples of the "true" class and 34 examples of the "fake" class, making 8 and 9 errors, respectively.

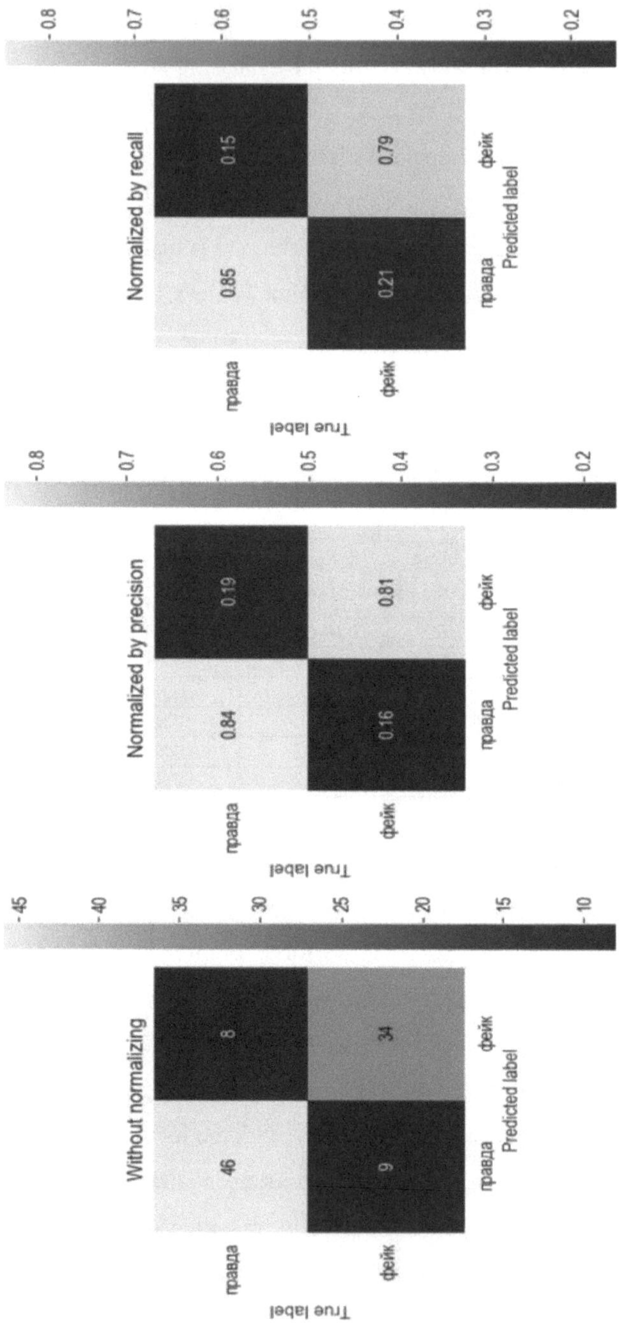

Fig. 8.10. Disparity matrices

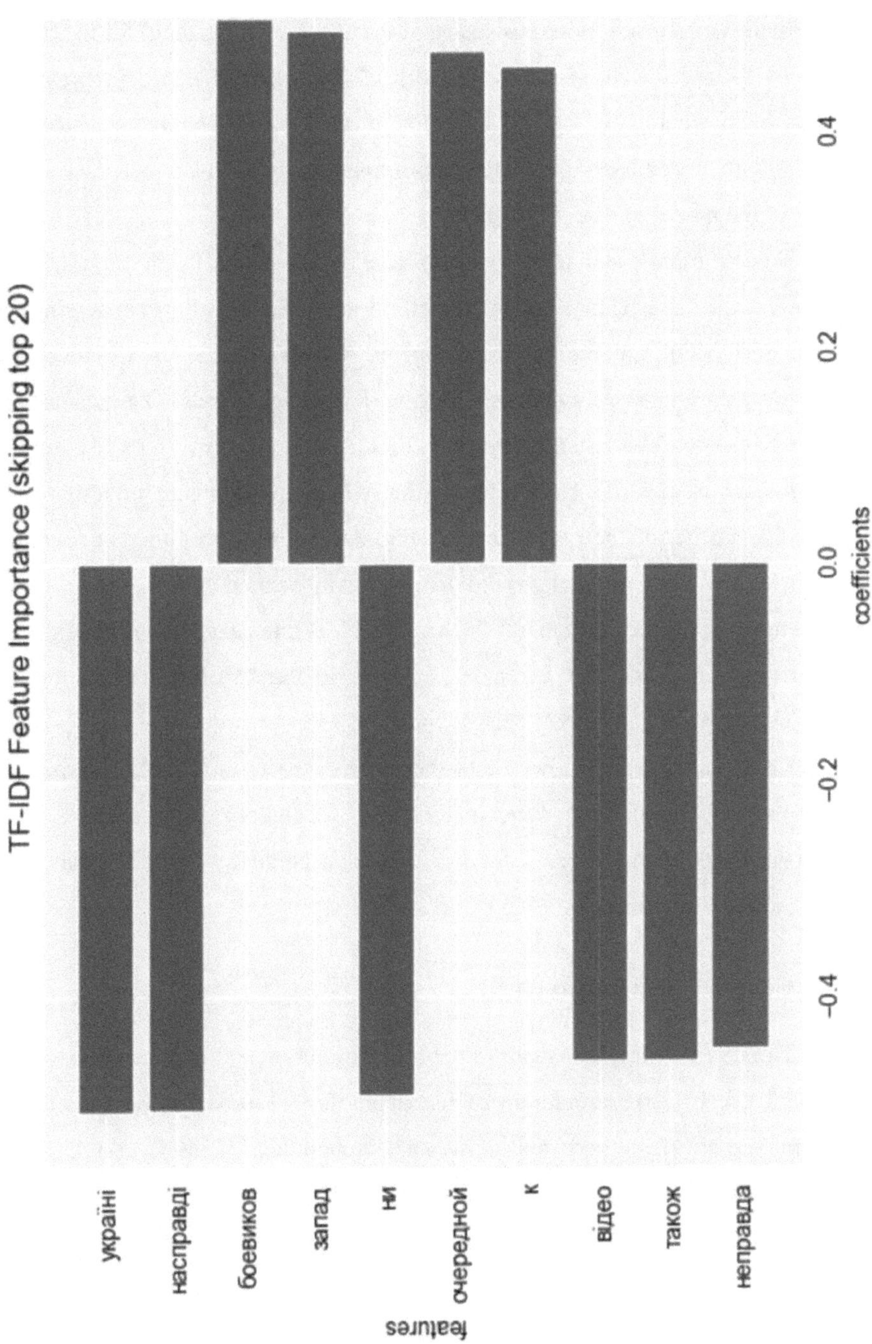

Fig. 8.11. The most essential words based on TF-IDF

In the normalised form, it is seen that the accuracy (precision) for the "fake" class is 81%, and the completeness (recall) is 79%, which is an acceptable result in a problem where it is vital to minimise missed fakes. The value of the Fβ-measure with an emphasis on recall is approximately 0.79, which indicates a good ability of the model to detect fake news.

To determine which terms (words) have the most significant impact on the decision of the classification model, a method was used that allows analysing the weight of TF-IDF features based on logistic regression coefficients, revealing which words are most strongly associated with a particular class. To increase the informativeness of the visualisation, the 20 most obvious terms (mostly common or frequently used words) were filtered, after which the following ten terms were displayed in order of their significance (Fig. 8.11). From this, we can conclude that positive values (on the right) indicate words associated with the "fake" class, for example: "boenikov", "zapad", "ocherednoy". While negative coefficients (on the left) reflect terms that are more inherent in the "truth" class, including: "Ukraine", "actually", "video", "also", "untrue".

Thus, the analysis showed that the model associates reliable information mainly with Ukrainian-language and neutral vocabulary. At the same time, disinformation texts often contain Russian-language words that are propagandistic or manipulative in nature.

8.3. Conclusions for Chapter 8

The research implemented an approach to automated fake news detection based on a hybrid representation of text data. The proposed system combines classical statistical methods and contextual embeddings (IBM Granite), which makes it possible to achieve a high level of classification accuracy by taking into account both frequency and semantic characteristics of texts. A preliminary analysis of the dataset structure was carried out using the EDA method, which made it possible to detect irrelevant records and missing values and identify the features of text data. The main stages of text pre-processing are presented, including text normalisation, noise removal, label unification, and duplicate removal, which ensured high-quality data preparation for model training.

For the binary classification task, the logistic regression method was used, which demonstrated stable results according to the main metrics: accuracy – 0.82, F1-measure for the “fake” and “true” classes – 0.80 and 0.84, respectively. The primary focus is on maximising the recall metric, which is critically important in the context of disinformation detection.

The proposed approach has shown its effectiveness and flexibility, and also provided a high level of interpretability of the results, which is an essential factor for the further use of the model in real media analysis systems and information security. Additional research will be aimed at expanding the dataset and creating new ensemble models for detecting sources of disinformation.

Chapter 9. Processing censoring inappropriate content in images, messages, and songs based on NLP, machine learning, sentiment and sarcasm analysis

The chapter is written based on publications and research [216-246].

9.1. Analyses of methods for sarcasm detection

On social networks and the official websites of various companies, it is vital to censor aggressive statements in texts and images, especially hate speech, in the comments. Natural language processing and machine learning methods are used to identify hate, particularly mentality analysis and sarcasm identification. Sarcasm is a statement that is the opposite of what you say, aiming to hurt someone's feelings or criticise something with humour. Sarcasm occurs when the literal meaning of words and what the speaker wants to say are different. The definition of sarcasm is spelt out in the Cambridge Dictionary. The literal meaning of thought and the content it carries become prophesied. With the help of positive words, a negative meaning is conveyed. The Oxford Dictionary defines sarcasm as "the use of irony to evoke or convey contempt." However, people use sarcasm daily to joke, be humorous, and criticise or make remarks about ideas, persons, or events. Sarcasm exists everywhere: in facial expressions, gestures, and even text. It is subjective, based on a situation, circumstance, people, language, or culture. Sarcasm detection is a very narrow area of study in NLP, a specific case of sentiment analysis where sarcasm is the focus instead of detecting sentiments across the spectrum. Therefore, the task of this field is to determine whether a given text is sarcastic or not. Detecting sarcasm is an exciting but challenging task in text since basic pointers such as intonations, facial expressions, and gestures are missing. The lyrics can be funny or disgusting, critical or praising, but everything can potentially convey sarcasm in one way or another [216].

The first problem is that sarcasm is unlimited, unlike sentiment analysis, where the mood categories are very well defined (love objectively has positive sentiments, hate negative feelings, no matter who you ask or what language you speak). Therefore, it is imperative that before starting to detect it, you have an idea of what sarcasm is. Sarcasm detection can benefit many areas of NLP interest, including market research, opinion research, and information categorisation. Sarcasm is a significant obstacle to improving the accuracy of mood analysis, especially on social media, as sarcasm relies heavily on the timbre of voice, facial expressions, and gestures that cannot be represented in the text. Recognising sarcasm in online text communication is difficult, as none of these signals are available. Understanding the actual mood of online conversations can help businesses process customer feedback and gather ideas to improve marketing efforts. Regarding protection, sentiment can be an essential signal for online information operations to identify problems or possible actions by attackers.

Sarcasm is widely used on social networks and on microblogging websites, where users mock or criticise in a way that even people find it difficult to understand if what is said is what is meant. Microblogging platforms are the central place for people to express their views and opinions on various topics and events. Short text messages are increasingly used for communication, primarily through social media platforms like Twitter. Due to insufficient or missing context, vague sarcasm in these messages can invert the statement's meaning, leading to confusion. Sarcasm is found on social media and websites, as these platforms often encourage trolling and criticism of others. Various studies have used Twitter, Reddit, and Facebook to detect sarcasm. However, Twitter remains the most popular medium, likely due to its ease of use. Twitter has become one of the most prominent web destinations for users to express their thoughts. Over the past few years, Twitter content has continued to grow, with hundreds of millions of tweets sent by more than 285 million active users daily. Many companies and organisations have become interested in this data to study people's opinions about political events, popular products or movies. However, due to the informal language used on Twitter and the character limit (i.e. 140 characters per tweet), it isn't easy to understand users' opinions and conduct such an analysis. In addition, the presence of sarcasm makes the task even more difficult. Some people are more sarcastic than others. However, sarcasm is generally very common, although it is difficult to recognise. In this case, modern sentiment and opinion analysis approaches are less effective when analysing data from such websites. The effectiveness of sentiment analysis can be significantly improved if sarcasm is detected in sarcastic statements. Therefore, there is a need for an effective way to detect sarcasm. Thus, to characterise the sarcasm on Twitter, the following was proposed:

- conflict between a negative situation and a positive mood;
- conflict between a favourable situation and a negative mood;
- Word Conversion Tweet;
- loves and dislikes contradictions;
- "Tweet conflicting" facts;
- The tweet contains positive vibes with a pair of antonyms.

The analysis and classification of sarcasm are essential to convey implicit information in the message that the person shares with others. In addition, the structure of the tweet can also be used to predict sarcasm. But there are some existing problems in the classification of sarcastic tweets:

- The nature of the tweets collected (Twitter limits the number of characters, resulting in more ambiguity);
- The collected tweets contain vague words, slang, and abbreviations that are more informal;
- Twitter has no predefined framework for recognising sarcasm.

However, most computational approaches to detecting sarcasm treat it as a purely linguistic matter, using information such as lexical cues and moods as predictable characteristics. But by including out-of-the-box information from the context of a tweet, such as the properties of the author, the audience, and the immediate communicative environment, it is possible to achieve a gain in accuracy compared to purely linguistic features in identifying this complex phenomenon. Recognising sarcastic language can be very useful for improving the automatic sentiment analysis of data collected from social networks. It also helps improve customer service efficiency and assistance by understanding consumers' intentions and actual opinions when reviewing their feedback or complaints. In textual classification, sarcasm detection is an essential tool with many implications for several areas, including safety, health, and sales. With sarcasm detection techniques, companies can analyse customers' feelings about their products. Social media sentiment analysis has been one of NLP's most targeted research topics over the past decade. Since sentiment analysis aims to automatically determine the polarity of the document, misinterpretation of irony and sarcasm is a big problem. Sarcasm usually reverses the polarity of the statement from positive or negative to its opposite, which worsens the results of this NLP task. Therefore, correctly identifying sarcasm can improve productivity. Most existing modern techniques are language-dependent, relying on language-specific lexical resources. Hashtags (#), for example, convey the exact meaning of the predicted sentences, so they can be a handy resource for classifying text. Hashtags like #sarcasm are essential for gathering information regarding a particular topic or event and obtaining data sets since they are clearly defined in their use of category tags in tweets. Most previous research has been conducted on datasets collected using sarcasm-related hashtags. Previous research has used machine learning techniques to predict sarcasm in tweets. This study will also use data collected from tags. With the rapid advancement of information technologies and the increasing ubiquity of the internet, there is a growing need to ensure a secure and comfortable online experience [217]. A vital element of this effort involves censoring inappropriate content, including profanity, offensive language, and violent or obscene imagery [218]. It is particularly relevant in protecting vulnerable groups, such as children, and providing all users with a positive online experience [219]. This research focuses on automatic detection and censorship of inappropriate content (text and images) on web pages. This process leverages modern artificial intelligence (AI) technologies to enhance internet safety and improve user comfort. The research subject encompasses the methods and technologies used to censor inappropriate content on web pages via a browser extension. It includes an analysis of existing content-filtering techniques and the development of novel algorithms and interface solutions aimed at optimising efficiency and user experience. The primary objective of this work is to design and implement an effective system for automatically censoring inappropriate content on web pages through a browser extension. This system will give users enhanced control over the content they encounter, creating a safer and more comfortable browsing experience. Central to this effort is developing a browser extension that uses AI technologies to detect and censor inappropriate text and images automatically. Research and Development Objectives:

1. Conduct a comprehensive review of existing approaches and technologies for censoring inappropriate content on web pages.
2. Explore methods for applying artificial intelligence to analyse text and images.
3. Identify critical components and functionalities for the censorship system and design its architecture.
4. Implement text and image analysis methods using pre-trained models and other AI techniques.
5. Develop a user-friendly interface for configuring censorship settings.
6. Test the extension across various web pages and optimise its performance to maximise efficiency and speed.

The innovative aspect of this work lies in its focus on personalisation, allowing users to customise censorship settings, such as defining a list of prohibited words and toggling between text and image filtering. It ensures a tailored, user-centric experience. The extension is designed to be compatible with all major web browsers, making it accessible to many users and enhancing its potential for broad adoption and practical utility across diverse user groups.

With the achievement of the goal, a program will be created to identify aggressive rhetoric in messages, images, news, and songs in comments on social networks (including for fakes, propaganda and disinformation), facilitating the perception of moods in online communication. It will also help improve customer service efficiency and assistance by understanding consumers' intentions and honest opinions when reviewing their feedback or complaints. In the defence sector, this will help to correctly analyse the mood of online conversations, which means it will prevent possible atrocities. Sarcasm detection can benefit many areas of NLP interest, including market research, opinion research, and information categorisation.

9.2. Technological advances in hate speech detection

The academic study of hate speech began in the early 2000s, spurred by the growing influence of the internet and social media, which introduced new forms of expression and interaction. Early research primarily focused on defining hate speech and examining its impact on individuals and society [1-3].

Defining the Concept of Hate Speech. In the seminal paper "The Concept of Hate Speech" (2003), the authors sought to define hate speech and outline its key characteristics, identifying elements such as aggression, discrimination, and incitement to hatred based on various sociocultural traits.

Social-Psychological Impact of Hate Speech. "The Psychology of Hate Speech" (2005) explored the psychological effects of hate speech on individuals and groups. This study examined the factors contributing to the acceptance and spread of hateful language, highlighting the broader social consequences of such behaviour.

Classification of Hate Speech. "A Taxonomy of Online Hate Speech" (2010) marked the first attempt to classify hate speech in online environments. The authors proposed a framework that categorised hate speech into various forms (such as racism, sexism, and homophobia), facilitating a deeper understanding and identification of online hostility.

These foundational studies provided the groundwork for further exploration into the nature of hate speech and the methods for mitigating its harmful effects [220-222]. In recent years, significant progress has been made in leveraging technology to detect hate speech in text and images. Key innovations include [223-225]:

1. Machine Learning as Classification Algorithms: Techniques such as Support Vector Machines, Random Forests, and neural networks have been applied to classify text and images, using labelled datasets to train models that automatically detect hate speech.

2. Natural Language Processing for Sentiment Analysis (NLP is used to evaluate the sentiment behind the text, identifying hostility or hateful intent) and Language Models (advanced models like BERT and GPT improve the understanding of context and semantics, enhancing the accuracy of hate speech detection).

3. Computer Vision for Image Recognition: CV algorithms, particularly deep learning models, enable the identification and classification of hate speech in visual content, improving accuracy in image-based data analysis.

4. Deep Learning based on Neural Networks: Through advanced feature extraction techniques, deep learning models address complex detection tasks and achieve high accuracy in hate speech classification.

5. Integration with Social Networks for APIs for Social Media: APIs have been developed for direct integration into social media platforms, enabling faster, more efficient content moderation by automating hate speech detection.

These technologies have revolutionised hate speech detection, making it faster, more efficient, and scalable. However, despite these advancements, several challenges persist in the field.

Challenges and Unresolved Issues. While technological advancements have improved hate speech detection, key challenges remain [225-228]:

1. False Classifications. The high rate of false positives and negatives is a persistent issue in ML-based detection systems. Improving the precision of algorithms to minimise errors is an ongoing research focus.

2. Adapting to Evolving Hate Speech. Language evolves and is influenced by shifting cultural and social dynamics. Detection systems must develop adaptive models capable of recognising new forms of hate speech as they emerge.

3. Multimodal Recognition. Integrating NLP and CV techniques needs enhancement to effectively detect hate speech in multimodal content (combining text and images).

4. Cultural Sensitivity. The concept of hate speech varies across cultures, so designing culturally aware detection models that adapt to different societal norms and sensitivities is essential.

5. Ethical Considerations. A crucial ethical concern is ensuring that hate speech detection systems are free from bias, discrimination, and privacy violations. Establishing ethical standards and guidelines for these systems is vital.

6. Recognising New Forms of Hostility. Hate speech is increasingly taking more subtle, coded forms, which require the development of more sophisticated algorithms to identify these emerging challenges.

7. Community Involvement. Engaging a diverse range of communities in developing and evaluating hate speech detection systems is critical to avoid narrow perspectives and ensure inclusivity in the solutions.

Therefore, despite significant progress in developing technological tools to identify and combat hate speech, further research is essential to address the remaining challenges. Improving classification techniques, expanding training datasets, and developing culturally adaptive models will create more effective and ethical systems. These advancements will provide all users with a safer and more equitable online environment.

9.3. Existing systems for detecting hostile/offensive speech

Numerous systems currently exist for detecting hostile or offensive speech in text, each employing various techniques to filter inappropriate content:

1. Google SafeSearch. Google SafeSearch filters inappropriate content from search results, including pornography, violence, and other unwanted material. SafeSearch uses advanced machine learning algorithms and artificial intelligence to identify and block inappropriate content. Its integration with other Google services makes it a reliable tool, particularly for families and educational institutions.

2. Net Nanny. Net Nanny is parental control software that allows parents to filter undesirable content, manage screen time, and monitor children's online activities. It uses content analysis technologies to block inappropriate material such as pornography and violence. Supporting multiple platforms (Windows, Mac, Android, iOS), Net Nanny offers customizable censorship settings tailored to family needs.

3. OpenDNS FamilyShield. OpenDNS FamilyShield is a free DNS-level service that automatically blocks pornographic and other undesirable content. Users configure their routers or devices to use OpenDNS servers, enabling network-wide content filtering without additional software.

4. K9 Web Protection. K9 Web Protection is a free tool that filters web content using Blue Coat technology, blocking pornography, violence, gambling, and other unwanted content. With customizable filtering levels and activity tracking, K9 Web Protection is famous among parents and educational institutions due to its robust filtering algorithms and detailed configuration options.

5. Adblock Plus. Although primarily known as an ad blocker, Adblock Plus also blocks inappropriate content. Users can add custom filters to block pornography and other unwanted material. Its open-source nature and community support allow users to create and share filters, expanding the tool’s functionality to meet their needs.

While these systems differ in their approaches, they all aim to create a safer and more comfortable internet environment. Our browser extension will combine the best features of these solutions while introducing new methods to maximise efficiency and user-friendliness. Existing Systems for Detecting Hostile/Offensive Speech in Text. Several systems specialise in detecting hostile or offensive speech in text:

1. Perspective API. Developed by Jigsaw, a subsidiary of Alphabet Inc., Perspective API is a machine learning-based tool that detects toxic language and harmful content in text. It is designed for scalability and allows developers to integrate its content moderation capabilities into various platforms, apps, or websites.

2. HateSonar. HateSonar uses machine learning and advanced natural language processing (NLP) techniques to detect hostile and offensive speech. It evaluates the text's context and meaning to identify different types of hate speech. HateSonar's API enables developers to automatically scan content and detect potential instances of hate, with adjustable thresholds for moderation.

3. OpenAI Content Policy. OpenAI's Content Policy defines the acceptable use of its models and services, prioritising safety, ethical standards, and respect for users' rights. It outlines prohibited content, including abusive, harmful, or rights-violating material, such as harassment and misinformation. The policy emphasises the need to avoid bias and commits to ongoing research to mitigate potential biases in AI models.

These systems rely on NLP techniques, machine learning algorithms, and large annotated datasets to detect hate speech and offensive content in text, representing key innovations in content moderation and online safety.

To compare existing solutions that perform similar tasks, we will evaluate the following three options: Net Nanny, K9 Web Protection and Norton Family (Table 9.1). Basic Comparison Criteria:

1. Platform Support:

- Net Nanny: Server/Desktop/Mobile (Windows, macOS, iOS, Android);
- K9 Web Protection: Desktop (Windows, macOS);
- Norton Family: Server/Desktop/Mobile (Windows, iOS, Android);
- Technical Characteristics and Programming Languages and Development Tools:
- Net Nanny: C++, Java, API for mobile platforms
- K9 Web Protection: C++, .NET
- Norton Family: Java, C, API for mobile platforms
- Compliance with General Requirements, Unification and Interoperability:
- Net Nanny: High unification across platforms, good interoperability
- K9 Web Protection: Limited unification (desktop platforms only)
- Norton Family: High unification across platforms, good interoperability

2. FURPS+ Quality Requirements:

- Net Nanny: Functionality (High), Usability (High), Reliability (High), Performance (Medium), Supportability (High);
- K9 Web Protection: Functionality (Medium), Usability (Medium), Reliability (Medium), Performance (High), Supportability (Medium);
- Norton Family: Functionality (High), Usability (High), Reliability (High), Performance (Medium), Supportability (High);

3. Performance and Efficiency in Task Execution:

- Net Nanny: High content filtering efficiency, but resource-intensive.
- K9 Web Protection: High performance but moderate filtering efficiency.
- Norton Family: High filtering efficiency but moderate performance due to the large data volumes for processing.

4. Cost and Maintenance:

- Net Nanny: High cost, significant maintenance expenses.

- K9 Web Protection: Free, low-maintenance costs.
- Norton Family: Moderate cost, average maintenance costs.

5. Additional Features:

- Net Nanny: Multilingual support, flexible settings.
- K9 Web Protection: No mobile versions, simple interface.
- Norton Family: Integration with other Norton products, detailed customisation options.

6. For the evaluation of features, we will use a Boolean assessment system (Yes/No):

Table 9.1. Assessment of Characteristics

Characteristic	Net Nanny	K9 Web Protection	Norton Family	Extension
Mobile Platform Support	Yes	No	Yes	No
High Unification	Yes	No	Yes	Yes
Interoperability	Yes	No	Yes	Yes
High Functionality	Yes	No	Yes	Yes
High usability	Yes	No	Yes	Yes
High reliability	Yes	Yes	Yes	Yes
High performance	Yes	Yes	Yes	Yes
High operational suitability	Yes	Yes	Yes	No
Low cost	No	Yes	No	Yes
Additional conveniences (customisation)	Yes	No	Yes	Yes

9.4. Current state of content censorship development on web pages

Several well-established solutions, including Net Nanny, K9 Web Protection, and Norton Family, characterise content censorship on web pages. Each of these systems has its strengths:

- Net Nanny: Offers high functionality and reliability but is associated with high costs and significant maintenance efforts.
- K9 Web Protection: Free of charge and highly performant, but provides limited functionality and lacks mobile versions.

- Norton Family: Well-integrated with other Norton products, offering high unification, though its performance is moderate, and it comes with a moderate cost.

Main Drawbacks of Existing Solutions:

- High costs for certain products limit accessibility.
- Limited functionality and absence of mobile versions in some systems.
- Performance issues when processing large amounts of data, leading to inefficiency

Description and Assessment of Similar Solutions. An analysis of existing solutions reveals notable shortcomings that warrant improvement. Specifically:

- The lack of mobile versions in some products restricts their usability across devices.
- High costs render many solutions less accessible to a broader audience.
- Many existing systems offer limited personalisation options, preventing users from fully customising the censorship process to their needs.

9.5. Methods and methodology

Description and Assessment of Similar Solutions. An analysis of existing solutions reveals notable shortcomings that warrant improvement. Specifically:

9.5.1. Business process modelling

Business Process Model and Notation is a standardised graphical notation designed to model business processes and illustrate the interactions between involved participants. BPMN diagrams simplify the creation of clear and consistent flowcharts for business processes, aiding in their analysis, optimisation, and automation. The primary objective of BPMN is to provide a transparent representation of a business process from start to finish, visualising the sequence of operations required at each stage. Its key advantage is flexibility, enabling the development of flowcharts that range from simple to highly complex. This standardised approach improves communication, understanding, and collaboration within teams, ultimately supporting the optimisation and automation of business processes across organisations [228].

For our project, we have developed three BPMN diagrams (Fig. 9.1-9.3), one of which explicitly illustrates the activation of the system's core functions. To begin, the user activates the extension and selects the desired function by clicking on the appropriate option. The available functions include:

- Hiding inappropriate text on websites.
- Hiding inappropriate text in images on websites.
- Hiding text based on a custom dictionary.

Once a function is selected, the system analyses and processes the content to conceal inappropriate material. The diagram also shows how the system's core functions can be deactivated once the process is complete.

To begin, the user must activate the extension. Then, they can turn off the desired function by selecting the appropriate option. The available functions include:

- Hiding inappropriate text on websites.
- Hiding inappropriate text in images on websites.
- Hiding text based on a custom dictionary.

Once a function is disabled, the system will restore all settings to their original state, completing the process. Additionally, the diagram illustrates the functionality for adding new entries to the custom dictionary.

To start, the user must activate the extension. They then enter a new word into the text field and click the "Add to Dictionary" button. Following this, they enable the function "Hide Inappropriate Text in Images on Websites." The system will process and conceal the inappropriate content accordingly. If necessary, the user can deactivate the extension.

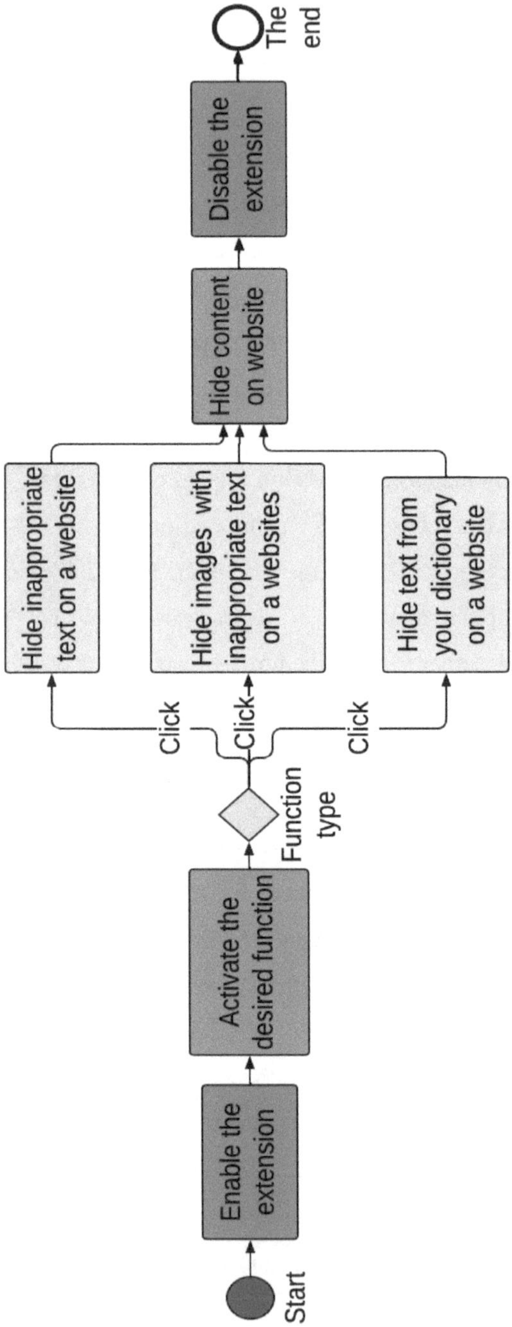

Fig. 9.1. BPMN Diagram

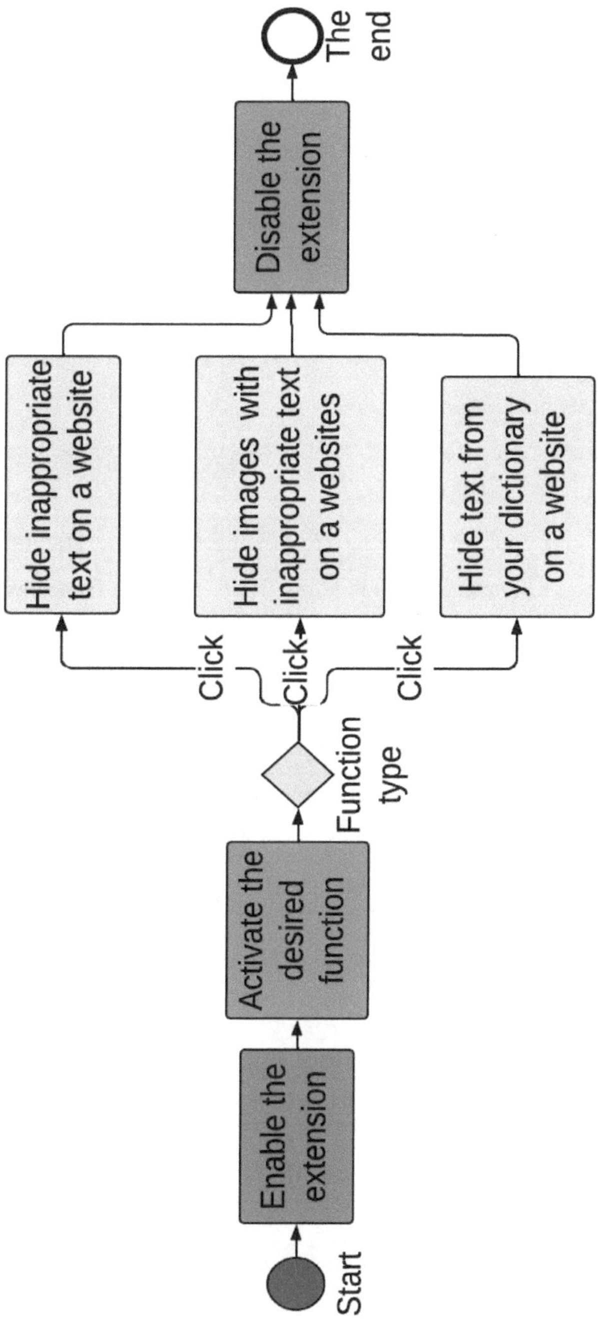

Fig. 9.2. BPMN Diagram

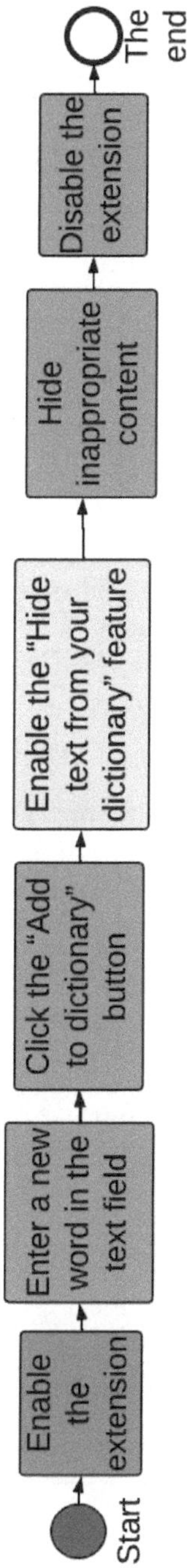

Fig. 9.3. BPMN Diagram

9.5.2. Project requirements modelling

Use Case Diagram provides a conceptual representation of the system, serving several vital purposes:

- Defining the typical boundaries and context of the software being modelled;
- Formulating general requirements for the functional behaviour of the designed system;
- Developing an initial conceptual model of the system to be further detailed into logical and physical models;
- Preparing initial documentation facilitates collaboration between system developers, clients, and users.

The key elements and concepts associated with the Use Case Diagram include Use Case, Actor, Interface, Association Relationship, Extension, Generalisation, and Inclusion [225]. The requirement formulation procedure for the system is shown in Table 9.2.

Table 9.2. Requirement Formulation Procedure for the System

Type of Requirements	Purpose	Content of Requirements
Business Requirements	*Define the goals of the business structure that the system will help achieve, as well as the problems it will solve.*	Key Business Requirements: 1. Provide the ability to log into the system. 2. Ensure users can select the required functions. 3. Enable the system to hide inappropriate website content, including text and images.
User Requirements	*Outline the tasks and actions that users can perform using the system.*	1. The user desires to receive statistics in a simple and easily understandable format. 2. The user wants the ability to add custom words to the dictionary. 3. The user expects the program to function reliably, efficiently, without interruptions, and to be easily accessible.
Functional Requirements	*Description of What the System Should Do*	1. Each user should have access to their history and results. 2. Each user must be able to activate or deactivate all functions.

		3. Activation should result in the changes being visible on the website, and deactivation should revert the changes.
Non-Functional Requirements	*Description of How the System Should Operate to Fulfil Its Functions*	1. The system must be cross-browser compatible. 2. It should be supported on the following operating systems: Windows, Linux, and macOS. 3. The system must be available 24/7, with technical maintenance scheduled during off-peak hours. 4. The system should be capable of handling at least 1,000 simultaneous users.

According to the subject area, we are constructing a Use Case Diagram using Rational Rose (see Fig. 9.4). This diagram illustrates the interaction between two key actors and various use cases for the browser extension:

Actors:

1. User: The individual who installs and uses the browser extension.

2. Extension: The system is responsible for censoring or concealing text, images, and individual words, as well as providing statistical reports.

Use Cases:

- Activate Extension: The user activates the extension to start using its features.
- Select Function: The user selects a specific function from the extension's interface.
- Hide Words from Dictionary: The extension hides words on websites that match those in the user's custom dictionary.
- Add to Dictionary: The user adds a new word to the dictionary.
- Enter Word: The user types the word into the designated field and clicks "Add to Dictionary."
- Remove from Dictionary: The user removes a word from the dictionary.
- Hide Inappropriate Text on Websites: The extension conceals inappropriate text found on websites.
- Analyse and Label Website Text: The extension analyses and labels text on websites.
- Hide Offensive Text: The extension hides text deemed offensive.

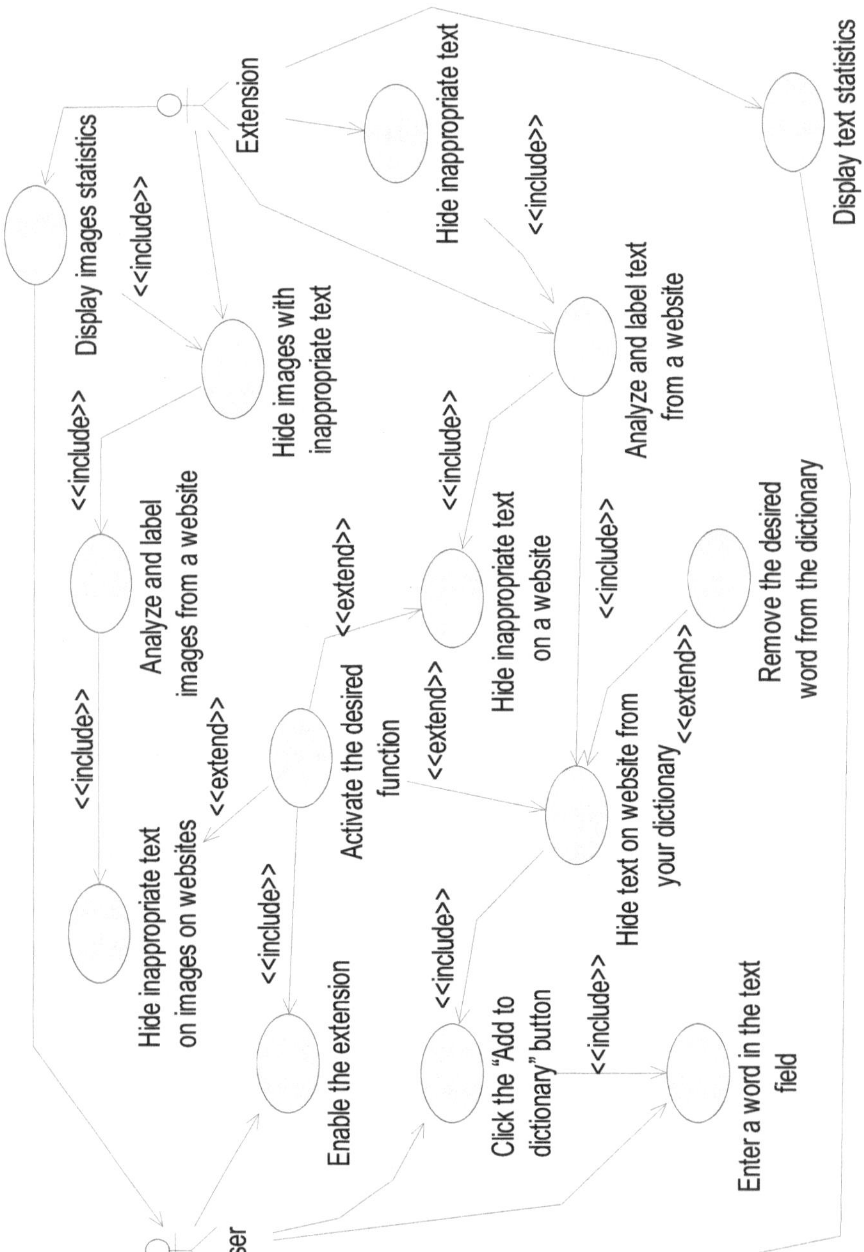

Fig. 9.4. Use Case Diagram

- Hide Images with Inappropriate Text: The extension conceals images containing unacceptable text.
- Display Text Statistics: The extension provides text visibility and censorship statistics.
- Analyse and Label Website Images: The extension processes and labels images on websites.
- Display Image Statistics: The extension shows image visibility and censorship statistics.

Initially, the user activates the browser extension and selects the desired function to enable it from the interface. For instance, if the user chooses the function "Hide Images with Inappropriate Text on Websites," the extension initiates a comprehensive scan of all images on the website. These images are processed by various AI models that extract and classify text. Following this, the extension re-scans the photos to ensure that those classified as containing inappropriate content are hidden. Once this process is complete, the extension provides the user with detailed statistics on the amount of hidden content. Similarly, if the function selected is to "Hide Inappropriate Text on Websites," the extension begins by scanning all text on the site. This text is sent to AI for classification, which labels it based on appropriateness. The extension then hides the text marked as inappropriate and presents the user with statistics detailing the extent of the content concealed. For the function "Hide Words on Websites from Your Dictionary," users can add specific words to a custom dictionary. It is done by entering the phrase into a designated field and pressing the "Add to Dictionary" button. With these words added, the extension will hide any occurrences of these terms on websites when the function is activated.

Each of these primary functions incorporates a hover effect, allowing users to temporarily view hidden content by hovering the mouse over it. When the mouse is moved away, the content reverts to being hidden. Upon deactivating any function, all previously hidden content becomes visible again, though statistics remain accessible. There is also a separate button to clear the statistics if needed.

9.5.3. *Modelling of domain objects*

A Cass diagram represents a static structural model of the designed system. It is considered a graphical representation of the structural relationships within the logical model of the system that are invariant over time. The diagram consists of elements that collectively reflect declarative knowledge about the domain. These elements are interpreted in terms of fundamental UML (Unified Modelling Language) concepts, such as classes, interfaces, and the relationships between them and their constituent components. By illustrating the system's components and interactions, the class diagram provides a comprehensive view of its architecture, facilitating a better understanding and documentation of its structure.

Description of system classes is shown in Table 9.3.

Table 9.3. Description of System Classes

Object Classes		Class Attributes		Class Methods	
Class Name	Purpose of the Class	Attribute Name	Attribute Content	Method Name	Action Content
User	An object that initiates all processes available in the extension	User_ID	User_ID	ActivateExtension	The user activates the extension
				ActivateDesiredFunction	The user enables the desired function.
		Login	Login	AddWordToDictionary	The user adds a required word to the dictionary
		Password	Password	DeactivateExtension	The user deactivates the extension
Extension	An object that initiates the process of all actions commanded by the User	ID_Extension	ID_Extension	ExtractTextOrImageFromSite	ExtractTextOrImageFromSite
		Extension Name	Extension Name	HideTextOrImageOnSite	HideTextOrImageOnSite
		Version	Version	HideDictionaryWordsOnSite	HideDictionaryWordsOnSite
				DeactivateCensorship	DeactivateCensorship
				DisplayStatistics	DisplayStatistics

According to the subject area, we are constructing a class diagram using Rational Rose (Fig. 9.5).

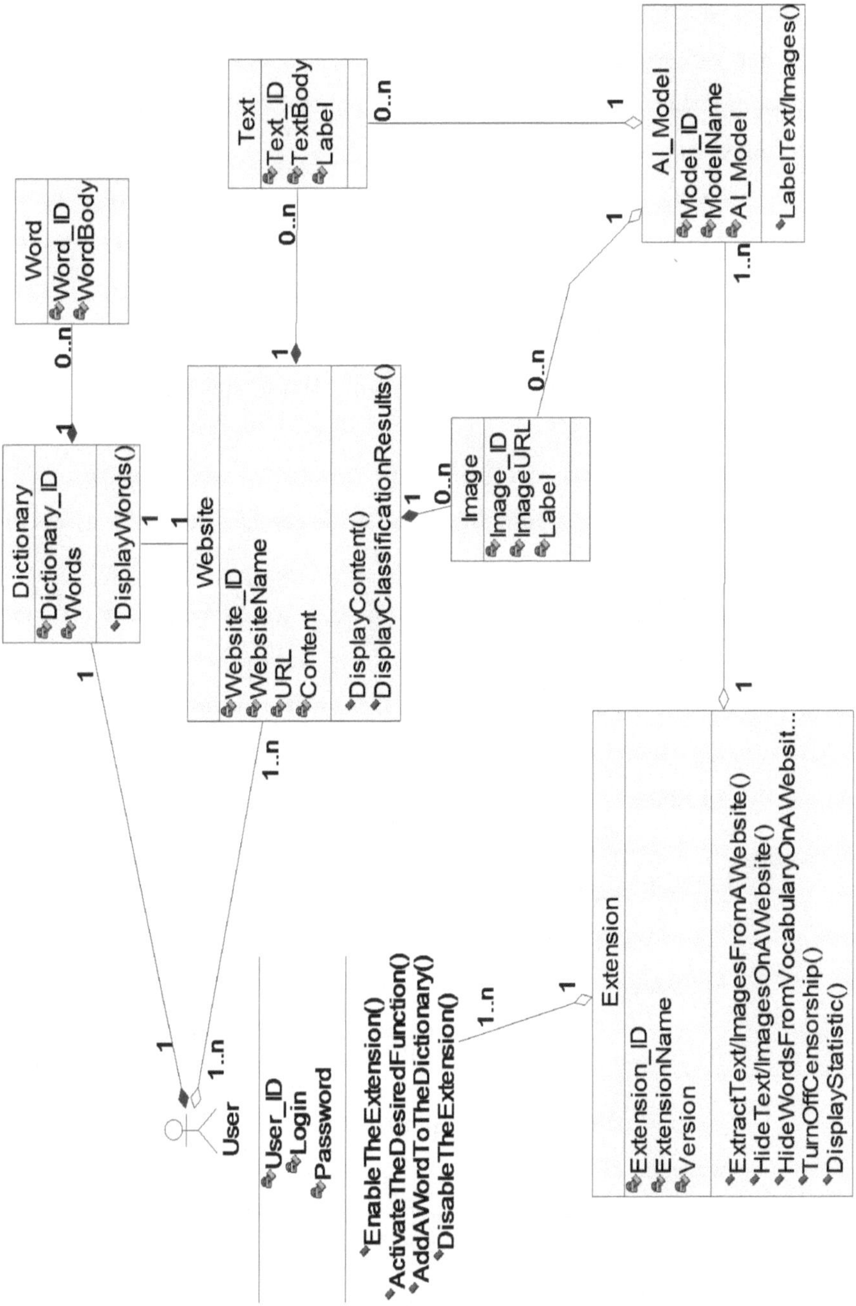

Fig. 9.5. Class Diagram

A class diagram illustrates the static structure of the system model, focusing on the primary classes and their relationships within the object-oriented paradigm. Each class is defined with specific attributes and methods, representing various system components.

1. User

- Attributes:
  - User_ID: Unique identifier for the user.
  - Login: User's login credentials.
  - Password: User's password.
- Methods:
  - ActivateExtension(): Activates the browser extension.
  - ActivateDesiredFunction(): Selects and activates a specific function.
  - AddWordToDictionary(): Adds a new word to the custom dictionary.
  - DeactivateExtension(): Deactivates the browser extension.

2. Extension

- Attributes:
  - Extension_ID: Unique identifier for the extension.
  - ExtensionName: Name of the extension.
  - Version: Version of the extension.
- Methods:
  - FilterText/ImageFromSite(): Filters text or images from a website.
  - HideText/ImageOnSite(): Hides text or pictures on the website.
  - HideText/WordsFromDictionary(): Hides text based on custom dictionary words.
  - DeactivateExtension(): Deactivates the extension.

o DisplayStatistics(): Displays statistics related to text and image censorship.

3. Dictionary Attributes:

o Dictionary_ID: Unique identifier for the dictionary.

o Words: A Collection of words in the dictionary.

o Methods: DisplayWords() - Displays the words contained in the dictionary.

4. Word Attributes: Word_ID (Unique identifier for the word) and WordText (Text of the word).

5. Website

- Attributes:

o Site_ID: Unique identifier for the website.

o SiteName: Name of the website.

o URL: URL of the website.

o Content: Content of the website.

- Methods:

o DisplayContent(): Displays the content of the website.

o DisplayClassificationResults(): Shows results of the content classification.

6. Text Attributes:

o Text_ID: Unique identifier for the text.

o TextType: Type of text (e.g., article, blog post).

o Label: Classification label for the text.

7. Image Attributes:

o Image_ID: Unique identifier for the image.

o ImageURL: URL of the image.

o Label: Classification label for the image.

8. AI Model Attributes:

o Model_ID: Unique identifier for the AI model.

o ModelName: Name of the AI model.

o Model: The actual AI model used for classification.

9. Methods: AssignLabelToText/Image() - Assigns classification labels to text or images.

This class diagram provides a detailed view of the system's static structure, highlighting how different components interact and contribute to the overall functionality of the browser extension.

9.5.4. Modelling of the problem-solving process in the project

An activity diagram is a graphical representation that outlines the activities that flow within a system. It is a specialised graph similar to a finite state machine, where vertices denote specific actions, and transitions occur when these actions are completed. Each action represents a fundamental unit of behaviour, processing inputs to produce outputs. Multiple actions are executed in an activity, and each can be performed numerous times during a single activity instance. Actions in the diagram must handle data, perform transformations, and may involve testing. Some actions might follow specific sequences, and higher levels of abstraction can introduce multiple logical threads and synchronisation mechanisms to ensure correct execution order [225]. For the given domain, the activity diagram is created using the Rational Rose environment (Fig. 9.6).

The diagram begins with the user activating the browser extension. Following activation, the user selects the desired function. The extension then reads the webpage's content and sends this data to the AI model. The AI model processes and classifies the data, returning the results to the extension. Based on these results, the extension generates statistics and hides any identified inappropriate content. Finally, the user deactivates the extension, concluding the process. Subsequently, the process of text censorship is modelled (Fig. 9.7a).

The activity diagram outlines the sequence of steps involved in text censorship on a website, divided into three main stages [225-234]:

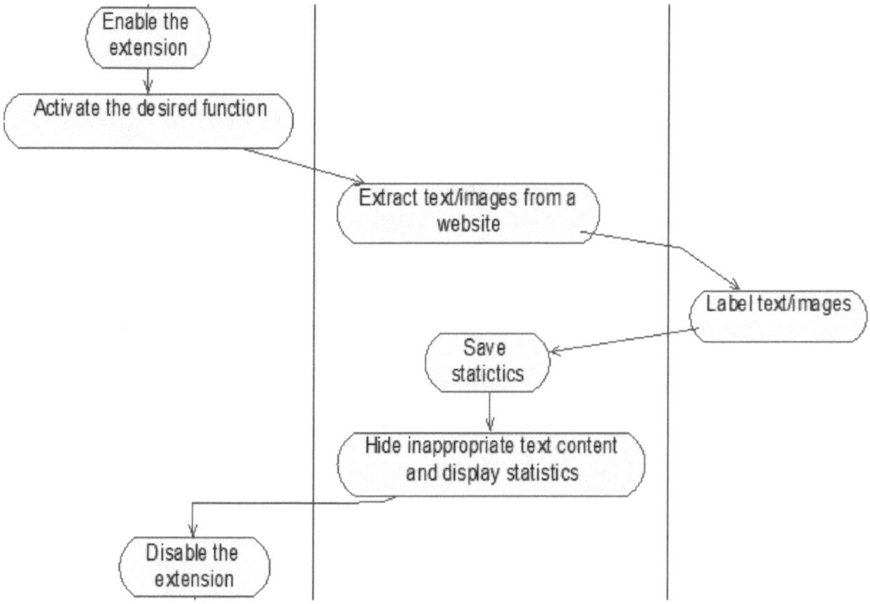

Fig. 9.6. Activity Diagram

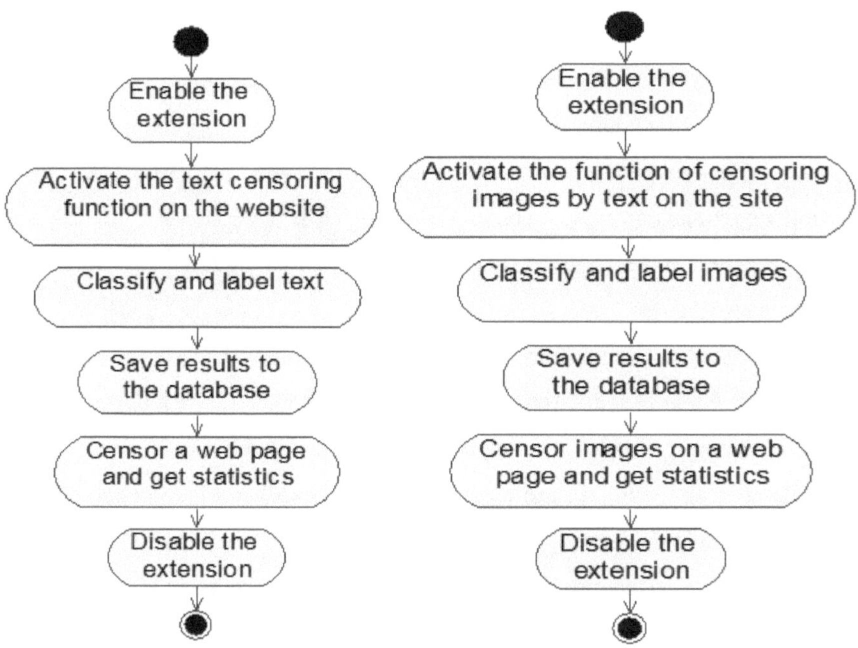

Fig. 9.7. Activity Diagrams

1. The preparation begins with the user activating the text censorship extension within their browser. Once the extension is active, the user must enable the text censorship function by selecting a designated button on the extension's interface.

2. Text Processing. Upon activation, the extension classifies and labels the text on the webpage. Each text piece is evaluated and labelled to determine if it should be censored. The results from this classification and labelling are then saved in a database, ensuring the system can use this information for future censorship decisions.

3. Text Censorship. In the censorship stage, the extension hides or obscures text on the webpage that has been identified as offensive. Alongside this, the database generates and stores statistics regarding the amount of censored text. The user can deactivate the extension at any point, stopping further text censorship on websites.

This diagram also models the process for image censorship, following a similar structured approach (Fig. 9.7b). This diagram illustrates the steps in censoring images on a website, guided by textual content. The process is segmented into three main stages:

1. The preparation process commences with activating the image censorship extension on the website. Following this, the user needs to enable the image censorship function by clicking a designated button provided by the extension.

2. Text Processing. Once the function is enabled, the extension classifies and labels the text found within images on the webpage. These labels are crucial for determining which images should be censored. The results of this classification and labelling are then saved in a database, which supports future image censorship decisions.

3. Image Censorship. In the censorship stage, the extension proceeds to hide or obscure images on the webpage identified as offensive. Along with censoring images, the extension collects and stores statistics on the number of images

censored in the database. Users can deactivate the image censorship extension anytime, halting further website image censorship.

Subsequently, the process for censoring text from the dictionary has been modelled (Fig. 9.8a). The diagram illustrates the processes for activating and deactivating the website extension and adding words to the dictionary.

Activation of the Website Extension. The process begins with the user activating the text censorship extension on the website. After activation, the user must enable the text censorship function, which prepares the extension to censor text based on predefined criteria.

Deactivation of the Website Extension. At any time, the user can choose to deactivate the extension. Upon deactivation, the extension ceases to perform any text censorship on the website, stopping further modifications to the site's content. Following the activation and deactivation processes, the diagram also models the steps for adding new words to the dictionary. Users can input words into the dictionary, which the extension will then use to identify and censor matching text on the website. The process for adding words to the dictionary has been modelled. The diagram illustrates adding words to a dictionary through a web extension (Fig. 9.8b).

First, you need to activate the Extension. Next, enter the desired word into the text field. The word will be added to the dictionary after clicking the "Add to Dictionary" button. After this, you can deactivate the Extension if needed.

The following diagram is an activity diagram. It describes the logic of the program in Fig. 9.9.

First, the program reads the file (dataset) and puts it into the Pandas object table. Then, stop words, numbers, punctuation marks, and references are removed (the last column of the table). None of these characters helps detect sarcasm in the text. Thus, after "cleaning up the text", the data is ready to build vectors for the future creation of models with neural networks. Neural networks are trained to detect sarcasm using scales and tokenised datasets. After testing all the created models, the results are returned as tables and graphs. Since the program has many functions that can confuse you, you need a diagram showing all the program's processes in time. The following sequence diagram (Fig. 9.10) shows that the text first passes through the "denoise" function. It removes stop words, numbers, and punctuation. Next, you need to select the properties from the tax. After extraction of properties, the set is divided into training and testing. The future model is trained during the training course, and its work is tested during test one. The result of the work is displayed on the screen.

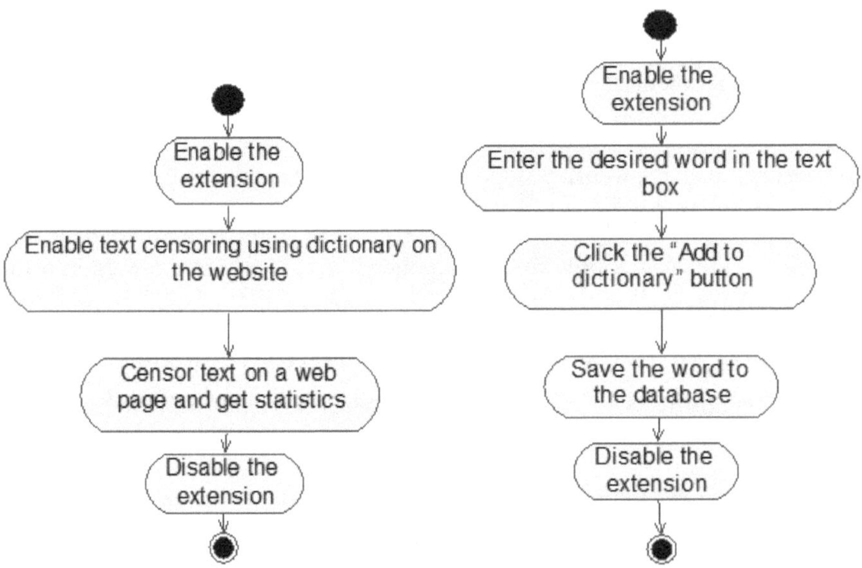

Fig. 9.8. Activity Diagrams

To build a class diagram, we have defined four main classes: Author, Text, ClassificationModel, and Result. The Result entity class is used to store information about the result of checking the text in the system after the destruction of objects of this class. The documentation section specifies an explanatory text: "Keeps information about the results of checking the text." This class has two attributes with a private visibility quantifier: author: String and date: Date, and the public (getResult(): String) visibility quantifier operation. The result is combined with the ClassificationModel class by the association relation.

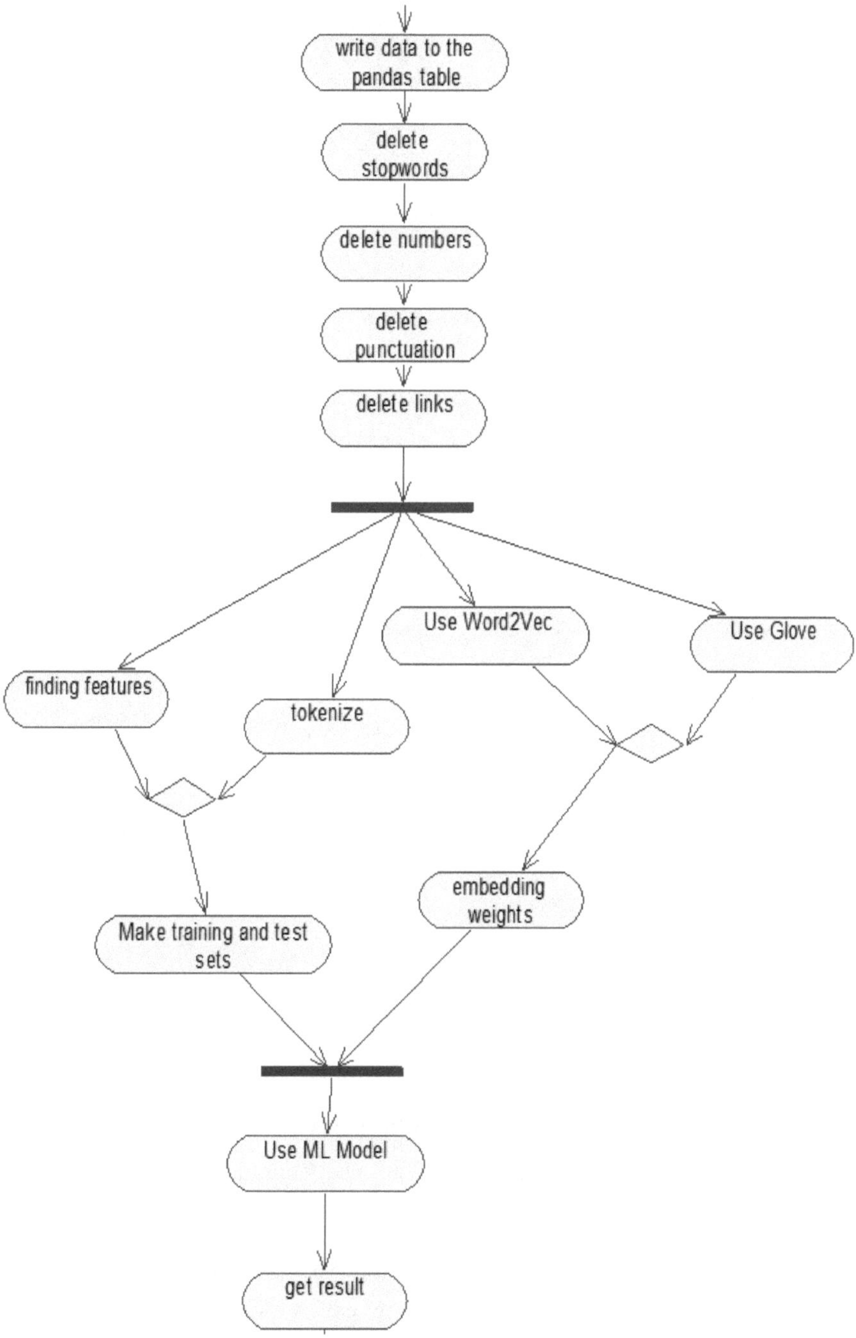

Fig. 9.9. Activity diagram

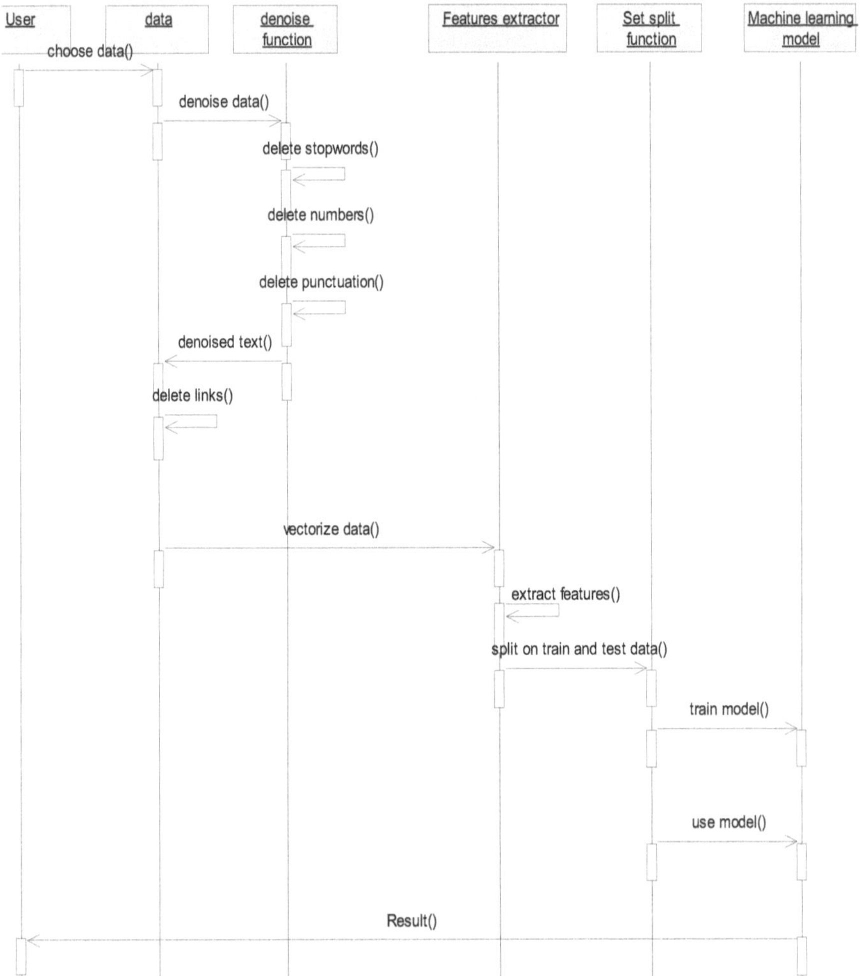

Fig. 9.10. Sequence diagram

The ClassificationModel class has two private attributes (name: String and supportedOS: List = ['Windows', 'MacOS']), six operations with the public visibility quantifier (checkText(), checkFormat(), returnResult(), reieveProblemReport(), denyTextChecking(), sendWarning()) and is associated with the Result and Text classes by association relations. reieveProblemReport – receive a message about the policy, denyTextChecking (if the language is unclear), sendWarning (notify the user about something, inability to check).

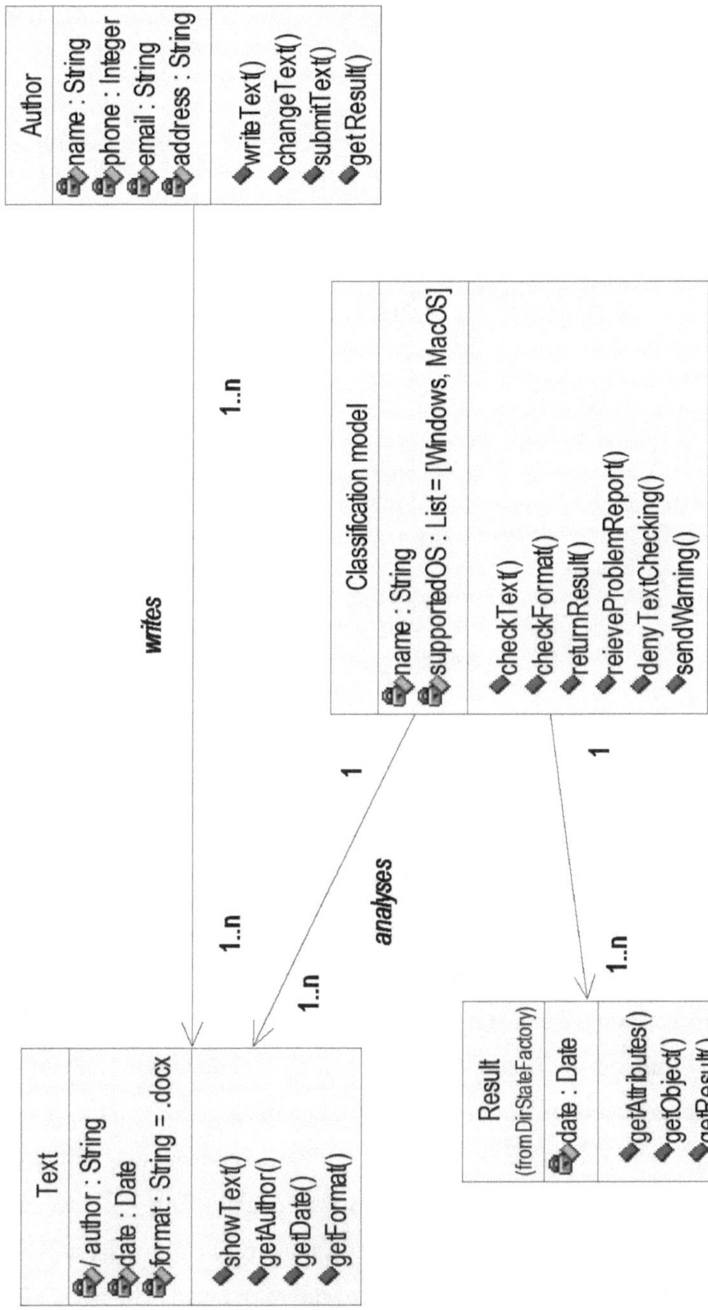

Fig. 9.11. Class diagram

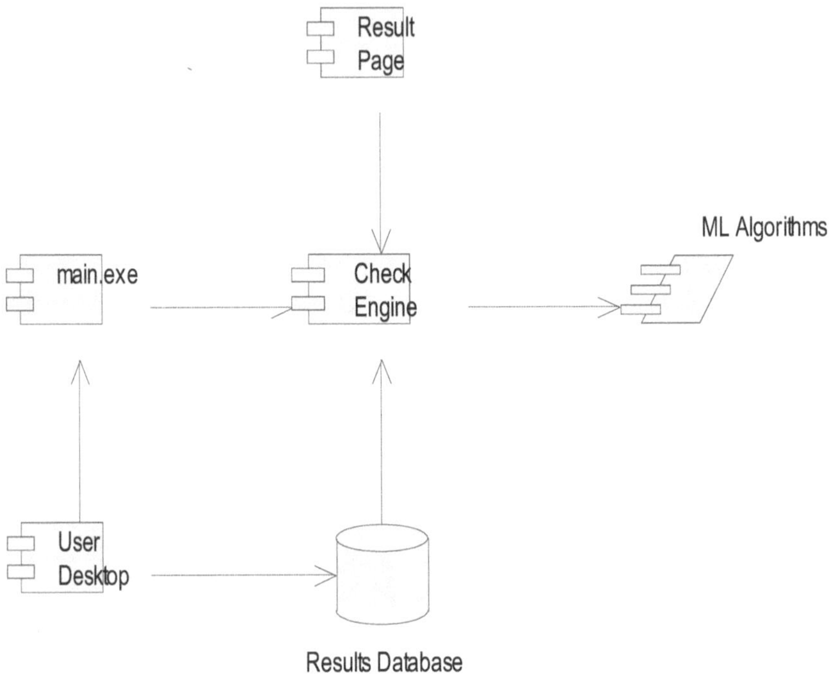

Fig. 9.12. Component Diagram

The Author class describes the author of the work and has four private attributes and four public operations. The basic operations for this class are the writeText() and submitText() operations. The author is related to the Text class by association relations. The Text class has three private attributes (author, date of writing, and format; the latter is set to .docx by default) and four operations, the main one being the text view – showText(). For the author attribute, the Derived (/) property is specified. This class is combined with the author class through an association relation. The multiplicity of all bonds and the names of the association bonds are indicated in Fig. 9.11. The component diagram is shown in Fig. 9.12. The User Desktop component is a type of program window, depending on the main.exe component (the main executable file) and the Results Database (a database that also contains the results of defining texts). The Result Page and Results Database components depend on the Check Engine component (a model for directly determining whether the text is sarcastic). The latter depends on the chosen machine learning algorithm. Methods for determining sarcasm in the text [234-246]:

1. Based on self-defined rules.
2. Based on the machine learning method.
3. Based on the machine/deep learning method.

The construction of rules for defining sarcasm is based on its features. For example, pragmatic (punctuation-related) features. The number of question marks can be a sign of sarcasm, the number of exclamation marks, the number of periods, words written in capital letters, words in quotation marks, and repeated vowels in text. Interjections (woo, oh, wow) and laughter expressions (lol, hahaha, hehe, rofl). It's good to focus only on parts of speech with some emotional meaning, such as nouns, adverbs, and adjectives, ADV+ADJ+N. Emoticons are commonly used in ironic or sarcastic expressions. Lexical properties such as TF-IDF can be extracted. Some properties can be extracted from hashtags because sometimes they express emotions. Three sets of features of a hashtag can be identified: a positive hashtag, a negative hashtag, and the coexistence of a positive and negative hashtag.

9.6. Experiments and results

9.6.1. Model construction for problem-solving

A dataset derived from Twitter was used to investigate the detection of hate speech (https://www.kaggle.com/datasets/mrmorj/hate-speech-and-offensive-language-dataset). The text in this dataset is categorised into three classes: hate speech, offensive language, and neither. Given the sensitive nature of this research, it is crucial to acknowledge that the dataset contains text that may be considered racist, sexist, homophobic, or otherwise offensive. The dataset consists of textual data and corresponding class labels: Class (hate, offensive, neither) and Text (Various text samples). Python and Google Colab were employed to train the model at this stage. The initial step involved connecting Google Drive to Google Colab to access the dataset and facilitate saving the trained model. The necessary libraries have been connected. NumPy (Numerical Python) is a high-level library for numerical computations in Python. It supports multi-dimensional arrays and various mathematical functions, enabling convenient and efficient operations involving numbers, arrays, linear algebra, statistics, and other mathematical computations. Pandas is a powerful library for data manipulation and analysis. It enables operations such as reading and writing data from various file formats, filtering, sorting, merging, aggregating, and visualising data. Pandas are widely used in scientific research, finance, business analytics, and many other fields to handle complex datasets. The dataset hate_speech.csv is read and displayed as follows (Fig. 9.14):

```
import numpy as np  import pandas as pd
df_offensive=pd.read_csv("/content/drive/MyDrive/hate_speech.c
sv") df_offensive.head()
```

	Unnamed: 0	count	hate_speech	offensive_language	neither	class	tweet
0	0	3	0	0	3	2	!!! RT @mayasolovely: As a woman you shouldn't...
1	1	3	0	3	0	1	!!!!! RT @mleew17: boy dats cold...tyga dwn ba...
2	2	3	0	3	0	1	!!!!!!! RT @UrKindOfBrand Dawg!!!! RT @80sbaby...
3	3	3	0	2	1	1	!!!!!!!!! RT @C_G_Anderson: @viva_based she lo...
4	4	6	0	6	0	1	!!!!!!!!!!!!! RT @ShenikaRoberts: The shit you...

Fig. 9.14. Results

Next, the unnecessary columns need to be removed.

```
df_offensive.drop(['Unnamed:
0','count','hate_speech','offensive_language','neither'],axis=
1,inplace=True) df_offensive.head()
```

Only the class and tweet columns were retained (Fig. 9.15). The values that the class column can take are 0, 1, and 2.

```
df_offensive['class'].unique()
```

Next, we replaced these values with 'hate_speech', 'offensive_speech', and 'no_hate'.

	class	tweet
0	2	!!! RT @mayasolovely: As a woman you shouldn't...
1	1	!!!!! RT @mleew17: boy dats cold...tyga dwn ba...
2	1	!!!!!!! RT @UrKindOfBrand Dawg!!!! RT @80sbaby...
3	1	!!!!!!!!! RT @C_G_Anderson: @viva_based she lo...
4	1	!!!!!!!!!!!!! RT @ShenikaRoberts: The shit you...

Fig. 9.15. Results

```
df_offensive["class"].replace({0: 'hate_speech'},
inplace=True) df_offensive["class"].replace({1:
'offensive_speech'}, inplace=True)
df_offensive["class"].replace({2:'no_hate' }, inplace=True)
```

We imported the Seaborn library and created a histogram to display the distribution of elements across the three labels: 'hate_speech', 'offensive_speech', and 'no_hate' (Fig. 9.16).

```
import seaborn as sns
sns.countplot(x=df_offensive["class"])
```

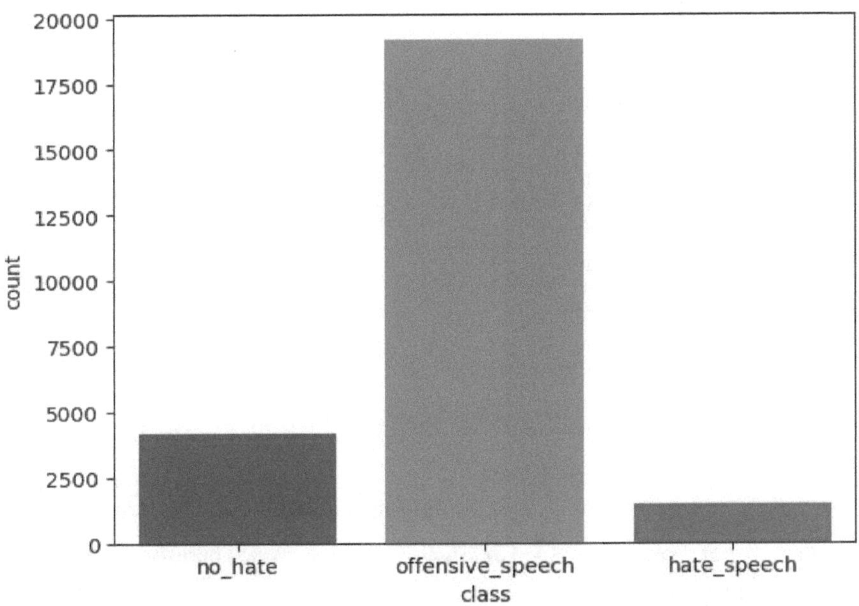

Fig. 9.16. Results

Subsequently, we rename the columns (Fig. 9.17).

```
df_offensive.rename(columns ={'class':'label'}, inplace =
True) df_offensive.rename(columns ={'tweet':'text'}, inplace =
True) df_offensive['label'].unique() df_offensive.head(50)
```

	label	text
0	no_hate	!!! RT @mayasolovely: As a woman you shouldn't...
1	offensive_speech	!!!!! RT @mleew17: boy dats cold...tyga dwn ba...
2	offensive_speech	!!!!!!! RT @UrKindOfBrand Dawg!!!! RT @80sbaby...
3	offensive_speech	!!!!!!!!! RT @C_G_Anderson: @viva_based she lo...
4	offensive_speech	!!!!!!!!!!!!! RT @ShenikaRoberts: The shit you...
5	offensive_speech	!!!!!!!!!!!!!!!!!!"@T_Madison_x: The shit just...
6	offensive_speech	!!!!!!"@__BrighterDays: I can not just sit up ...

Fig. 9.17. Result

Next, we import the re-library using regular expressions (regex) to clean the data (Fig. 9.18).

```
import re
def clean_text(text):
    text = re.sub('RT ', '', text)
    text = re.sub('https?://\S+|www\.\S+', '', text)     text
= re.sub('@\w*\s*:*', '', text)     text = re.sub('&\W*\w*;*',
'', text)
    text = re.sub('!*', '', text)     text = re.sub('\n', '',
text)     text = re.sub('\[.*?\]', '', text)
    text = re.sub('<.*?>+', '', text)
    return text.strip().lower()
df_offensive['text']=df_offensive['text'].apply(clean_text)
df_offensive.head(50)
```

FastText requires the text to be in a specific format. The template is as follows: __label__offensive_speech. She looks like a train. Therefore, we convert all text to this format (Fig. 9.18).

```
#templates
```

```
#__label__offensive_speech she look like a tranny
#__label__offensive_speech the shit you hear ab... #labeling
df=df_offensive
df['label'] = '__label__' + df['label'].astype(str) df.head()
# Fig. 13a
df['category_text'] = df['label'] + ' ' + df['text']
df.head(5)  # Fig. 13b
```

	label	text
0	no_hate	as a woman you shouldn't complain about cleani...
1	offensive_speech	boy dats cold...tyga dwn bad for cuffin dat ho...
2	offensive_speech	dawg you ever fuck a bitch and she start to c...
3	offensive_speech	she look like a tranny
4	offensive_speech	the shit you hear about me might be true or it...
5	offensive_speech	" the shit just blows me..claim you so faithfu...
6	offensive_speech	" i can not just sit up and hate on another bi...
7	offensive_speech	cause i'm tired of you big bitches coming for ...
8	offensive_speech	" you might not get ya bitch back thats that "
9	offensive_speech	" hobbies include: fighting mariam"bitch
10	offensive_speech	" keeks is a bitch she curves everyone " lol i...
11	offensive_speech	" murda gang bitch its gang land "
12	offensive_speech	" so hoes that smoke are losers ? " yea ... go...
13	offensive_speech	" bad bitches is the only thing that i like "
14	offensive_speech	" bitch get up off me "
15	offensive_speech	" bitch nigga miss me with it "
16	offensive_speech	" bitch plz whatever "
17	offensive_speech	" bitch who do you love "
18	offensive_speech	" bitches get cut off everyday b "

Fig. 9.18. Results

9.6.2. Dataset partitioning

Parting the dataset into training and testing sets is critical for assessing and enhancing machine learning models. This approach helps identify overfitting and fine-tune hyperparameters and objectively evaluates the model's performance on new data. Next, we will divide the dataset into training and testing subsets.

```
from sklearn.model_selection import train_test_split train,
test = train_test_split(df, test_size=0.3)
```

The code provided splits the dataset into training (X_train, y_train) and testing (X_test, y_test) subsets using the train_test_split() function. The parameter test_size=0.30 specifies that 30% of the data will be allocated for testing, allowing for evaluating the model's performance. The random_state=0 parameter is used to seed the random number generator for reproducibility. It ensures that the dataset is split similarly each time the code is executed with the same random_state value. The execution of this code results in four variables: X_train (training features), X_test (testing features), y_train (training target values), and y_test (testing target values). These datasets can be used to train the model on the training data and assess its performance on the test data.

```
test.to_csv("speech.test", columns=["category_text"],
index=False, header=False) train.to_csv("speech.train",
columns=["category_text"], index=False, header=False)
```

The provided code saves data from two DataFrames (train and test) as CSV files. Specifically, it extracts the "category_text" column from each DataFrame and saves it to a separate CSV file – the code train.to_csv("speech.train", columns=["category_text"], index=False, header=False) saves the data from the train DataFrame to a file named "speech.train". The columns=["category_text"] parameter specifies that only the "category_text" column should be saved.

The parameters index=False and header=False indicate that the row indices and column headers should be excluded from the saved file. Similarly, test.to_csv("speech.test", columns=["category_text"], index=False, header=False) saves the data from the test DataFrame to a file named "speech.test", including only the "category_text" column.

This format for saving data in CSV files facilitates easy reading and processing in subsequent stages.

9.6.3. Training the model

We are installing the necessary library for training, fasttext, using the following command (Fig. 9.19):

```
pip install fasttext
```

```
Looking in indexes: https://pypi.org/simple, https://us-python.pkg.dev/colab-wheels/public/simple/
Collecting fasttext
  Downloading fasttext-0.9.2.tar.gz (68 kB)
     ━━━━━━━━━━━━━━━━━━━━━━━━━━━━━━━━━━━━━━━━ 68.8/68.8 kB 2.9 MB/s eta 0:00:00
  Preparing metadata (setup.py) ... done
Collecting pybind11>=2.2 (from fasttext)
  Using cached pybind11-2.10.4-py3-none-any.whl (222 kB)
Requirement already satisfied: setuptools>=0.7.0 in /usr/local/lib/python3.10/dist-packages (from fasttext) (67.7.2)
Requirement already satisfied: numpy in /usr/local/lib/python3.10/dist-packages (from fasttext) (1.22.4)
Building wheels for collected packages: fasttext
  Building wheel for fasttext (setup.py) ... done
  Created wheel for fasttext: filename=fasttext-0.9.2-cp310-cp310-linux_x86_64.whl size=4393441 sha256=393fbdb15d376
  Stored in directory: /root/.cache/pip/wheels/a5/13/75/f811c84a8ab36eedbaef977a6a58a98990e8e0f1967f98f394
Successfully built fasttext
Installing collected packages: pybind11, fasttext
Successfully installed fasttext-0.9.2 pybind11-2.10.4
```

Fig. 9.19. Result

We proceed with the following steps:

```
import fasttext
model = fasttext.train_supervised(input="speech.train")
model.test("speech.test")
```

This code utilises the fasttext library to train a text classification model using the training dataset "speech.train" and evaluates its performance on the test dataset "speech.test":

- Import fasttext — This line imports the fasttext library, which provides functionalities for training and classifying text.
- Model = fasttext.train_supervised(input="speech.train") — This line trains the model using the "speech.train" dataset. The model learns to classify text based on the provided categories.

• Model.test("speech.test") — This line tests the trained model using the "speech.test" dataset. The test() method computes performance metrics, such as accuracy, recall, and F1-score, and outputs the test results.

The model's accuracy is shown as 89% (Fig. 9.20).

```
(3716, 0.8942411194833154, 0.8942411194833154)
```

Fig. 9.20. Results

Next, we perform predictions. For this, we classify an artificially provided text (Fig. 9.21):

```
strings ="""nigga"""
result = " ".join(line.strip() for line in strings.split
lines()) print((result))
model.predict(result)#as it should be - Fig. 9.21
strings ="""i hate that black person"""
result = " ".join(line.strip() for line in
strings.splitlines()) print(repr(result))
model.predict(result)#as it should be - Fig. 9.20
```

```
nigga
(('__label__hate_speech',), array([0.95959681]))
```

Fig. 9.21. Results

```
strings ="""just brought some bread and went home""" result =
" ".join(line.strip() for line in strings.splitlines())
print(repr(result))
model.predict(result)#as it should be - Fig. 9.22
strings ="""you ugly bstard don`t show your face to anybody"""
result = " ".join(line.strip() for line in
strings.splitlines()) print(repr(result))
model.predict(result)#as it should be - Fig. 9.23
```

```
'just brought some bread and went home'
(('__label__no_hate',), array([0.81684661]))
```

Fig. 9.22. Result

```
'you ugly bstard don`t show your face to anybody'
(('__label__hate_speech',), array([0.60036236]))
```

Fig. 9.23. Result

```
strings ="""you are not that intelligent machine""" result = "
".join(line.strip() for line in strings.splitlines())
print(repr(result))
model.predict(result)#unlucky - Fig. 9.24
strings ="""I can not just sit up and HATE on another bitch ..
I got too much shit going on """ result = "
".join(line.strip() for line in strings.splitlines())
print(repr(result))  model.predict(result)#unlucky - Fig. 9.25
```

```
'you are not that intelligent machine'
(('__label__offensive_speech',), array([0.45037791]))
```

Fig. 9.24. Result

```
'I can not just sit up and HATE on another bitch .. I got too much shit going on'
(('__label__offensive_speech',), array([0.99653608]))
```

Fig. 9.25. Result

After testing, we will save the model to Google Drive:

```
model.save_model('/content/drive/My Drive/model.bin')
```

9.6.4. Model building with alternative methods

In addition to the previously described approach, models will be constructed using alternative methodologies and data processing techniques. Specifically, various text-cleaning methods will be applied to enhance the robustness of the models. WordNetLemmatizer is a tool utilised to lemmatise words in Python. Lemmatisation refers to reducing a word to its base form, known as a lemma. WordNetLemmatizer employs WordNet, a lexical database of the English language that encompasses syntactic and semantic relationships among words. By leveraging this database, WordNetLemmatizer determines the base form of a word, representing its semantic meaning.

For example, the word "running" would be lemmatised to "run" by WordNetLemmatizer. This process is beneficial for standardising words, reducing vocabulary size during text processing, enabling more effective search for similar words, and performing other linguistic operations. WordNetLemmatizer is a component of the NLTK (Natural Language Toolkit) library in Python, which offers a range of tools for text processing and language analysis.

Following this, regular expressions (regex) will be employed to identify patterns and replace unnecessary data within the dataset. Additionally, text cleaning will be performed using the alternative method described above.

```
import nltk
nltk.download('wordnet')
def preprocess(textdata): #Cleaning
     processedText = []
     wordLemm = WordNetLemmatizer()# Creates Lemmatizer.
    urlPattern        = r"((http://)[^ ]*|(https://)[^ ]*|(
www\.)[^ ]*)" #regex patterns.
    userPattern       = '@[^\s]+'
    alphaPattern      = "[^a-zA-Z0-9]"
    sequencePattern   = r"(.)\1\1+"
    seqReplacePattern = r"\1\1"
    newlinepattern = '\n'
    for tweet in textdata:
        tweet = tweet.lower()
        tweet = re.sub(urlPattern,' URL',tweet)
        tweet = re.sub(userPattern,' USER', tweet)
        tweet = re.sub(alphaPattern, " ", tweet)
        tweet = re.sub(newlinepattern, " ", tweet)
        tweet = re.sub(sequencePattern, seqReplacePattern,
tweet)
        tweetwords = ''
        for word in tweet.split():
                if len(word)>1:
                    word = wordLemm.lemmatize(word) #
Lemmatization of words.
                    tweetwords += (word+' ')
                    processedText.append(tweetwords)
            return processedText t = time.time()
corpus = preprocess(dt_transformed['tweet'])
```

```
print(f'Text Preprocessing complete.')
print(f'Time Taken: {round(time.time()-t)} seconds')
```

Result after cleaning is shown in Fig. 9.26.

CountVectorizer simplifies the use of text data directly in machine learning and deep learning models, such as text classification (converting text into numerical data). The text is transformed into a sparse matrix. Since the words "is" and "my" appeared twice, the counts for these specific words are 2 and 1, respectively, for the rest (Fig. 29.7a).

```
['rt USER a woman you shouldn complain about cleaning up your house amp a man you should always take the trash out ',
 'rt USER boy dat cold tyga dwn bad for cuffin dat hoe in the 1st place ',
 'rt USER dawg rt USER you ever fuck bitch and she start to cry you be confused a shit ',
 'rt USER USER she look like tranny ',
 'rt USER the shit you hear about me might be true or it might be faker than the bitch who told it to ya 57361 ',
 'USER the shit just blow me claim you so faithful and down for somebody but still fucking with hoe 128514 128514 128514 ',
 'USER can not just sit up and hate on another bitch got too much shit going on ',
 '8220 USER cause tired of you big bitch coming for u skinny girl 8221 ',
 'amp you might not get ya bitch back amp thats that ',
 'USER hobby include fighting mariam bitch ',
 'keeks is bitch she curve everyone lol walked into conversation like this smh ',
 'murda gang bitch it gang land ',
 'so hoe that smoke are loser yea go on ig ',
 'bad bitch is the only thing that like ',
 'bitch get up off me ',
 'bitch nigga miss me with it ',
 'bitch plz whatever ',
 'bitch who do you love ',
 'bitch get cut off everyday ',
 'black bottle amp bad bitch ',
 'broke bitch cant tell me nothing ',
 'cancel that bitch like nino ',
 'cant you see these hoe wont change ',
 'fuck no that bitch dont even suck dick 128514 128514 128514 the kermit video bout to fuck ig up ',
 'got ya bitch tip toeing on my hardwood floor 128514 URL ',
 'her pussy lip like heaven door 128524 ',
 'hoe what it hitting for ',
 'met that pussy on ocean dr gave that pussy pill 128524 ',
 'need trippy bitch who fuck on hennessy ',
 'spend my money how want bitch it my business ',
 'txt my old bitch my new bitch pussy wetter ',
 'say im back to the old me but my old bitch would get excited 128524 ',
 'if you aint bout that murder game pussy nigga shut up ',
 'if you re toe ain done you pussy stink ',
```

Fig. 9.26 Result

```
cv = CountVectorizer(max_features = 2000)
X = cv.fit_transform(corpus).toarray()
```

We are splitting the data set into the Test/Training set

```
X_train, X_test, y_train, y_test = train_test_split(X, y, test_size = 0.20, random_state = 0)
```

```
Creating the models:
classifier_np = GaussianNB() #Naive Bayes
classifier_np.fit(X_train, y_train)
classifier_dt = DecisionTreeClassifier(criterion = 'entropy',
random_state = 0) classifier_dt.fit(X_train, y_train)
#Decision Tree
classifier_rf = RandomForestClassifier(n_estimators = 10,
criterion = 'entropy', random_state = 0)
classifier_rf.fit(X_train, y_train) #Random Forest
classifier_knn = KNeighborsClassifier(n_neighbors = 5, metric
= 'minkowski', p = 2) classifier_knn.fit(X_train, y_train)
#KNN
classifier_lr = LogisticRegression(
solver='lbfgs',max_iter=1000,random_state = 0)
classifier_lr.fit(X_train, y_train) #Logistic Regression
```

Testing the model with arbitrary text (Fig. 9.27b):

```
def predict(vectoriser, model, text):
    textdata =
vectoriser.transform(preprocess(text)).toarray()
    sentiment = model.predict(textdata)
    data = []
    for text, pred in zip(text, sentiment):
        data.append((text,pred))
        df = pd.DataFrame(data, columns = ['tweet','class'])
    df = df.replace([0,1,2], ["Hate","Offensive","Neither"])
    return df
test_data = ["Making the Confusion Matrix for each model"]
result=predict(cv,classifier_lr,test_data) print(result) #
Fig. 20b
Determining the accuracy of different methods (Fig. 26):
rf_score = accuracy_score(y_test, y_pred_rf)
lr_score = accuracy_score(y_test, y_pred_lr)
dt_score = accuracy_score(y_test, y_pred_dt)
np_score = accuracy_score(y_test, y_pred_np)
knn_score = accuracy_score(y_test, y_pred_knn)
```

	hello	is	james	my	name	notebook	python	this
0	1	2	1	2	1	1	1	1

	tweet	class
0	Making the Confusion Matrix for each model	Neither

Fig. 9.27. Example with eight unique words

9.6.5. Testing and implementation of the project

To initiate extension testing in real-time, navigate to a website, such as Instagram (Fig. 9.28).

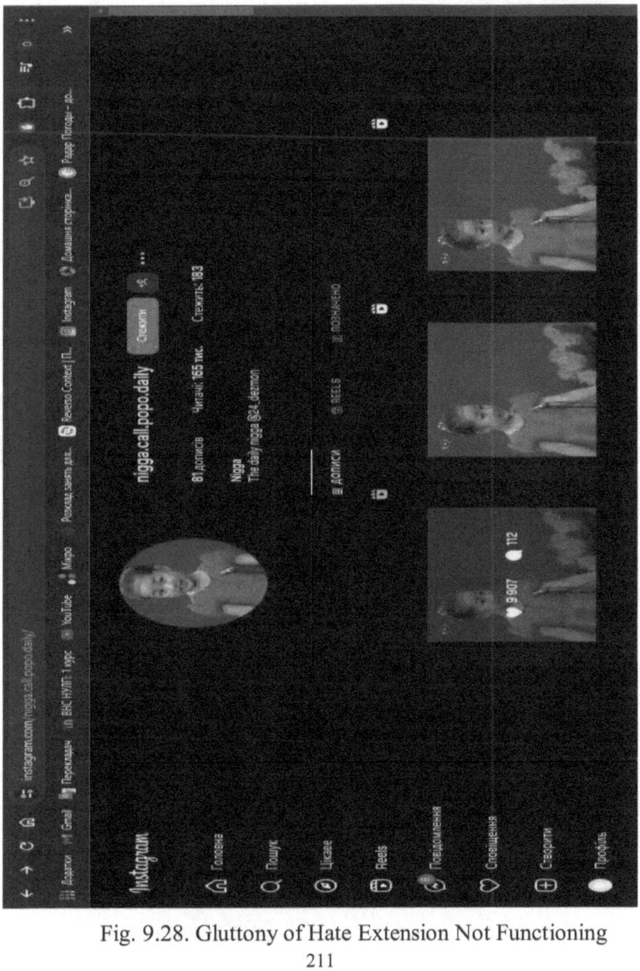

Fig. 9.28. Gluttony of Hate Extension Not Functioning

Upon enabling the "Hide words" feature, it is evident that certain words have been obscured (Fig. 9.29). The extension was tested by accessing the Wikipedia section on "Profanity" (Fig. 9.30).

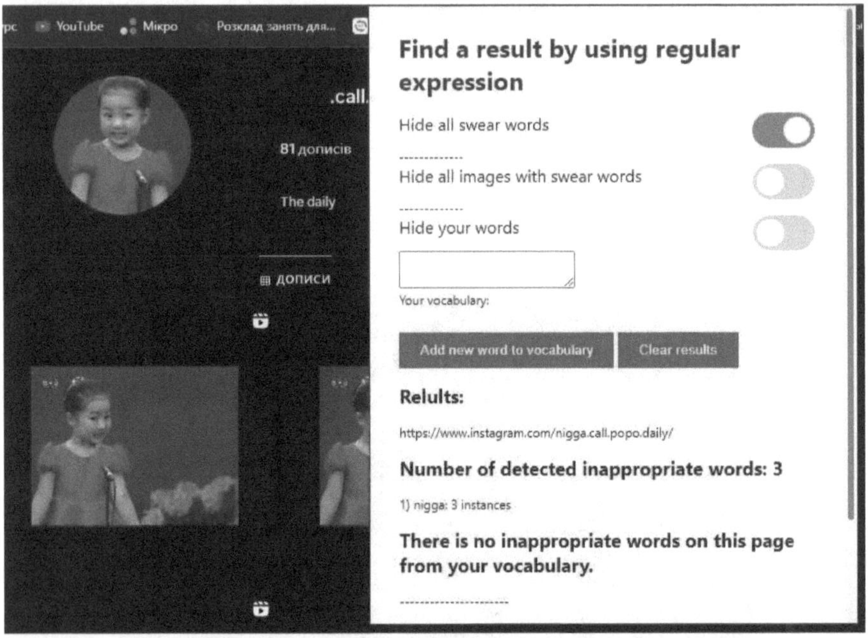

Fig. 9.29. Result of Gluttony of Hate Extension Operation

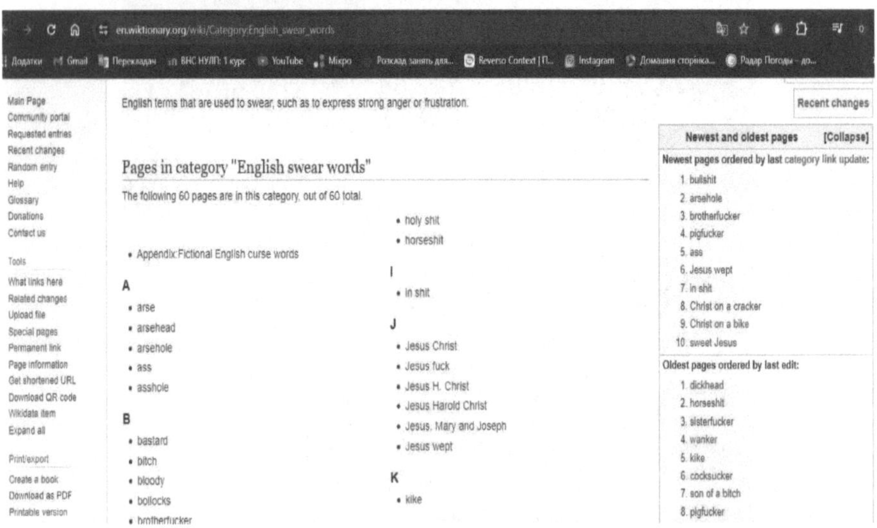

Fig. 9.30. Absence of Gluttony of Hate Extension Operation

The same function was activated, resulting in the extension obscuring nearly all content on the website (Fig. 9.31).

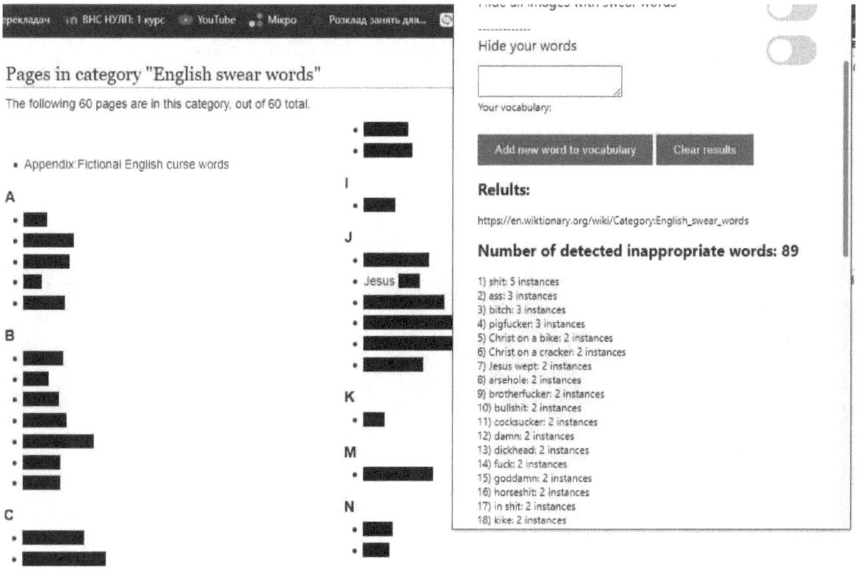

Fig. 9.31. Results of the Gluttony of Hate Extension Operation

A test website featuring images was opened (Fig. 9.32).

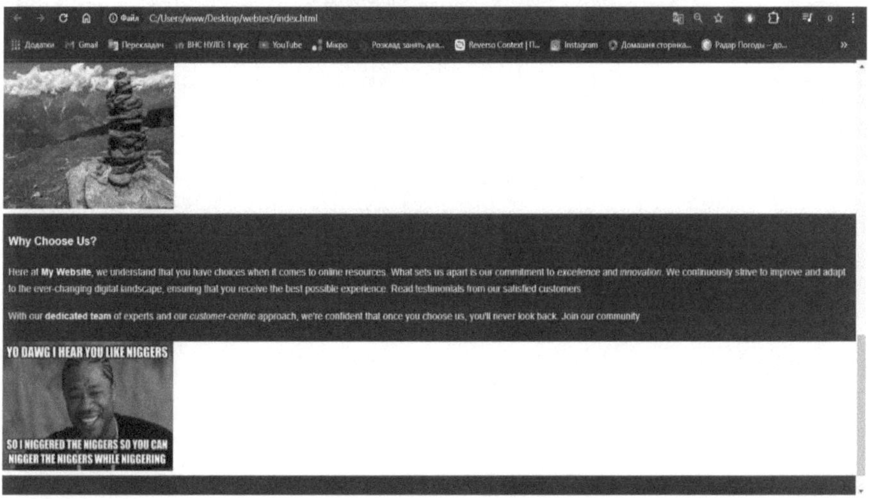

Fig. 9.32. Without the Gluttony of Hate Extension

The function to hide images was activated. It is observed that the specific image that was required is no longer displayed (Fig. 9.33).

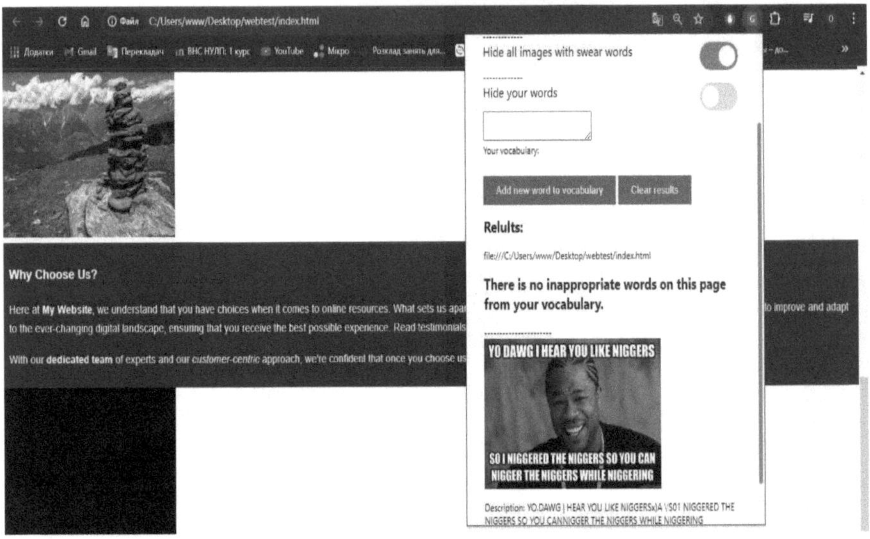

Fig. 9.33. Results of the "Gluttony of Hate" extension.

Furthermore, a word was incorporated into the dictionary, and the dictionary functionality was evaluated (Fig. 9.34-9.35).

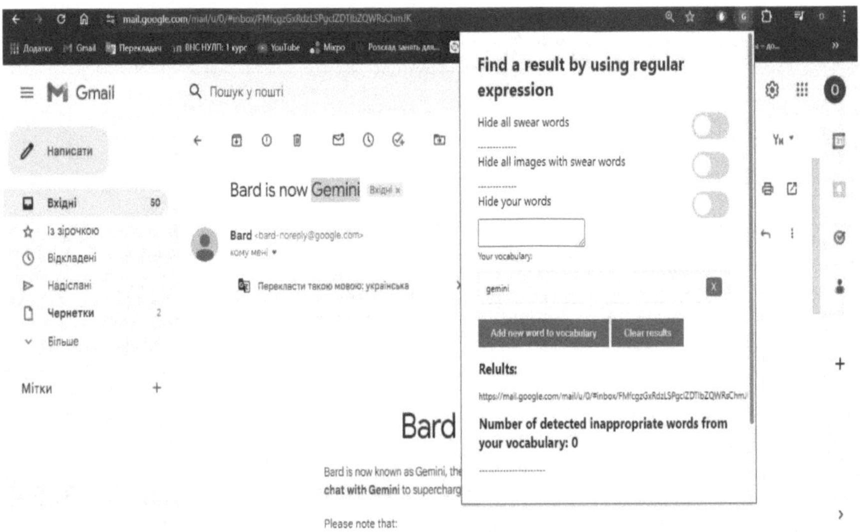

Fig. 9.34. With the "Gluttony of Hate" extension disabled

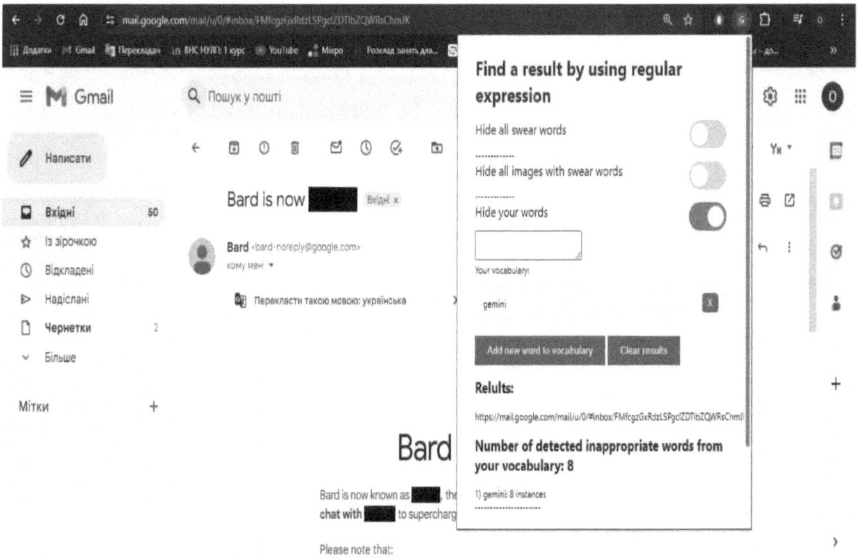

Fig. 9.35. Results of the "Gluttony of Hate" extension implementation

LSTM model hyperparameters(32, dropout=0.4, recurrent_dropout=0.4, kernel_regularizer=l2(0.01)).

Table 9.4. Epochs for machine learning

#	X s Y ms/step		Train			Val			t, X s Y ms/step	Train		Val	
	155	620	F1	Precision	Recall	F1	Precision	Recall		accuracy	loss	accuracy	loss
1	1s 7	4s 6	0.871	0.879	0.864	0.846	0.862	0.833	28- 45	0.820	0.235	0.885	0.046
2	1s 5	3s 5	0.884	0.869	0.901	0.861	0.850	0.875	18- 28	0.896	0.050	0.886	0.042
3	1s 6	4s 6	0.899	0.877	0.923	0.862	0.843	0.881	18- 29	0.912	0.043	0.888	0.047
4	1s 6	4s 6	0.904	0.881	0.928	0.854	0.838	0.871	18- 29	0.922	0.039	0.883	0.051
5	1s 6	4s 6	0.9059	0.882	0.93	0.855	0.838	0.875	18- 29	0.925	0.038	0.883	0.057

155/155 - 1s - 6ms/step - accuracy: 0.8862 - loss: 0.0418, and Accuracy on the test set: 0.8862215280532837 (Fig. 9.36). Accuracy estimates for various classifiers, such as Random Forest (0.879), Logistic Regression (0.904), Decision

Tree (0.878), Naive Bayes (0.315), and KNN (0.832), with class 2 indicating no hate speech, class 1 indicating offensive speech, and class 0 indicating hate speech was performed. Overall AUC estimates for various classifiers, such as Random Forest (0.89), Logistic Regression (0.92), Decision Tree (0.80), Naive Bayes (0.61), and KNN (0.82), were performed.

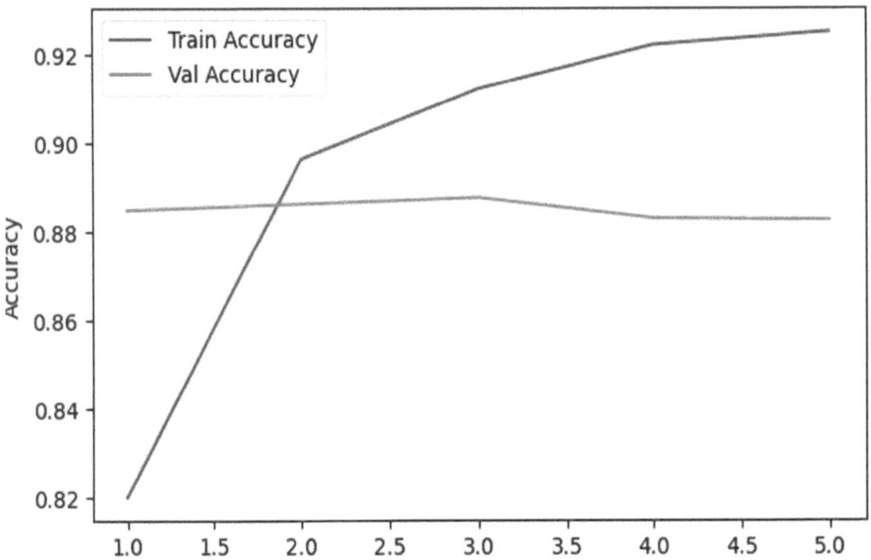

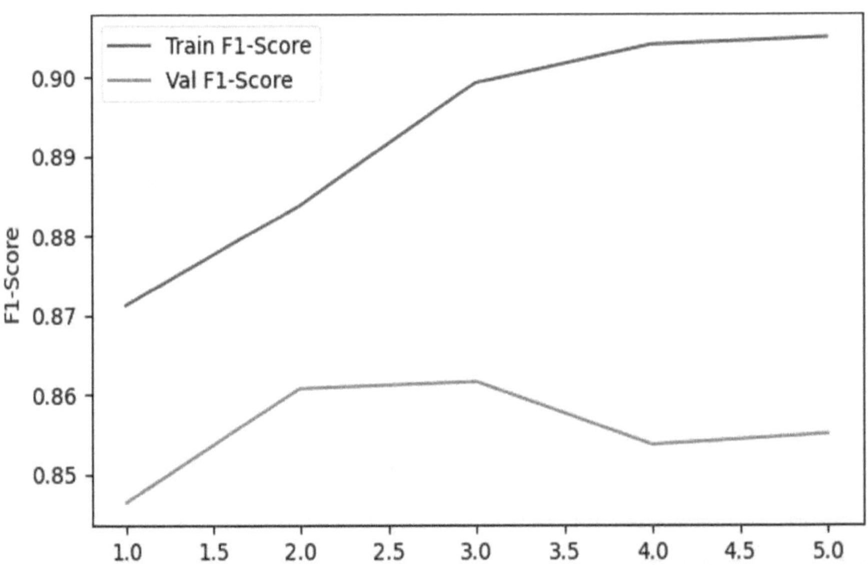

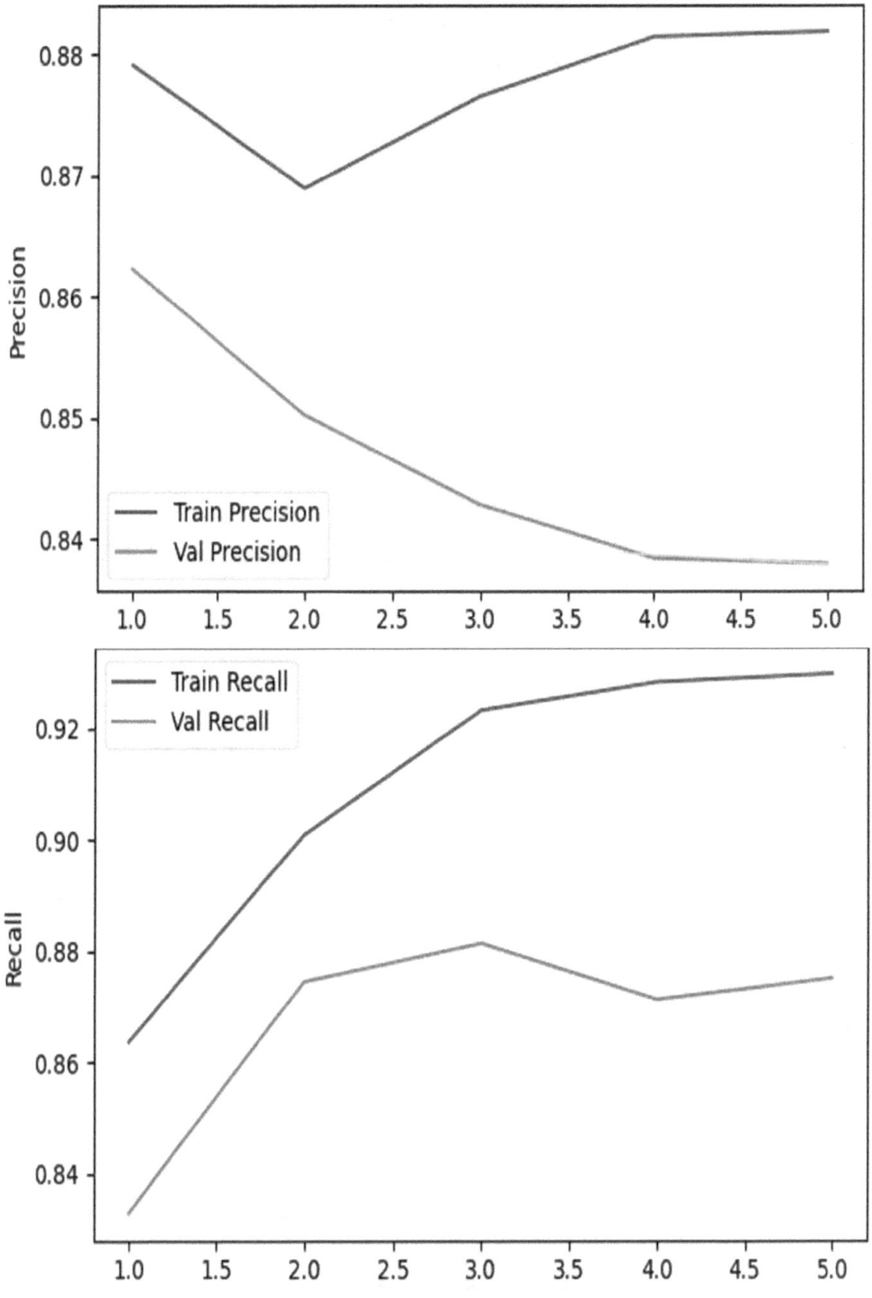

Fig. 9.36. Result for the LTSM model.

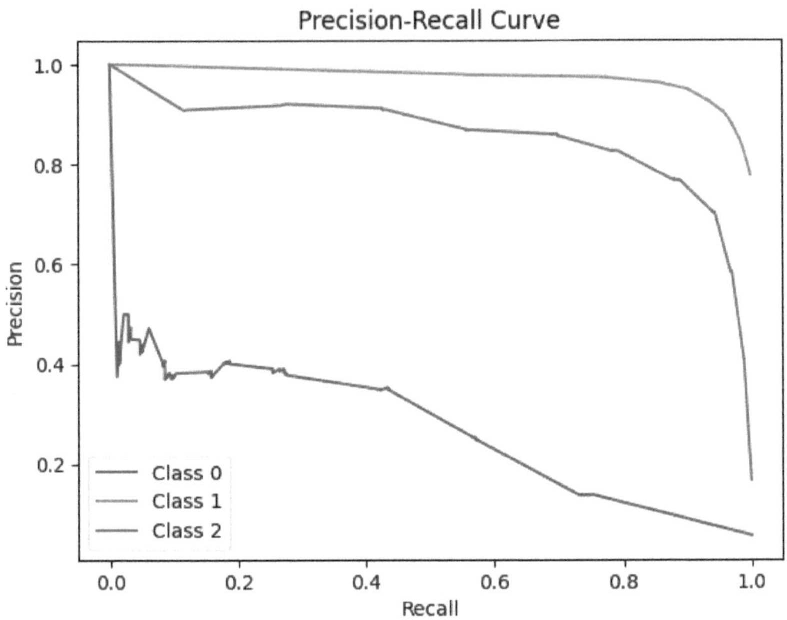
Precision-Recall Curve
1.0
0.8
0.6
0.4
0.2
Precision
Class 0
Class 1
Class 2
0.0
0.2
0.4
0.6
0.8
1.0
Recall

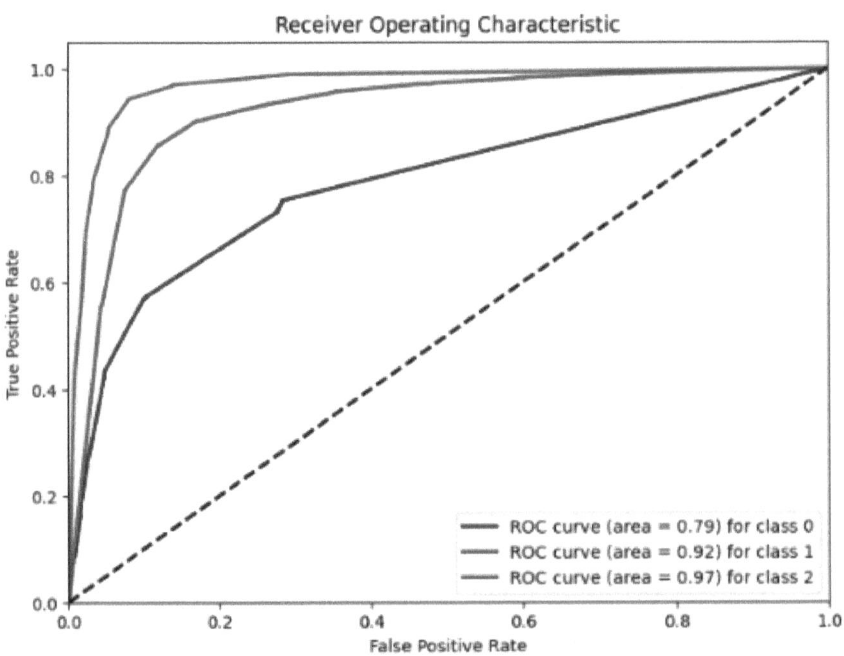
Receiver Operating Characteristic
1.0
0.8
0.6
0.4
0.2
0.0
True Positive Rate
ROC curve (area = 0.79) for class 0
ROC curve (area = 0.92) for class 1
ROC curve (area = 0.97) for class 2
0.0
0.2
0.4
0.6
0.8
1.0
False Positive Rate

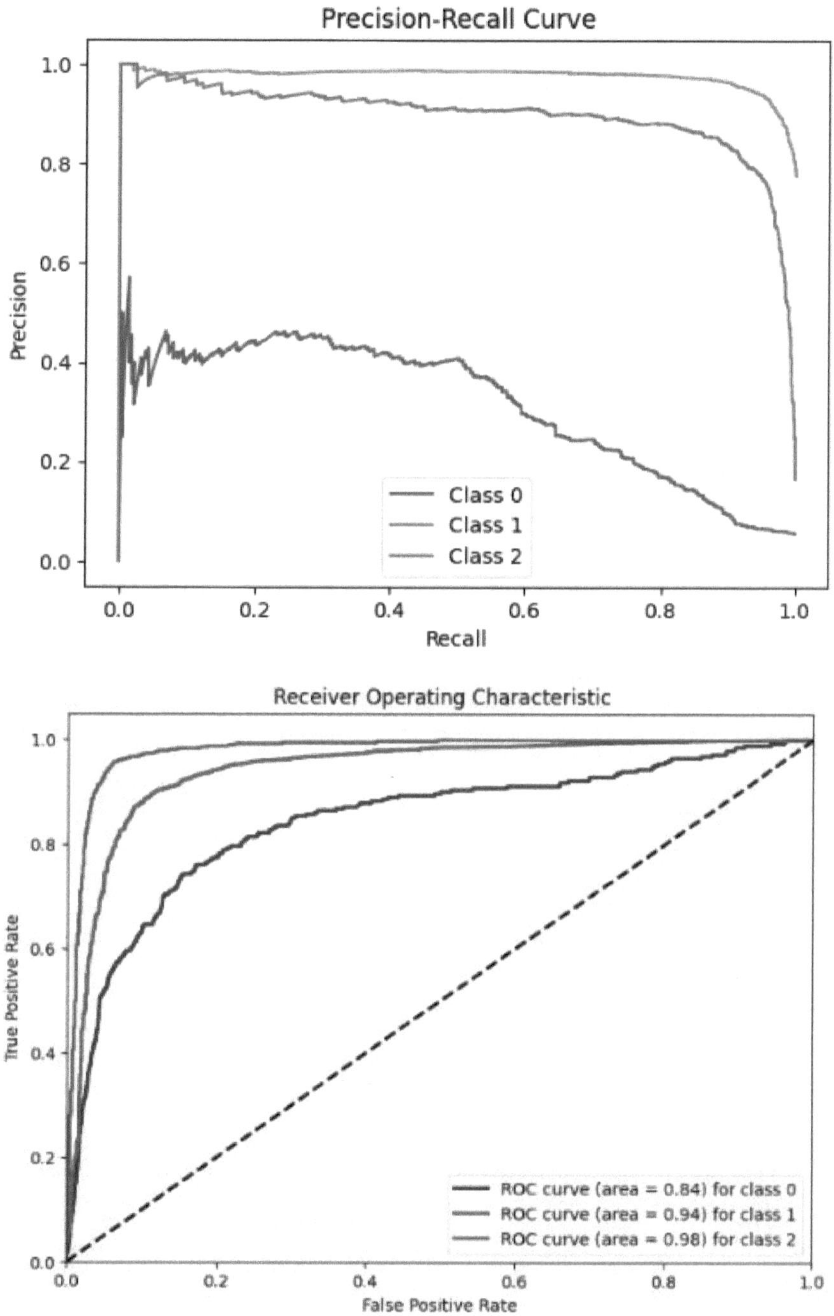

Fig. 9.37. Results for the Random Forest classifier

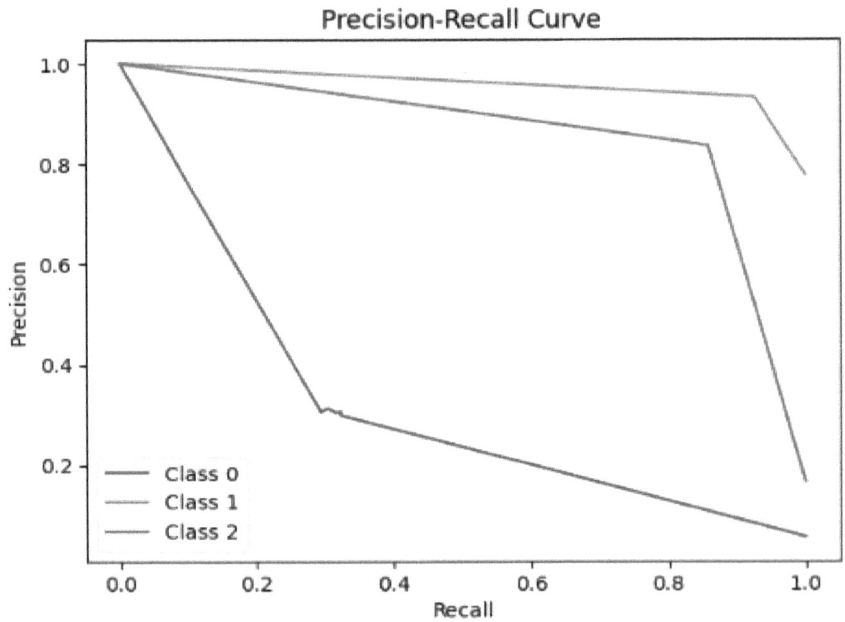

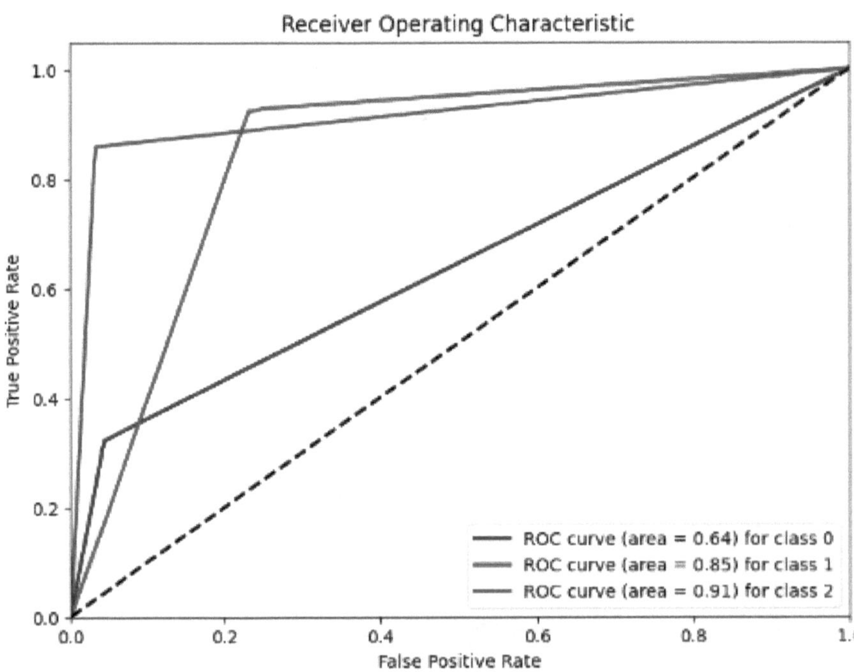

Fig. 9.39. Results for the Decision Tree classifier

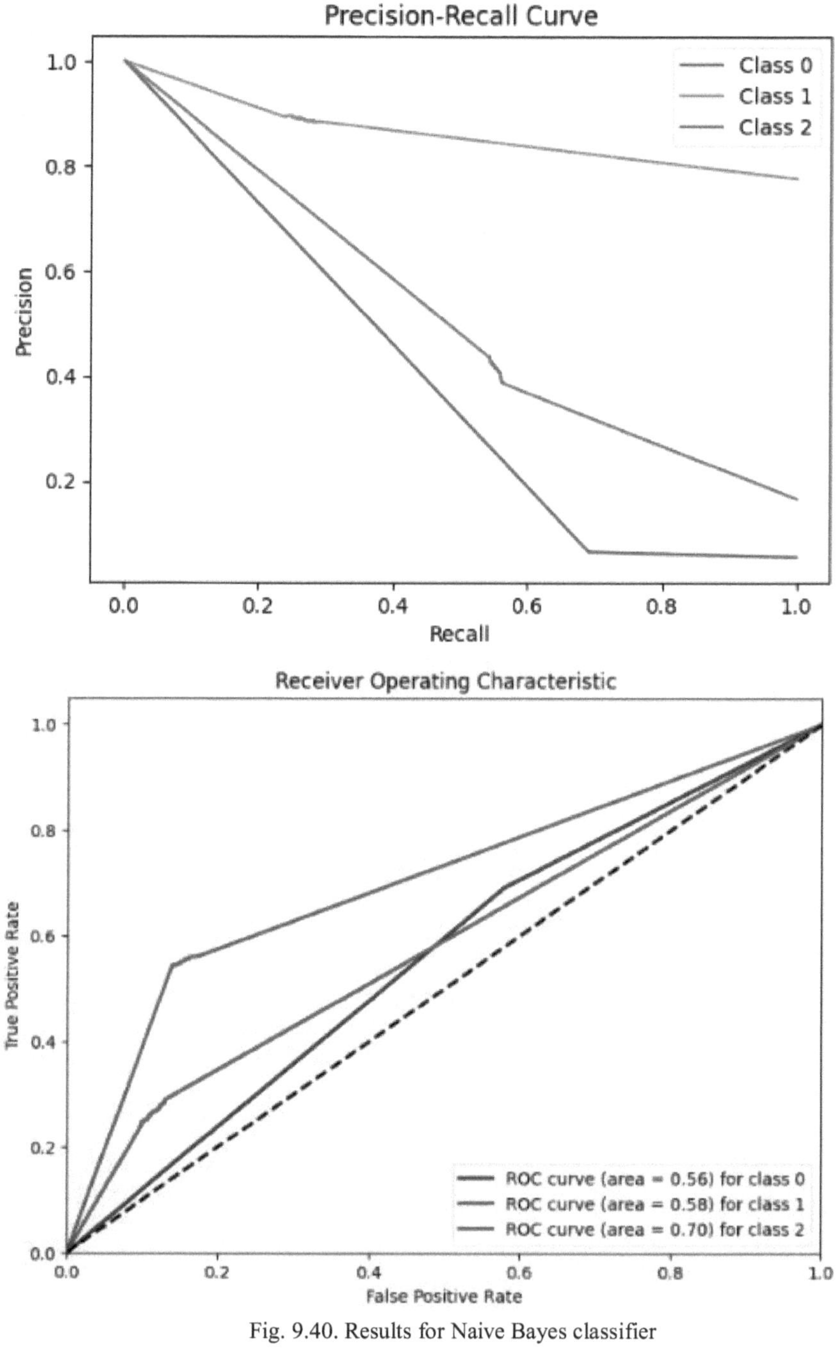

Fig. 9.40. Results for Naive Bayes classifier

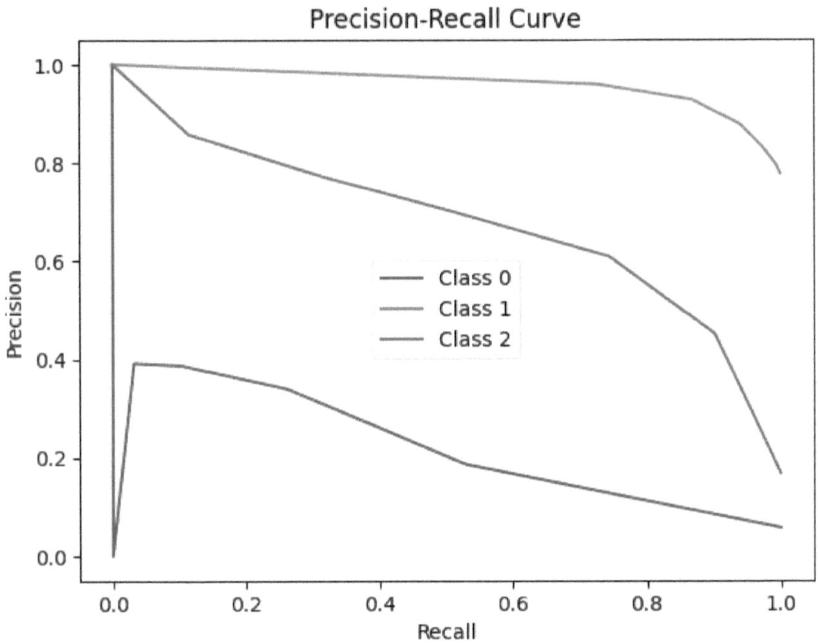

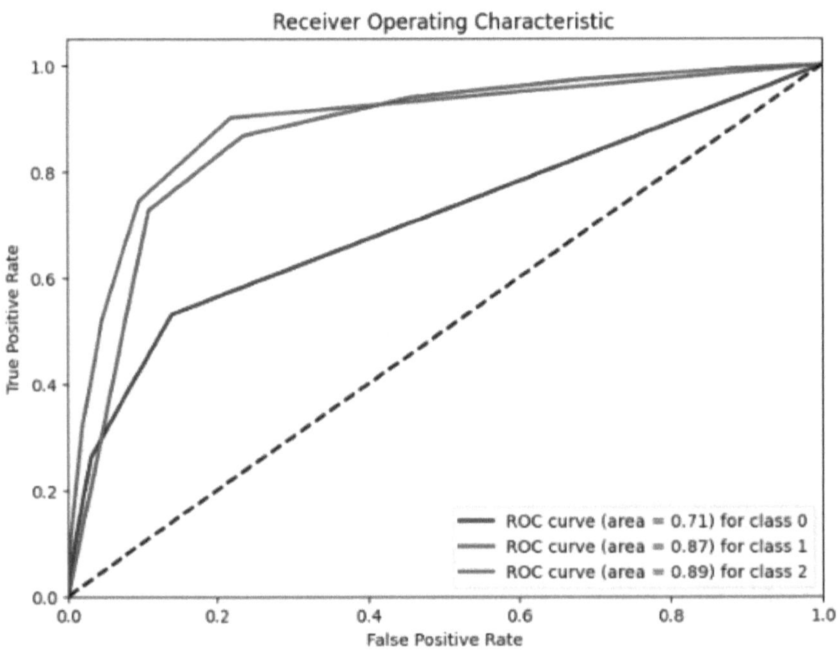

Fig. 9.41. Results for the KNN classifier

9.7. Conclusion for Chapter 9

These research directions aim to improve the accuracy, effectiveness, and ethical standards of hate speech detection systems, thereby enhancing their ability to identify and mitigate harmful content across online platforms. This research focused on employing information technology to censor inappropriate content in text and images on web pages. The study examined various methodologies and approaches to business process modelling, particularly emphasising the application of BPMN. BPMN is an invaluable tool for visualising and analysing business processes, as it effectively delineates the various stages and interactions within a process, enhancing understanding and facilitating communication among stakeholders.

A critical aspect of requirements modelling is the development of UML Use Case Diagrams. These diagrams are essential for visualising user and functional requirements, helping to identify primary use cases and critical system functions. Use Case Diagrams clearly define requirements and interactions between users and the system, ensuring that all functional aspects are comprehensively addressed.

A UML Class Diagram was developed to outline the entities responsible for executing the core processes of the project. This diagram offers a structured representation of the primary objects and their relationships within the system, which is vital for the subsequent software development and implementation stages. Furthermore, UML Activity Diagrams were employed to detail the primary subprocesses and actions. These diagrams facilitate an in-depth examination of individual process steps, illustrating the sequence of actions and interactions among system components. Using UML Activity Diagrams improves understanding of process logic and structure, significantly aiding the implementation and testing phases. In summary, integrating BPMN methodology with UML diagrams enables effective modelling, analysis, and development of business processes. This approach ensures a clear comprehension of requirements and system functionality, providing a solid foundation for successful project implementation, thereby enhancing quality and reducing the risk of misalignment with client expectations.

The study also covered several critical aspects of information technology and data analysis. It reviewed fundamental concepts and practical applications, including data processing, preparation for analysis, data splitting into training and testing sets, and various machine learning algorithms such as Naive Bayes, Decision Trees, Random Forests, Logistic Regression, and KNN. Performance metrics such as the Confusion Matrix, classification report, and accuracy were also evaluated. Understanding these concepts and employing appropriate algorithms and metrics are essential for practical data analysis, ranging from text classification to outcome prediction. This knowledge supports informed decision-making based on comprehensive data analysis. The project achieved substantial progress through multiple stages, from research and analysis to model training and extension development. Emphasising accuracy, usability, and performance led to the creation of a functional and efficient solution for detecting hate speech.

Chapter 10. Identifying sources and participants of propaganda in tiktok using machine learning

The chapter is written based on publications and research [247-257].

10.1. Analyses of recent research and publications

The modern information space is constantly transforming under the influence of technological progress, but these changes bring not only new opportunities but also unprecedented challenges. One of the most acute and socially significant problems of today is the rapid spread of disinformation, fake news, and propaganda. The methods and tools available today, designed to detect such content, often demonstrate insufficient efficiency, as they lack the time to adapt to new, increasingly complex techniques for generating disinformation. This situation creates serious risks for public trust, can destabilise political processes, and undermine the foundations of information security both at the level of individual citizens and entire states. It is to counteract these complex threats that the development of a system for identifying sources of disinformation and propaganda, as well as their potential participants, is being initiated.

Comments, as a tool for spreading propaganda, can serve as a channel for promoting a specific ideological or political narrative. For example, bots or coordinated accounts leave messages that repeat the same messages, and disinformation is placed in comments under the guise of "the opinions of ordinary people". Therefore, it is essential to develop tools to identify potential participants in the spread of propaganda and disinformation, as well as the source itself.

Given the growth of information warfare in social networks, especially in the context of military aggression and hybrid threats, there is a need for automated solutions for monitoring and detecting propaganda. Comments in the online space play a dual role in the processes of information influence: on the one hand, they can be a channel for the spread of propaganda through bot activity and manipulative messages; on the other, a source for studying the mechanisms of information influence and a possible tool for countering disinformation. For the classification of comments and reviews in the Ukrainian language, such language models as BERT, DistilBERT, RoBERTa, XLM-RoBERTa, and Ukr-RoBERTa are used. The authors chose the RoBERTa transformer model for research and classification.

RoBERTa is an optimised BERT model retrained with an improved training methodology, more data, and hardware resources, as proposed in [247]. It improves BERT by carefully and intelligently optimising the training hyperparameters for BERT. RoBERTa uses the same architecture as BERT. However, unlike BERT, it only trains the generation of the missing token during pretraining (BERT was also pretrained to predict the following sentence). That is, RoBERTa without the concept of predicting the following sentence is similar to BERT and uses dynamic masking.

The scientific paper [248] presents the use of different algorithms for the multi-class and cross-lingual task of fake news detection using the RoBERTa model. The results of the macro F1-score evaluation using the pre-trained RoBERTa model are 28.60% for the monolingual task in English.

Scientists [249] conducted a study of the problem of automatic fake news detection in Urdu. The article presents the use of various word embedding models, such as RoBERTa, ALBERT, XLM-RoBERTa, and Multilingual BERT. Model RoBERTa is trained on Urdu news data from Pakistani newspapers and gives an accuracy of 92%. It is built on BERT, trained with larger mini-batches and learning rates.

The study [250] describes the fine-tuning of the BERT, DistilBERT, XLM-RoBERTa and Ukr-RoBERTa models for sentiment analysis of Ukrainian language reviews, since transformer models demonstrate better understanding of the context and show high efficiency in solving natural language processing tasks. The dataset for the study consists of approximately 11,000 user comments in Ukrainian on various topics. The authors proposed to classify text data into two classes: positive and negative. After pre-processing the text, the dataset was divided into training and test samples in a ratio of 80:20. The effectiveness of the classification models was evaluated using metrics such as accuracy, recall, precision, and F1-score. According to the research results, the XLM-RoBERTa model achieved the highest accuracy of 91.32%. However, considering the time required to train the model and all classification metrics, Ukr-RoBERTa is a more optimal choice.

The study [251] proposes a framework that allows you to quickly create corpora for classifying Ukrainian-language news with minimal data annotation efforts. The results of testing on this set showed that the ukr-RoBERTa, ukr-ELECTRA, and XLM-R large models demonstrate the highest accuracy rates. At the same time, XLM-R large and ukr-ELECTRA perform better in processing longer texts, while ukr-RoBERTa shows an advantage in classifying short text fragments.

The scientific paper [252] presents EMOBENCH-UA, the first annotated corpus for emotion recognition in Ukrainian-language texts. The annotation scheme was adapted from English-language research in this field [253], taking into account instructions and cultural features. The data was collected through crowdsourcing on the Toloka.ai platform, which made it possible to ensure high-quality labelling. During the research, various approaches to analysing this corpus were evaluated – from basic linguistic models and translated synthetic sets to modern large language models (LLM). The results of the experiments demonstrate the complexity of the task of emotional classification for languages with limited resources, particularly Ukrainian, and indicate the need for further development of models and training materials focused explicitly on the Ukrainian language context.

The article [254] addresses the problems of sentiment analysis in Ukrainian social networks, where users frequently switch encodings between Russian and other languages. Authors present COSMUS (COde-Switched MUltilingual Sentiment for Ukrainian Social media) – a corpus of 12,224 texts collected from

Telegram channels, product review sites, and open datasets annotated with positive, negative, neutral, and mixed sentiment classes, as well as language tags (Ukrainian, Russian, with code-switching). Fine-tuning UkrRoBERTa using GPT-4o-based data augmentations provides a maximum accuracy of 73.6%, which exceeds the baseline levels of mBERT.

The scientific paper [255] presents LiBERTa Large – the first BERT Large model that was fully trained from scratch exclusively on the Ukrainian-language corpus. By using large-scale multilingual corpora with a significant proportion of Ukrainian texts, the model forms a solid foundation for solving natural language processing problems in Ukrainian. The results show that LiBERTa Large outperforms both existing multilingual and monolingual models pre-trained in Ukrainian, and demonstrates performance comparable to or better than models based on knowledge transfer from English.

The authors [256] propose a conceptual model of the information warfare system, identify its weaknesses, and suggest an improvement mechanism, in particular through the creation and dissemination of content on social media, expanding audience coverage on WhatsApp, and utilising IT, advanced technologies, and AI for faster threat detection. The proposed approach aims to reduce the vulnerability of state institutions and society to disinformation and propaganda, increase the responsiveness of countermeasures, and improve the effectiveness of risk assessment in the sphere of national security.

The article [257] describes a method for detecting sources of disinformation based on ensemble machine learning models. The authors used two types of text embeddings and corresponding classification models – linear and logistic regression. At the final stage, an ensemble of models was applied, which allowed the combination of their predictive capabilities and increased the accuracy from 71% to 78%.

Based on the analysis of scientific papers, the authors selected the RoBERTa language model for the study. To test the model, a dataset of comments was manually collected, which will be used for training and classification.

10.2. Classification and clustering model

A dataset of comments was manually collected for training and testing the system. Comments were selected from videos containing trigger tags, such as #ukraine, #zelensky, #crimea, etc. Since the bot specialises in detecting russian propaganda, those comments that promote russian narratives, such as denial of Ukraine's independence and sovereignty, denial of the legitimacy of the Ukrainian government, justification of aggression, cruel treatment of the Armed Forces of Ukraine and Ukrainians, etc., were marked as propaganda. Thus, about 700 comments in Ukrainian and 1,300 comments in russian were collected and labelled for the classification model. More than 6,000 and 10,000 comments in Ukrainian and Russian, respectively, were collected for the clustering model.

The data sets have the following form (see Table 10.1 and Table 10.2).

If there is propaganda in the comment, the value of the field "Propaganda" is equal to 1, otherwise, it is 0.

Table 10.1. Description of the dataset for the classification model

Column name	Data type	Description
Comment_ID	Integer	Comment identifier
Comment	String	Comment text
Propaganda	Bool	Presence or absence of propaganda features

A custom scraper was used to collect comments. However, due to certain functional limitations of this scraper, the auxiliary tool TTCommentExporter was used. In addition, the generated dataset contained not only Ukrainian and russian, but also others. Therefore, a software module was created that automatically separates comments by language features. After that, an algorithm for pre-processing data from the dataset was developed.

Table 10.2. Description of the dataset for the clustering model

Column name	Data type	Description
Comment_ID	Integer	Comment identifier
Comment	String	Comment text

The data pre-processing algorithm contains the following steps:

Step 1. Reading the comment. The comment is sent by the user to the Telegram bot or downloaded from an Excel file (during the training stage).

Step 2. Determining the language of the comment. Using the langdetect library, it is determined whether the comment is written in Ukrainian or russian. The choice of the transformer model (UA_model or RU_model) depends on this.

Step 3. Tokenization. The AutoTokenizer from the corresponding Hugging Face model is used. The text is converted into a sequence of tokens, taking into account:

• maximum size (truncation to 128 tokens);

• automatic padding;

• conversion to tensor (return_tensors='pt').

Step 4. Obtaining the embedding. From the AutoModel model (e.g. youscan/ukr-roberta-base), the CLS embedding (the first vector of the last layer) is extracted, which is considered a representation of the entire text.

Step 5. Extracting custom features.

Step 6. Scaling the features. Before merging, the custom features are normalised using StandardScaler() in order to avoid scale imbalance (CLS embedding has a different scale).

Step 7. Merging the features. The final feature is formed as a horizontal concatenation.

Step 8. Feeding to the classifier / clusterer.

Step 9. Saving. Embeddings or merged vectors can be saved as .npy or .pkl for reuse; the trained model (KMeans, StandardScaler) is also saved using joblib.

The system implemented language models for comments in Ukrainian and russian:

• UA_model – for processing Ukrainian comments;

• RU_model – for processing russian comments.

The development of the models took place in two stages: experiments with classification with a teacher and the final transition to clustering without a teacher.

The primary process of the system's operation includes the following stages:

• Model training. Training a machine learning model on data. It includes text vectorisation, clustering, and testing the effectiveness of the model.

• User interface creation. Developing a graphical interface where users can send links to video materials that need to be analysed and display the results of the analysis.

• Comment clustering. The process in which the system accepts a link provided by the user, receives comments, generates data sets, and determines which comments are propaganda and which are not. Includes vectorisation, model application, and result calculation.

• Result display. Visualisation of analysis results, including the percentage of propaganda. Fig. 10.1 shows a UML activity diagram that describes the basic process of the system.

Classification model. For the classification model, data collection and preparation were carried out, namely, a small corpus of comments was manually collected and marked, where each text was marked as:

• 1 – propaganda;

• 0 – not propaganda.

The next stage was to calculate embeddings. For this, the comments were processed through youscan/ukr-roberta-base for the Ukrainian language, and for each comment, a representation was made in the form of a CLS vector. In addition, the following manual set of features was manually extracted for each comment:

- the presence of flags RU/UA;
- the proportion of capital letters;
- the number of character repetitions;
- the number of emojis;
- the length of the text, etc.

After that, the features were scaled using StandardScaler and combined with the CLS vector to form the final feature vector. The next stage was training the classifier. For this, the RandomForestClassifier model was selected and trained on the collected vectors. Parameters were obtained via GridSearchCV with cross-validation (cv=5). The model was trained to determine whether the text contains propaganda. Results for the classification model are as follows:

- Recall for propaganda (1) – 100%;
- Recall for non-propaganda (0) – only 5%;
- Due to sample imbalance, the model tended to label almost everything as "propaganda".

In addition, an analysis of the criteria and parameters that can influence the identification of sources of disinformation and propaganda, as well as their potential participants, was conducted. Among the criteria that make it possible to identify sources of disinformation, one can single out certain propaganda narratives, as well as the language in which the comment is written (the vast majority of comments are written primarily in russian). Another criterion for identifying potential participants in propaganda is the fakeness of the account itself and, accordingly, all posts and comments of this participant. These criteria can be described as a set:

$$K = \{L, F_u, F_p\},$$

where L is the language, F_u is the fakeness of the account and F_p is the fakeness of posts.

Clustering model. For the clustering model, the RoBERTa language model was used separately for the Ukrainian (UA_model) and russian (RU_model) language classes. During the collection of comments and their labelling, it was found that many comments are “grey”, that is, neutral or not unambiguously propagandistic. The same structure was implemented for the two models (UA_model and RU_model) using the corresponding RoBERTa language model, performing vectorisation and feature extraction, as well as training the KMeans clusterer (2 clusters).

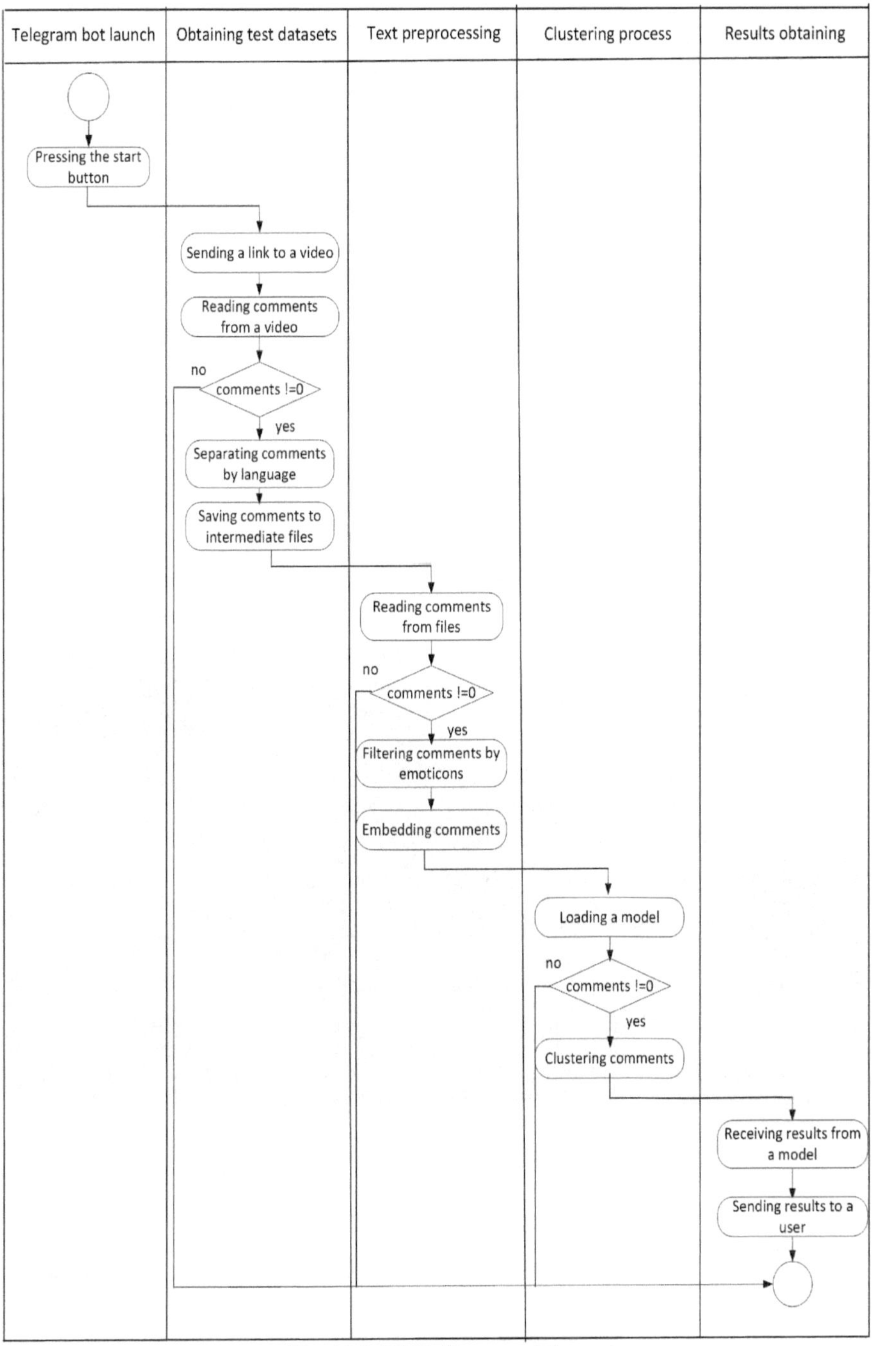

Fig. 10.1. UML diagram of the system

The K-Means clustering algorithm divides all vectors into two groups without knowing the actual labels. After clustering, the system analyses the content of each cluster by the frequency of propaganda phrases. For each cluster, the following is calculated:

• the proportion of texts containing keywords;

• the proportion of propaganda emojis.

Accordingly, the cluster with the highest "propaganda score" is considered to correspond to the "Propaganda" class. For new texts, the following occurs:

• vectorization (CLS + features);

• prediction of belonging to one of the clusters;

• determination of whether it is propaganda, based on comparison with the propaganda cluster.

Fig. 10.2 shows an example of using a Telegram bot to detect the presence of propaganda in comments.

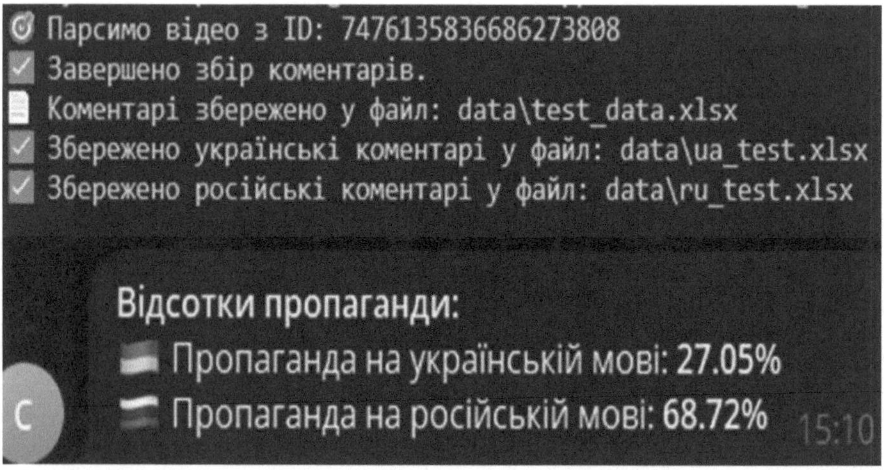

Fig. 10.2. The result of the clustering model

In the process of research, a system was developed that allows for analysing and classifying comments from videos on the TikTok network as propaganda or neutral. It will allow for determining the source of the spread of propaganda, fakes, and disinformation.

10.3. Conclusion for Chapter 10

As a result of the research, an effective system was developed for automatic detection of propaganda in comments to TikTok videos. The use of modern transformer models (RoBERTa), machine learning algorithms (classification and clustering), as well as the development of a full-fledged software package with a graphical interface, made it possible to implement a complete cycle of data analysis, from collection to visualisation of results. The structure of the system assumes a modular architecture: individual components are responsible for text vectorisation, manual feature extraction, pre-processing, clustering, decision-making, and user interaction. Experiments showed high sensitivity of the classification model to detect propaganda messages, and accordingly, to track potential participants in disinformation and propaganda. However, due to the imbalance of the sample, limitations in accuracy were identified for neutral content. The clustering model allowed for better work with "grey zones" - ambiguous comments.

Additionally, an analysis was conducted of parameters that allow us to identify not only propaganda, but also potential sources of its distribution. These parameters include the use of characteristic propaganda narratives, the language of comments (mostly Russian), and signs of fake accounts - the same type of posts, low level of profile authenticity, etc. The created system can be integrated into platforms for monitoring the information space, which will significantly strengthen the capabilities of state and public institutions in countering hybrid threats in the information sphere.

References

1. V. Vysotska, O. Markiv, D. Svyshch, L. Chyrun, S. Chyrun, R. Romanchuk,. (2024). Fake News Identification Based on NLP, Big Data Analysis and Deep Learning Technology. 199-204. 10.1109/TCSET64720.2024.10755902.
2. Altheneyan, et al. "Big data ML-based fake news detection using distributed learning." IEEE Access 11 (2023): 29447-29463.
3. Thota, et al. "Fake news detection: a deep learning approach." SMU Data Science Review 1.3 (2018): 10.
4. M. F. Mridha, et al. "A comprehensive review on fake news detection with deep learning." IEEE access 9 (2021): 156151-156170.
5. K., Hiramath, et al. "Fake news detection using deep learning techniques." Advances in Information Technology. IEEE, 2019.
6. E. Qawasmeh, et al. "Automatic identification of fake news using deep learning." Social networks analysis, Management and Security, 2019.
7. R. R., Karwa, et al. "Automated hybrid Deep Neural Network model for fake news identification and classification in social networks." Journal of Integrated Science and Technology 10.2 (2022): 110-119.
8. T. Chauhan, et al. "Optimisation and improvement of fake news detection using deep learning approaches for societal benefit." Int. Journal of Information Management Data Insights 1.2 (2021): 100051.
9. S. R. Sahoo, and B. B. Gupta. "Multiple features based approach for automatic fake news detection on social networks using deep learning." Applied Soft Computing 100 (2021): 106983.
10. D.-H. Lee, et al. "Fake news detection using deep learning." Journal of Information Processing Systems 15.5 (2019): 1119-1130.
11. Ahmed, et al. "Analysis of text feature extractors using deep learning on fake news." Engineering, Technology & Applied Science Research 11.2 (2021): 7001-7005.
12. Shupta, et al. "An Adaptive Approach to Detecting Fake News Based on Generalised Text Features," CEUR Workshop Proceedings, Vol-3387, 2023, pp. 300-310.
13. R. A. Dar, Dr. R. Hashmy, "A Survey on COVID-19 related Fake News Detection using Machine Learning Models," CEUR Workshop Proceedings, Vol-3426, 2023, 36-46.
14. Mykytiuk, et al. "Technology of Fake News Recognition Based on Machine Learning Methods," CEUR Workshop Proceedings, Vol-3387, 2023, pp. 311-330.
15. Afanasieva, et al. "Application of Neural Networks to Identify of Fake News, CEUR Workshop Proceedings," Vol-3396, 2023, 346-358.
16. V. Vysotska, et al. "NLP Tool for Extracting Relevant Information from Criminal Reports or Fakes/Propaganda Content," International Conference on Computer Sciences and Information Technologies (CSIT), 2022, pp. 93-98, doi: 10.1109/CSIT56902.2022.10000563.
17. V.-A. Oliinyk, et al. "Propaganda Detection in Text Data Based on NLP and Machine Learning," CEUR workshop proceedings, Vol-2631, 2020, pp. 132-144. https://ceur-ws.org/Vol-2631/paper10.pdf
18. Dataset. URL: https://www.kaggle.com/datasets/clmentbisaillon/fake-and-real-news-dataset
19. Dataset. URL: https://dx.doi.org/10.21227/b5bt-5244
20. Dataset. URL: https://www.kaggle.com/datasets/algord/fake-news
21. Dataset. URL: https://www.kaggle.com/code/coshgunrahimli/fake-news-90-accuracy
22. Dataset. URL: https://www.kaggle.com/code/mayankjagtap/fake-news-analysis-by-mayank
23. Dataset. URL: https://www.kaggle.com/code/kkhandekar/real-or-fake-simple-bidirectional-rnn
24. Dataset. URL: https://www.kaggle.com/datasets/mrisdal/fake-new.
25. Dataset. URL: https://www.kaggle.com/code/therealsampat/fake-news-detection/inPortland State University, "Criminal Justice Policy Research Institute: Portland Crime Data," September 2012, www.pdx.edu/crime-data.
26. V. Vysotska, S. Mazepa, L. Chyrun, O. Brodyak, I. Shakleina and V. Schuchmann, "NLP Tool for Extracting Relevant Information from Criminal Reports or Fakes/Propaganda Content," 2022 IEEE 17th International Conference on Computer Sciences and Information Technologies (CSIT), Lviv, Ukraine, 2022, pp. 93-98, doi: 10.1109/CSIT56902.2022.10000563.
27. US Department of Justice, Federal Bureau of Investigation. "Uniform Crime Report Handbook", Federal Bureau of Investigation 1000 Custer Hollow Road Clarksburg, August 2004.
28. R. G. Plecas, "Introduction to Criminal Investigation: Processes, Practices and Thinking," Darryl Plecas, University of the Fraser Valley: BCcampus, 2017.

29. G. Akash Desai, "Criminal Investigation Tracker with Suspect Prediction," IJESC, 2017.
30. S. J. Nitin Sakhare, "Criminal Identification System Based On Data Mining," Recent Trends in Engineering & Technology, p. 1, 2014, Elsevier Publication.
31. Data Preprocessing in Data Mining - GeeksforGeeks. (n.d.). Retrieved from GeeksforGeeks: https://www.geeksforgeeks.org/data-
32. Himmiche, "AI meets criminology: an nlp tool for criminal investigations", AL Akhawayn University 2021.
33. Marokhovskaya, "Semantic analysis in Python," Access: https://isto ries.media/workshops/2021/12/07/semanticheskii-analiz-v-python/
34. N. Sharonova, I. Kyrychenko, I. Gruzdo, and G. Tereshchenko, "Generalized Semantic Analysis Algorithm of Natural Language Texts for Various Functional Style Types," CEUR Workshop Proceedings, Vol-3171, 2022, pp. 16-26.
35. S. Albota, "Modelling the Impact of the Pandemic on Online Communication: Textual Semantic Analysis," CEUR Workshop Proceedings, Vol-3171, 2022, pp. 471-486.
36. N. Romanyshyn, "Stylistic and Conceptual Function of Epithet in Poetic Discourse: an Experience of "Tropes" Text Semantics Analysis Program Application," CEUR Workshop Proceedings, Vol-3171, 2022, pp. 514-535.
37. V. Hryhorovych, "Analysis of Scientific Texts by Semantic Inverse-Additive Metrics for Ontology Concepts," CEUR Workshop Proceedings, Vol-3171, 2022, pp. 801-816.
38. V.Starko, "Implementing Semantic Annotation in a Ukrainian Corpus," CEUR Workshop Proceedings, Vol-2870, 2021, pp. 435-447.
39. V. Hryhorovych, "Construction of Semantic Metric for Measuring the Distance between Ontology Concepts," CEUR Workshop Proceedings, Vol-2870, 2021, pp. 498-510.
40. S. Albota, "Linguistically Manipulative, Disputable, Semantic Nature of the Community Reddit Feed Post," CEUR Workshop Proceedings, Vol-2870, 2021, pp. 769-783.
41. N. Bondarchuk, and I. Bekhta, "Quantitative Characteristics of Lexical-Semantic Groups Representing Weather in Weather News Stories (Based on British Online Press)," CEUR Workshop Proceedings, Vol-2870, 2021, pp. 799-810.
42. V. Starko, "Semantic Annotation for Ukrainian: Categorization Scheme, Principles, and Tools," CEUR workshop proceedings, Vol-2604, 2020, pp. 239-248.
43. PyAnswer, https://pyanswer.site/zadacha-chastotnyj-analiz/
44. M. Das, et. al. "A Comparative Study on TF-IDF Feature Weighting Method and Its Analysis Using Unstructured Dataset," CEUR Workshop Proceedings, Vol-2870, 2021, pp. 98-107.
45. Berko, et. al. "The text classification based on Big Data analysis for keyword definition using stemming," IEEE 16th International conference on computer science and information technologies, Lviv, 22–25 September, 2021, pp. 184–188.
46. Boyer, L. Dolamic, and N. Grabar, "Automated Detection of Health Websites' HONcode Conformity: Can N-gram Tokenization Replace Stemming?," SHTI, 2015, 216, pp. 1064.
47. M. Chaudhary, "TF-IDF Vectorizer scikit-learn," Access mode: https://medium.com/@cmukesh8688/tf-idf-vectorizer-scikit-learn-dbc0244a911a
48. Z. Saaya, and T. Hong, "The development of trust matrix for recognizing reliable content in social media," International Journal of Computing, 18(1), 2019, pp. 60-66.
49. S. Mazepa, et. al. "An Ontological Approach to Detecting Fake News in Online Media," International Conference on Advanced Computer Information Technologies, 2021, pp. 531-535.
50. M. Dyvak, A. Melnyk, S. Mazepa, M. Stetsko, "An Ontological Approach to Detecting Irrelevant and Unreliable Information on Web-Resources and Social Networks," Future Intent-Based Networking, Springer, Cham, 2022, pp. 481-492.
51. V. Oliinyk, V. Vysotska, Y. Burov, K. Mykich, V. B. Fernandes, "Propaganda Detection in Text Data Based on NLP and Machine Learning," CEUR workshop proceedings, Vol-2631,2020,pp.132-144.
52. V. Husak, et. al. "Information System for Recommendation List Formation of Clothes Style Image Selection According to User's Needs Based on NLP and Chatbots," CEUR workshop proceedings, Vol-2604, 2020, pp. 788-818.
53. N. Sharonova, et. al. "Generalized Semantic Analysis Algorithm of Natural Language Texts for Various Functional Style Types," CEUR Workshop Proceedings, Vol-3171, 2022, pp. 16-26.
54. V. Lytvyn, et. al. "Peculiarities of Generation of Semantics of Natural Language Speech by Helping Unlimited and Context-Dependent Grammar," CEUR workshop proceedings, Vol-2604, 2020, 536-551.

55. O. Bisikalo, Y. Ivanov, and N. Karevina, "Encoding of Natural Language Information on the Basis of the Power Set," Computer Sciences and Information Technologies, 2018, pp. 17–20.
56. O. Bisikalo, I. Bogach, and V. Sholota, "The Method of Modelling the Mechanism of Random Access Memory of System for Natural Language Processing," Advanced Trends in Radioelectronics, Telecommunications and Computer Engineering, 2020, pp. 472–477.
57. O. Bisikalo, and O. Vasilevskyi, "Evaluation of uncertainty in the measurement of sense of natural language constructions," International Journal of Metrology and Quality Engineering, 2017, 8.
58. V. Vysotska, S. Holoshchuk, and R. Holoshchuk, "A comparative analysis for English and Ukrainian texts processing based on semantics and syntax approach," CEUR Workshop Proceedings, Vol- 2870, 2021, pp.311-356.
59. V. Bobicev, O. Kanishcheva, and O. Cherednichenko, "Sentiment Analysis in the Ukrainian and Russian News," Conference on Electrical and Computer Engineering, 2017, pp. 1050-1055.
60. N. Khairova, A. Kolesnyk, O. Mamyrbayev, and K. Mukhsina, "The Aligned Kazakh-Russian Parallel Corpus Focused on the Criminal Theme," CEUR Workshop Proceedings, Vol-2362,2019, pp.116-125.
61. O. Levchenko, and M. Dilai, "Key Colour Terms in the Ukrainian Prose Fiction of the 21st Century," CEUR Workshop Proceedings, Vol-3171, 2022, pp. 49-60.
62. V. Vysotska, O. Markiv, S. Teslia, Y. Romanova, and I. Pihulechko, "Correlation Analysis of Text Author Identification Results Based on N-Grams Frequency Distribution in Ukrainian Scientific and Technical Articles," CEUR Workshop Proceedings,Vol-3171,2022,pp.277-314.
63. V. Starko and A. Rysin, "VESUM: A Large Morphological Dictionary of Ukrainian As a Dynamic Tool," CEUR Workshop Proceedings, Vol-3171, 2022, pp. 61-70.
64. M. Shvedova, N. Prydvorova, and I. Skibina, "Normalization of Early Modern Ukrainian in GRAC: the Case of Lesia Ukrainka's Works," CEUR Workshop Proceedings, Vol-3171, 2022, pp. 71-80.
65. Dmytriv, et. al. "Comparative Analysis of Using Different Parts of Speech in the Ukrainian Texts Based on Stylistic Approach," CEUR Workshop Proceedings, Vol-3171, 2022, pp. 546-560.
66. Y. Hlavcheva, O. Kanishcheva, M. Vovk, and M. Glavchev, "Using Topic Modeling for Automation Search to Reviewer," CEUR Workshop Proceedings, Vol-3171, 2022, pp. 81-90.
67. Z. Kunch, A. Serednytska, I. Vasylyshyn, H. Horodylovska, and I. Farion, "The Peculiarities of Spelling Rules in Formal, Informal Handwriting and Internet Communication," CEUR Workshop Proceedings, Vol-3171, 2022, pp. 91-103.
68. N. Hrytsiv, et. al., "Sylvia Plath's I felt-Narrative Label of The Bell Jar in Ukrainian Translation: Tagging Textness Features," CEUR Workshop Proceedings, Vol-3171, 2022, pp. 240-255.
69. S. Kubinska, et. al., "Ukrainian Language Chatbot for Sentiment Analysis and User Interests Recognition based on Data Mining," CEUR Workshop Proceedings, Vol-3171, 2022, pp. 315-327.
70. N. Borysova, et. al., "Gender Classification of Surnames: Ukrainian aspect, CEUR Workshop Proceedings," Vol-3171,2022, pp.354-364.
71. Mandziy, U. Yurlova, and M. Dilai, "English-Ukrainian Parallel Corpus of IT Texts: Application in Translation Studies," CEUR Workshop Proceedings, Vol-3171, 2022, pp. 724-736.
72. Datsyshyn, et. al., "Neologisms with the Prefix Anti- in the Ukrainian Online Media in the Covid-19 Pandemic Period," CEUR Workshop Proceedings, Vol-3171, 2022, pp. 192-211.
73. O. Cherednichenko, and O. Kanishcheva, "Readability Evaluation for Ukrainian Medicine Corpus(UKRMED)," CEUR Workshop Proceedings, Vol-2870, 2021, pp. 402-412.
74. O. Cherednichenko, N. Babkova, O. Kanishcheva, "Complex Term Identification for Ukrainian Medical Texts," CEUR Workshop Proceedings, Vol-2255, 2018, pp. 146-154.
75. O. Synchak, and V. Starko, "Ukrainian Feminine Personal Nouns in Online Dictionaries and Corpora," CEUR Workshop Proceedings, Vol-3171, 2022, pp. 775-790.
76. O. Levchenko, N. Romanyshyn, D. Dosyn, "Method of Automated Identification of Metaphoric Meaning in Adjective + Noun Word Combinations (Based on the Ukrainian Language)," CEUR Workshop Proceedings, Vol-2386, 2019, pp. 370-380.
77. V. Shyrokov, ""Accuracy" vs "Unambiguity" in Linguistics," CEUR Workshop Proceedings, Vol-2870, 2021, pp. 1-5.
78. Public opinion in a situation of total disinformation (fake news problem). International Scientific Journal of media and communications in Central Asia, (5) https://doi.org/10.62499/ijmcc.vi5.57
79. V. Vysotska, K. Przystupa, L. Chyrun, S. Vladov, Yu. Ushenko, D. Uhryn, Dmytro, Z. Hu. (2024). Disinformation, Fakes and Propaganda Identifying Methods in Online Messages Based on NLP and Machine

Learning Methods. International Journal of Computer Network and Information Security. 16. 57-85. 10.5815/ijcnis.2024.05.06.
80. Hartmann, Y. Golovchenko, and I. Augenstein, "Mapping (dis-)information flow about the MH17 plane crash,"/ arXiv. https://arxiv.org/abs/1910.01363.
81. Mykytiuk, V. Vysotska, O. Markiv, L. Chyrun, and Y. Pelekh, "Technology of Fake News Recognition Based on Machine Learning Methods," CEUR Workshop Proceedings 3387 (2023): 311-330.
82. Khairova, A. Galassi, F. Lo Scudo, B. Ivasiuk, and I. Redozub, "Unsupervised approach for misinformation detection in Russia-Ukraine war news," CEUR Workshop Proceedings 3722 (2024): 21-36.
83. V. Vysotska, "Information technology for recognizing propaganda, fakes and disinformation in textual content based on NLP and machine learning method," Radio Electronics, Computer Science, Control 2 (2024):126-141. https://doi.org/10.15588/1607-3274-2024-2-13.
84. V. A. Oliinyk, V. Vysotska, Y. Burov, K. Mykich, and V. B. Fernandes, "Propaganda Detection in Text Data Based on NLP and Machine Learning," CEUR Workshop Proceedings 2631 (2020): 132-144.
85. V. Vysotska, L. Chyrun, S. Chyrun, and I. Holets, "Information technology for identifying disinformation sources and inauthentic chat users' behaviours based on machine learning," CEUR Workshop Proceedings 3723 (2024): 427-465.
86. Brennen, "Making sense of lies, deceptive propaganda, and fake news." Journal of Media Ethics 32.3 (2017): 179-181. https://doi.org/10.1080/23736992.2017.1331023
87. T. Stephen, "The role of digital and social media marketing in consumer behavior." Current opinión in Psychology 10 (2016): 17-21. https://doi.org/10.1016/j.copsyc.2015.10.016
88. Aldwairi, and A. Alwahedi, "Detecting fake news in social media networks." Procedia Computer Science 141 (2018): 215-222. https://doi.org/10.1016/j.procs.2018.10.171
89. V. Prokopenko, "Legal nature of pages in social networks. Legal newspaper-online version." https://yur-gazeta.com/publications/practice/zahist-intelektualnoyi-vlasnosti-avtorske-pravo/pravova-priroda-storinok-u-socialnih-merezhah.html
90. Bjola "Propaganda in the digital age," Global Affairs 3(3), (2017): 189-191. https://doi.org/10.1080/23340460.2017.1427694.
91. R. A. Dar, and Dr. R. Hashmy, "A Survey on COVID-19 related Fake News Detection using Machine Learning Models," CEUR Workshop Proceedings, Vol-3426, 2023, pp. 36-46.
92. Propaganda Definitions. https://propaganda.qcri.org/annotations/definitions.html.
93. Shupta, O. Barmak, A. Wierzbicki, and T. Skrypnyk, "An Adaptive Approach to Detecting Fake News Based on Generalized Text Features," CEUR Workshop Proceedings 3387 (2023): 300-310.
94. J. Garcia-Marín, and A. Calatrava, "The Use of Supervised Learning Algorithms in Political Communication and Media Studies: Locating Frames in the Press," Pamplona 31(3) (2018): 175-188. https://doi.org/10.15581/003.31.3.175-188.
95. texty.org.ua. How Texty detects and makes sense of manipulative news. https://medium.com/@texty.org.ua/how-texty-detects-and-makes-sense-of-manipulative-news-1f43d33936eb.
96. Nginx. https://fgz.texty.org/.
97. Afanasieva, N. Golian, V. Golian, A. Khovrat, and K. Onyshchenko, "Application of Neural Networks to Identify of Fake News," CEUR Workshop Proceedings 3396 (2023): 346-358.
98. Wierzbicki, A. Shupta, and O. Barmak, "Synthesis of model features for fake news detection using large language models," CEUR Workshop Proceedings 3722 (2024): 50-65.
99. Jain, et al., "A smart system for fake news detection using machine learning." 2019 International conference on issues and challenges in intelligent computing techniques (ICICT). Vol. 1. IEEE, 2019. https://doi.org/10.1109/ICICT46931.2019.8977659
100. S. Yang, et al., "Unsupervised fake news detection on social media: A generative approach." Proceedings of the AAAI conference on artificial intelligence. Vol. 33. No. 01. 2019. https://doi.org/10.1609/aaai.v33i01.33015644
101. Shu, et al. "Fake news detection on social media: A data mining perspective." ACM SIGKDD explorations newsletter 19.1 (2017): 22-36. https://doi.org/10.1145/3137597.3137600
102. O'Brien, Machine learning for detection of fake news. https://dspace.mit.edu/handle/1721.1/119727
103. S. Aphiwongsophon, and P. Chongstitvatana, "Detecting fake news with machine learning method." 2018 15th international conference on electrical engineering/electronics, computer, telecommunications and information technology (ECTI-CON). IEEE, 2018. https://doi.org/10.1109/ECTICon.2018.8620051

104.A. Tanvir, et al. (2019). "Detecting fake news using machine learning and deep learning algorithms." 2019 7th international conference on smart computing & communications (ICSCC). IEEE, 2019. https://doi.org/10.1109/ICSCC.2019.8843612
105.Reis, et al. "Supervised learning for fake news detection." IEEE Intelligent Systems 34.2 (2019): 76-81. https://doi.org/10.1109/MIS.2019.2899143
106.Sukailo, and N. Korshun, "The influence of NLU and generative AI on the development of cyber defense systems." Cyber security: education, science, technology 2.18 (2022): 187-196.
107.Martseniuk, V. Kozachok, O. Bohdanov, and Z. Brzhevska, "Analysis of Methods for Detecting Misinformation in Social Networks Using Machine Learning." Electronic Professional Scientific Journal «Cybersecurity: Education, Science, Technique» 2(22), (2023): 148–155. https://doi.org/10.28925/2663-4023.2023.22.148155
108.What Is Natural Language Processing (NLP)? https://www.oracle.com/eg/artificial-intelligence/what-is-naturallanguage-processing/.
109.Introduction to Information Retrieval BM25, BM25F, and User Behavior Chris Manning and Pandu Nayak. https://web.stanford.edu/class/cs276/handouts/lecture12-bm25etc.pdf
110.Understanding TF-IDF and BM-25. https://kmwllc.com/index.php/2020/03/20/understanding-tf-idfand-bm-25/.
111.T. T. T. Pham, T. D. Pham, and V. C. Ta, "Evaluation of GAN-based Models for Phishing URL Classifiers," International Journal of Computer Network and Information Security 15(2) (2023):1-14. https://doi.org/10.5815/ijcnis.2023.02.01.
112.M. Meligy, H. M. Ibrahim, and M. F. Torky, "Identity Verification Mechanism for Detecting Fake Profiles in Online Social Networks," International Journal of Computer Network and Information Security 9(1) (2017): 31-39. https://doi.org/10.5815/ijcnis.2017.01.04.
113.Gao, "A Preliminary Study of Fake Fingerprints," International Journal of Computer Network and Information Security 6(12) (2014): 1-8. https://doi.org/10.5815/ijcnis.2014.12.01.
114.Soufyane, B. A. Abdelhakim, and M. B. Ahmed "An intelligent chatbot using NLP and TF-IDF algorithm for text understanding applied to the medical field." Emerging Trends in ICT for Sustainable Development: The Proceedings of NICE2020 International Conference. Cham: Springer International Publishing, 2021. https://doi.org/10.1007/978-3-030-53440-0_1
115.Y. Lv, and C. Zhai. "A log-logistic model-based interpretation of TF normalization of BM25." Advances in Information Retrieval: 34th European Conference on IR Research, ECIR 2012, Barcelona, Spain, April 1-5, 2012. Proceedings 34. Springer Berlin Heidelberg, 2012. https://doi.org/10.1007/978-3-642-28997-2_21
116.L., Mishchenko, I., Klymenko, and V. Tkachenko, "The Fake News Recognition Method Based on Naïve Bayes with Improved TF-IDF Algorithm." In: Kazymyr, V., et al. Mathematical Modeling and Simulation of Systems. MODS 2023. Lecture Notes in Networks and Systems 1091 (2024). Springer, Cham. https://doi.org/10.1007/978-3-031-67348-1_12
117.Mishchenko, and I. Klymenko, "Recognizing fake news based on natural language processing using the BM25 algorithm with fine-tuned parameters." Eastern-European Journal of Enterprise Technologies 6(2(126)) (2023) 33–40. https://doi.org/10.15587/1729-4061.2023.293513
118.V. Lande, et al. "Spoken language identification based on the transcript analysis." Digital Scholarship in the Humanities 38.2 (2023): 586-595. https://doi.org/10.1093/llc/fqac052
119.Soufyane, B. A. Abdelhakim, and M. B. Ahmed. "An intelligent chatbot using NLP and TF-IDF algorithm for text understanding applied to the medical field." Emerging Trends in ICT for Sustainable Development: The Proceedings of NICE2020 International Conference. Cham: Springer International Publishing, 2021. https://doi.org/10.1007/978-3-030-53440-0_1
120.Jiang, et al., "Naive bayes text categorization algorithm based on tf-idf attribute weighting." Proceedings of the 2018 2nd International Conference on Computer Science and Artificial Intelligence. 2018. https://doi.org/10.1145/3297156.3297256
121.S. Wang, L. Jiang, and C. Li. "Adapting naive Bayes tree for text classification." Knowledge and Information Systems 44 (2015): 77-89. https://doi.org/10.1007/s10115-014-0746-y
122.S. Mazumder, and T. Barui. "Discovering topics from the titles of the Indian LIS theses." Library Philosophy and Practice (e-journal) (2021): 1-23.
123.H. Fan, and Y. Qin. "Research on text classification based on improved tf-idf algorithm." 2018 International Conference on Network, Communication, Computer Engineering (NCCE 2018). Atlantis Press, 2018. https://doi.org/10.2991/ncce-18.2018.79

124. C., Liu, et al. "Research of text classification based on improved TFIDF algorithm." 2018 IEEE International Conference of Intelligent Robotic and Control Engineering (IRCE). IEEE, 2018. https://doi.org/10.1109/IRCE.2018.8492945
125. W. Dai. "Improvement and implementation of feature weighting algorithm TF-IDF in Text classification." 2018 International Conference on Network, Communication, Computer Engineering (NCCE 2018). Atlantis Press, 2018. https://doi.org/10.2991/ncce-18.2018.94
126. K. Izzah, and A. S. Girsang, "Modified TF-Assocterm weighting method for text classification on news dataset from twitter." IAENG International Journal of Computer Science 48.1 (2021): 142-151. https://www.iaeng.org/IJCS/issues_v48/issue_1/IJCS_48_1_15.pdf
127. S. Alammary, "Arabic questions classification using modified TF-IDF." IEEE Access 9 (2021): 95109-95122. https://doi.org/10.1109/ACCESS.2021.3094115
128. T. Dogan, and A. K. Uysal. "On term frequency factor in supervised term weighting schemes for text classification." Arabian Journal for Science and Engineering 44 (2019): 9545-9560. https://doi.org/10.1007/s13369-019-03920-9
129. Sharifani, et al. "Operating Machine Learning across Natural Language Processing Techniques for Improvement of Fabricated News Model." International Journal of Science and Information System Research 12.9 (2022): 20-44. https://papers.ssrn.com/sol3/papers.cfm?abstract_id=4251017
130. J.-Y., Yoo, and D. Yang. "Classification scheme of unstructured text document using TF-IDF and naive bayes classifier." Advanced Science and Technology Letters 111.50 (2015): 263-266. https://web.archive.org/web/20180604105217id_/http://onlinepresent.org/proceedings/vol111_2015/50.pdf
131. H. Hairani, et al. "The abstract of thesis classifier by using naive Bayes method." 2021 International Conference on Software Engineering & Computer Systems and 4th International Conference on Computational Science and Information Management (ICSECS-ICOCSIM). IEEE, 2021. https://doi.org/10.1109/ICSECS52883.2021.00063
132. S. Xu, "Bayesian Naive Bayes classifiers to text classification." Journal of Information Science 44.1 (2018): 48-59. https://doi.org/10.1177/016555151667794
133. Lande, and A. Feher. "OSINT Time Series Forecasting Methods Analysis." Theoretical and Applied Cybersecurity 5.1 (2023). https://doi.org/10.20535/tacs.2664-29132023.1.287750
134. Word Representation in Natural Language Processing Part II. https://towardsdatascience.com/wordrepresentation-in-natural-language-processing-part-ii-1aee2094e08a
135. V. Gangadharan, et al. "Paraphrase detection using deep neural network based word embedding techniques." 2020 4th International Conference on Trends in Electronics and Informatics (ICOEI)(48184). IEEE, 2020. https://doi.org/10.1109/ICOEI48184.2020.9142877
136. Egger, "Text Representations and Word Embeddings: Vectorizing Textual Data." Applied Data Science in Tourism: Interdisciplinary Approaches, Methodologies, and Applications. Cham: Springer International Publishing, 2022. 335-361. https://doi.org/10.1007/978-3-030-88389-8_16
137. How to use tf idf vectorizer. https://www.projectpro.io/recipes/use-tf-df-vectorizer.
138. H. Zhao, R. Wang, and K. Chen. "Syntax in end-to-end natural language processing." Proceedings of the 2021 Conference on Empirical Methods in Natural Language Processing: Tutorial Abstracts. 2021. https://doi.org/10.18653/v1/2021.emnlp-tutorials.6
139. M. Bender, "Linguistic fundamentals for natural language processing: 100 essentials from morphology and syntax." Springer Nature, 2022. https://doi.org/10.1007/978-3-031-02150-3
140. A., Salloum, R. Khan, and K. Shaalan. "A survey of semantic analysis approaches." Proceedings of the International Conference on Artificial Intelligence and Computer Vision (AICV2020). Springer International Publishing, 2020. https://doi.org/10.1007/978-3-030-44289-7_6
141. D. H. Maulud, et al. "State of art for semantic analysis of natural language processing." Qubahan academic journal 1.2 (2021): 21-28. https://doi.org/10.48161/qaj.v1n2a44
142. K. Singh, and M. Shashi. "Vectorization of text documents for identifying unifiable news articles." International Journal of Advanced Computer Science and Applications 10.7 (2019). https://doi.org/10.14569/IJACSA.2019.0100742
143. TF-IDF from scratch in python on a real-world dataset. https://towardsdatascience.com/tf-idf-for-documentranking-from-scratch-in-python-on-real-world-dataset-796d339a4089.
144. V. Vysotska, R. Holoshchuk, S. Goloshchuk, O. Voloshynskyi, M. Shevchenko, V. Panasyuk, "Predicting the Effects of News on the Financial Market Based on Machine Learning Technology." 2023 IEEE 5th International Conference on Advanced Information and Communication Technologies (AICT) (pp. 152-157). IEEE. (2023, November). https://doi.org/10.1109/AICT61584.2023.10452706

145.Robertson, H. Zaragoza, and M. Taylor. "Simple BM25 extension to multiple weighted fields." Proceedings of the thirteenth ACM international conference on Information and knowledge management. (2004): 42-49. https://doi.org/10.1145/1031171.1031181
146.V. Vysotska, S. Mazepa, L. Chyrun, O. Brodyak, I. Shakleina, and V. Schuchmann, "NLP tool for extracting relevant information from criminal reports or fakes/propaganda content." 2022 IEEE 17th International Conference on Computer Sciences and Information Technologies (CSIT) (pp. 93-98). IEEE. (2022, November). https://doi.org/10.1109/CSIT56902.2022.10000563
147.Vo, and K. Lee. "Where are the facts? searching for factchecked information to alleviate the spread of fake news." arXiv preprint arXiv:2010.03159 (2020). https://arxiv.org/abs/2010.03159
148.V. Vysotska, S. Voloshyn, O. Markiv, O. Brodyak, N. Sokulska, and V. Panasyuk, "Tone Analysis of Regional Articles in English-Language Newspapers Based on Recurrent Neural Network Bi-LSTM." 2023 IEEE 5th International Conference on Advanced Information and Communication Technologies (AICT) (pp. 1-6). IEEE. (2023, November). https://doi.org/10.1109/AICT61584.2023.10452700
149.Propaganda detection. https://www.kaggle.com/datasets/vladimirsydor/propaganda-detection-our-data.
150.Fake News Detection, https://www.kaggle.com/code/ilaydadu/fake-news-detection-with-nlp-and-lstm.
151.Fake News Detection, https://www.kaggle.com/code/superrajdoor/fake-news-detection-with-lstm-and-nlp-prorew1/input%20//
152.M. Nazarkevych, V. Vysotska, V. Liakh, Vladyslav Ye. Leheza, N. Naconechnyi. (2024). Methods of Identifying Fake News in Social Networks. 10.32388/6H9WKK.
153.Public opinion in a situation of total disinformation (fake news problem). International Scientific Journal of media and communications in Central Asia, (5) https://doi.org/10.62499/ijmcc.vi5.57
154.Hobbs R. Teach the conspiracies. Knowledge Quest. 2017. Vol. 46. №1. P. 16–24.
155.Kertysova K. Artificial intelligence and disinformation: How AI changes the way disinformation is produced disseminated, and can be countered. Security and Human Rights. 2018. Vol. 29. №1. P. 55-81.
156.Nazarkevych, M., Lytvyn, V., & Demchyk, D. (2024, February). Ensemble Methods of Determining the Effective Activity of Enterprises. In IEEE International Conference on Advanced Trends in Radioelectronics, Telecommunications and Computer Engineering (pp. 160-183). Cham: Springer Nature Switzerland.
157.Nazarkevych, M., Levush, P., & Pankovych, B. (2021, May). Improving the Efficiency of Information Collection Based on the Development of a Chatbot with a Parser. In 2021 IEEE 12th International Conference on Electronics and Information Technologies (ELIT) (pp. 125-129). IEEE.
158.Mazepa, V. Vysotska, D. Ivanchyshyn, L. Chyrun, V. Schuchmann and Y. Ryshkovets, "Relationships Knowledge Graphs Construction Between Evidence Based on Crime Reports," 2022 IEEE 17th International Conference on Computer Sciences and Information Technologies (CSIT), Lviv, Ukraine, 2022, pp. 165-171, doi: 10.1109/CSIT56902.2022.10000587.
159.S. Pemberton, "Social harm future(s): Exploring the potential of the social harm approach," Crime, Law and Social Change, vol. 48, 2007, pp. 27–41.
160.S. V. Nath, "Crime Pattern Detection Using Data Mining," International Conference on Web Intelligence and Intelligent Agent Technology Workshops, 2006, pp. 41–44.
161.H. Chen, W. Chung, J. J. Xu, G. Wang, Y. Qin, and M. Chau, "Crime data mining: a general framework and some examples," computer, vol. 37(4), 2004, pp. 50–56.
162.M. Keyvanpour, M. Javideh, and M. Ebrahimi, "Detecting and investigating crime by means of data mining: A general crime matching framework," Procedia CS, vol. 3, 2011, pp. 872–880.
163.D. Kuang, P. J. Brantingham, and A. L. Bertozzi, "Crime topic modeling," Crime Science, vol. 6(1), 2017, p. 12.
164.M. D. Choudhury, E. Kiciman, M. Dredze, G. Coppersmith, and M. Kumar, "Discovering Shifts to Suicidal Ideation from Mental Health Content in Social Media," Human Factors in Computing Systems, CHI, New York, NY, USA, 2016, pp. 2098–2110.
165.Mohler, J. Carter, and R. Raje, "Improving social harm indices with a modulated hawkes process," International Journal of Forecasting, vol. 34(3), 2018, pp. 431 – 439.
166.R. Eshleman, D. Jha, and R. Singh, "Identifying individuals amenable to drug recovery interventions through computational analysis of addiction content in social media," IEEE International Conference on Bioinformatics and Biomedicine, BIBM, 2017, pp. 849–854.
167.Clark, and C. D. Manning, "Improving Coreference Resolution by Learning Entity-Level Distributed Representations," Annual Meeting of the Association for Computational Linguistics, 2016, pp. 643–653.
168.Riedel, and J. Jarvis, "The decline of arrest clearances for criminal homicide: Causes, correlates, and third parties," Criminal Justice Policy Review, vol. 9(3-4), 1999, pp. 279–306.

169. Y. Chi, Y. Qin, R. Song, and H. Xu, "Knowledge graph in smart education: A case study of entrepreneurship scientific publication management," Sustainability, vol. 10(4), 2018, p. 995.
170. T. Elyezjy, and A. M. Elhaless, "Investigating crimes using text mining and network analysis," International Journal of Computer Applications, vol. 126, 2015, pp. 19-25.
171. R. Pandey, P. J. Brantingham, C. D. Uchida, and G. Mohler, "Building knowledge graphs of homicide investigation chronologies," Data Mining Workshops, 2020, pp. 790-798.
172. R. Pandey, "Text Mining for Social Harm and Criminal Justice Applications," PhD Thesis, 2020, http://dx.doi.org/10.7912/C2/2375.
173. R. Pandey, and G. O. Mohler, "Evaluation of crime topic models: topic coherence vs spatial crime concentration," IEEE International Conference on Intelligence and Security Informatics, 2018. pp. 76-78.
174. Himmiche, "AI meets criminology: an nlp tool for criminal investigations", AL Akhawayn University 2021.
175. Vysotska, S. Holoshchuk, and R. Holoshchuk, "A comparative analysis for English and Ukrainian texts processing based on semantics and syntax approach," CEUR Workshop Proceedings, Vol-2870, 2021, pp. 311-356.
176. Lenko, V. Pasichnyk, N. Kunanets, and Y.Shcherbyna,"Knowledge Representation and Automated Formal Reasoning in Description Logic ALC," CEUR Workshop Proceedings, Vol-2917, 2021, pp. 26-39.
177. Y. Burov, "Knowledge Based Situation Awareness Process Based on Ontologies," CEUR Workshop Proceedings, Vol-2870, 2021, 413-423.
178. Bomba, M. Nazaruk, N. Kunanets, and V. Pasichnyk, "Modeling the Dynamics of Knowledge Potential of Agents in the Educational Social and Communication Environment," Advances in Intelligent Systems and Computing, Springer, Cham, vol. 1080, 2020, pp. 17-24.
179. Bublyk, O. Rybytska, A. Karpiak, and Y. Matseliukh, "Structuring the fuzzy knowledge base of the IT industry impact factors," Computer sciences and information technologies, 2018, pp. 21–24.
180. Khavalko, I. Bilyk, O. Hasko, and I. Protsyk, "Architecture of Online Automated Knowledge Testing Systems," CEUR Workshop Proceedings, Vol-3171, 2022, pp. 1583-1593.
181. S. Lupenko, et. al., "The axiomatic-deductive strategy of knowledge organization in onto-based e-learning systems for Chinese image medicine," CEUR Workshop Proceedings, Vol. 2255, 2018,126-134.
182. R. Miroshnyk, I. Matviy, Y. Voytsekhovska, Y. Kis, I. Bahlai,'Current Trends in Knowledge Management: Problems and Challenges, ' CEUR Workshop Proceedings, Vol-3171, 2022, pp. 1708-1718.
183. Berko, et. al., "Application of ontologies and meta-models for dynamic integration of weakly structured data," International Conference on Data Stream Mining and Processing,2020,pp.432-437.
184. Shubin, A. Kozyriev, V. Liashik, and G. Chetverykov, "Methods of Adaptive Knowledge Testing Based on the Theory of Logical Networks," CEUR Workshop Proceedings, 2870, 2021,pp.1184-1193.
185. S. Mazepa, S. Banakh, A. Melnyk, S. Pugach, O.Yavorska, N.Golota, "An Ontological Approach to Detecting Fake News in Online Media," Advanced Computer Information Technologies, 2021, pp. 531-535.
186. M. Dyvak, A. Melnyk, S. Mazepa, M. Stetsko, "An Ontological Approach to Detecting Irrelevant and Unreliable Information on Web-Resources and Social Networks," Future Intent-Based Networking, Springer, Cham, 2022, pp. 481-492.
187. Nataliia, and M. Halyna, "Application of the 'Smart City' data domain thesaurus as the tool for representing knowledge while improving the problem-oriented Web search effectiveness," Computer Sciences and Information Technologies, 2019, pp. 31-34.
188. Mykich, and Y. Burov, "Algebraic framework for knowledge processing in systems with situational awareness," Advances in Intelligent Systems and Computing, vol. 512, 2017, pp. 217-227.
189. Burov, K. Mykich, and I. Karpov, "Building a Versatile Knowledge-Based System Based on Reasoning Services and Ontology Representation Transformations," Computer Sciences and Information Technologies, 2020, 2, pp. 255–260.
190. Савенко П.О., Соляр Т.Я. Перетворення Фур'є й Лапласа в задачах апроксимації: монографія / НАН України, Ін-т приклад. проблем мех. і мат. ім. Я. С. Підстригача. — Львів: Інститут прикладних проблем механіки і математики ім. Я. С. Підстригача, 2019. — 382 с.
191. Stanley F.Chen, Joshua T. Goodman. An Empirical Study of Smoothing Techniques for Language Modeling. ACL '96: Proceedings of the 34th annual meeting on Association for Computational Linguistics, 310 – 318
192. Jurafsky, D., & Martin, J. H. Speech and Language Processing: An Introduction to Natural Language Processing, Computational Linguistics, and Speech Recognition (3rd ed.). – 2023
193. Milad Vazan. Deep Learning: From Basics to Building Deep Neural Networks with Python. – https://arxiv.org/abs/2205.01069
194. The Propaganda War for Ukraine. – https://www.dw.com/en/the-propaganda-war-for-ukraine/a-64282924.

195.Natural Language Processing with Python and spaCy: A practical introduction. –https://dokumen.pub/natural-language-processing-with-python-and-spacy-a-practical-introduction-1718500521-9781718500525.html
196.Mane, S., Kundu, S., & Sharma, R. A Survey on Online User Aggression: Content Detection and Behavioral Analysis on Social Media. – https://dl.acm.org/doi/10.1145/3711125
197.Measuring the Prevalence of Anti-Social Behavior in Online Communities. – https://dl.acm.org/doi/10.1145/3555552
198.Особливості інформаційних каналів соціальних мереж під час російсько-української війни. – https://er.nau.edu.ua/items/bdda70b3-2db1-4a56-a0c4-bafed7870a40
199.Продакт-плейсмент як сучасний прийом маркетингу. – https://economyandsociety.in.ua/index.php/journal/article/view/3472
200.Wardle, C., & Derakhshan, H. (2017). Information Disorder: Toward an Interdisciplinary Framework for Research and Policy Making. Council of Europe report DGI09. 118 p.
201.Tajrian, M., Rahman, A., Kabir, M.A. & Islam, M. R. (2023). A Review of Methodologies for Fake News Analysis. IEEE Access, 11, 73879-73893, https://doi.org/10.1109/ACCESS.2023.3294989.
202.Mohammed, S., Al-Aaraji, N., & Al-Saleh, A. (2024). Knowledge Rules-based Decision Tree Classifier model for effective fake accounts detection in social networks. International Journal of Safety and Security Engineering, 14(4), 1243-1251. https://doi.org/10.18280/ijsse.140421.
203.Sudhakar, M., & Kaliyamurthie, K.P. (2024). Detection of fake news from social media using support vector machine learning algorithms. Measurement: Sensors, 32(101028). https://doi.org/10.1016/j.measen.2024.101028.
204.Kozik, R., Kula, S., Choraś, M. & Wozniak, M. (2022). Technical solution to counter potential crime: Text analysis to detect fake news and disinformation. Journal of Computational Science, 60(101576). https://doi.org/10.1016/j.jocs.2022.101576.
205.Battal, B., Yıldırım, B., Dinçaslan, Ö., & Cicek, G. (2024). Fake News Detection with Machine Learning Algorithms. Celal Bayar University Journal of Science. 20(3), 65-83. https://doi.org/10.18466/cbayarfbe.1472576.
206.Abdulaziz, A., & Marwan, A. (2020). An Empirical Comparison of Fake News Detection using different Machine Learning Algorithms. International Journal of Advanced Computer Science and Applications (IJACSA), 11(9), 146-152. http://dx.doi.org/10.14569/IJACSA.2020.0110917.
207.Wang, W. Y. (2017). "Liar, Liar Pants on Fire": A New Benchmark Dataset for Fake News Detection. In Proceedings of the 55th Annual Meeting of the Association for Computational Linguistics. 2, 422–426.
208.Alikhashashneh, E., Nahar, K., Abual-Rub, M., & Alkhaldy, H. (2024). A robust method for detecting fake news using both machine and deep learning algorithms. Indonesian Journal of Electrical Engineering and Computer Science. 36, 1816-1826. https://doi.org/10.11591/ijeecs.v36.i3.pp1816-1826.
209.Shu, K., Sliva, A., Wang, S., Tang, J., & Liu, H. (2017). Fake News Detection on Social Media: A Data Mining Perspective. ACM SIGKDD Explorations Newsletter. 19(1), 22–36. https://doi.org/10.1145/3137597.3137600.
210.Su, Q., Wan, M., Liu, X., & Huang, C.-R. (2020). Motivations, methods and metrics of misinformation detection: An NLP perspective. Natural Language Processing Research. 1, 1–13. https://doi.org/10.2991/nlpr.d.200522.001.
211.Huang, J. (2020). Detecting Fake News With Machine Learning. Journal of Physics: Conference Series. 1693. https://doi.org/10.1088/1742-6596/1693/1/012158.
212.Jouhar, J., Pratap, A., Tijo, N., & Mony, M. (2024). Fake News Detection using Python and Machine Learning. Procedia Computer Science. 233, 763-771. https://doi.org/10.1016/j.procs.2024.03.265.
213.Shu, X. (2024). BERT and RoBERTa for Sarcasm Detection: Optimizing Performance through Advanced Fine-tuning. Applied and Computational Engineering. 97, 1-11. https://doi.org/10.54254/2755-2721/97/20241354.
214.Lozynska, O., Markiv, O., Vysotska, V., Romanchuk, R., & Nazarkevych, M. (2024). Information technology for developing and populating a disinformation dataset using intelligent deepfakes and clickbait search. Herald of Khmelnytskyi National University. Technical Sciences. 343(6(1)), 158-167. https://doi.org/10.31891/2307-5732-2024-343-6-24.
215.Komorowski, M., Marshall, D., Salciccioli, J., & Crutain, Y. (2016). Exploratory Data Analysis. Secondary Analysis of Electronic Health Records. 185-203. https://doi.org/10.1007/978-3-319-43742-2_15.
216.Tverdokhlib, V. Vysotska, O. Nagachevska, Yu. Ushenko, D. Uhryn, Yu. Tomka. (2025). Intelligent Processing Censoring InappropriateContent in Images, News, Messages and Articleson Web Pages Based on

Machine Learning. International Journal of Image, Graphics and Signal Processing. 17. 107-164. 10.5815/ijigsp.2025.01.08.
217.Purnima, T., & Rao, C. K. (2024). Automated Detection of Offensive Images and Sarcastic Memes in Social Media Through NLP. International Journal of Advanced Computer Science & Applications, 15(7).
218.Jani, K., Chaudhuri, M., Patel, H., & Shah, M. (2020). Machine learning in films: an approach towards automation in film censoring. Journal of Data, Information and Management, 2, 55-64.
219.Gongane, V. U., Munot, M. V., & Anuse, A. D. (2022). Detection and moderation of detrimental content on social media platforms: current status and future directions. Social Network Analysis and Mining, 12(1), 129.
220.Einwiller, S. A., & Kim, S. (2020). How online content providers moderate user-generated content to prevent harmful online communication: An analysis of policies and their implementation. Policy & Internet, 12(2), 184-206.
221.Galli, F., Loreggia, A., & Sartor, G. (2022, May). The Regulation of Content Moderation. In International Conference on the Legal Challenges of the Fourth Industrial Revolution (pp. 63-87). Cham: Springer International Publishing.
222.Yang, E., & Roberts, M. E. (2021, March). Censorship of online encyclopedias: Implications for NLP models. In Proceedings of the 2021 ACM Conference on Fairness, Accountability, and Transparency (pp. 537-548).
223.Chen, T. M. (2021). Automated content classification in social media platforms. In Securing Social Networks in Cyberspace (pp. 53-71). CRC Press.
224.Gorwa, R., Binns, R., & Katzenbach, C. (2020). Algorithmic content moderation: Technical and political challenges in the automation of platform governance. Big Data & Society, 7(1), 2053951719897945.
225.Tverdokhlib, O., Vysotska, V., Pukach, P., & Vovk, M. (2024). Information Technology for Identifying Hate Speech in Online Communication Based on Machine Learning. In Data-Centric Business and Applications: Modern Trends in Financial and Innovation Data Processes 2023. Volume 1 (pp. 339-369). Cham: Springer Nature Switzerland.
226.Marsoof, A., Luco, A., Tan, H., & Joty, S. (2023). Content-filtering AI systems–limitations, challenges and regulatory approaches. Information & Communications Technology Law, 32(1), 64-101.
227.Levshun, D., Tushkanova, O., & Chechulin, A. (2023). Two-model active learning approach for inappropriate information classification in social networks. International Journal of Information Security, 22(6), 1921-1936.
228.BPMN diagram. URL: https://iampm.club/ua/blog/shho-take-bpmndiagrama-i-navishho-vona-potribna-z-prikladami-2/.
229.Choosing Python or R for Data Analysis? An Infographic. URL: https://www.datacamp.com/community/tutorials/r-orpython-for-data-analysis.
230.Naïve Bayes classifiers. URL: https://www.ibm.com/topics/naive-bayes.
231.What is a Decision Tree? URL: https://www.ibm.com/topics/decision-trees.
232.Understand Random Forest Algorithms With Examples? URL: https://www.analyticsvidhya.com/blog/2021/06/understanding-random-forest/.
233.Logistic Regression. URL: https://towardsdatascience.com/logistic-regression-detailedoverview-46c4da4303bc.
234.What is fastText? URL: https://fasttext.cc/.
235.Python for NLP. URL: https://stackabuse.com/python-for-nlp-working-withfacebook-fasttext-library/.
236.Train Python Code Embedding with FastText. URL: https://medium.com/nerd-for-tech/train-python-code-embeddingwith-fasttext-1e225f193cc.
237.Tundis, A., Mukherjee, G., & Mühlhäuser, M. (2021). An algorithm for the detection of hidden propaganda in mixed-code text over the internet. Applied Sciences, 11(5), 2196.
238.R. Alam, et al. "Social media content categorization using supervised based machine learning methods and natural language processing in bangla language." 11th International Conference on Electrical and Computer Engineering (ICECE). IEEE, 2020.
239.V. Vysotska, et al. "NLP tool for extracting relevant information from criminal reports or fakes/propaganda content." 2022 IEEE 17th International Conference on Computer Sciences and Information Technologies (CSIT). IEEE, 2022.
240.W. H. Bangyal, et al. "Detection of Fake News Text Classification on COVID-19 Using Deep Learning Approaches." Computational and mathematical methods in medicine 2021.1 (2021): 5514220.
241.Haider, and A. Gandomi. "When big data made the headlines: Mining the text of big data coverage in the news media." International Journal of Services Technology and Management 27.1-2 (2021): 23-50.
242.Kratzwald, et al. "Deep learning for affective computing: Text-based emotion recognition in decision support." Decision support systems 115 (2018): 24-35.

243. V. Vysotska, et al. "Tone Analysis of Regional Articles in English-Language Newspapers Based on Recurrent Neural Network Bi-LSTM." 2023 IEEE 5th International Conference on Advanced Information and Communication Technologies (AICT). IEEE, 2023, pp. 158-163.
244. S. Voloshyn, et al. "Sentiment Analysis Technology of English Newspapers Quotes Based on Neural Network as Public Opinion Influences Identification Tool." Proceedings of the IEEE 17th International Conference on Computer Sciences and Information Technologies (CSIT), 2022, pp. 83-88, doi: 10.1109/CSIT56902.2022.10000627.
245. Hasan, et al. "Leveraging textual information for social media news categorization and sentiment analysis." Plos one 19.7 (2024): e0307027.
246. V. Vysotska, et al. "Sentiment Analysis of Information Space as Feedback of Target Audience for Regional E-Business Support in Ukraine." CEUR Workshop Proceedings, Vol-3426, 2023, 488-513.
247. Liu, Y., Ott, M., Goyal, N., Du, J., Joshi, M., Chen, D., Levy, O., Lewis, M., Zettlemoyer, L., & Stoyanov, V. (2019). Roberta: A robustly optimized Bert pretraining approach. arXiv preprint arXiv:1907.11692. DOI: 10.48550/arXiv.1907.11692.
248. Arif, M., Tonja, A. L., Ameer, I., Kolesnikova, O., Gelbukh, A., Sidorov, G., & Meque, A. G. M. (2022). CIC at CheckThat! 2022: Multi-class and Cross-lingual Fake News Detection. CEUR Workshop Proceedings (pp. 434 – 443).
249. Kalraa, S., Verma, P., Sharma, Y., & Chauhan, G. S. (2021). Ensembling of Various Transformer Based Models for the Fake News Detection Task in the Urdu Language. Proceedings of the Forum for Information Retrieval Evaluation.
250. Prytula, M. (2024). Fine-tuning BERT, DistilBERT, XLM-RoBERTa, and Ukr-RoBERTa models for sentiment analysis of Ukrainian language reviews. Artificial Intelligence, 29(2), 85–97. https://doi.org/10.15407/jai2024.02.085
251. Panchenko, D., Tytarenko, S., et al. (2022). Evaluation and Analysis of the NLP Model Zoo for Ukrainian Text Classification. In Information and Communication Technologies in Education, Research, and Industrial Applications (pp. 109–123). Springer. https://doi.org/10.1007/978-3-031-20834-8_6.
252. Dementieva, D., Babakov, N., & Fraser, A. (2025, May 29). EmoBench-UA: A Benchmark Dataset for Emotion Detection in Ukrainian. arXiv preprint. https://doi.org/10.48550/arXiv.2505.23297.
253. Saif M. Mohammad (2022). Ethics Sheet for Automatic Emotion Recognition and Sentiment Analysis. Computational Linguistics, 48(2), 239–278. https://doi.org/10.48550/arXiv.2109.08256.
254. Shynkarov, Y., Solopova, V., & Schmitt, V. (2025). Improving Sentiment Analysis for Ukrainian Social Media Code-Switching Data. In Proceedings of UNLP-2025 Workshop (COSMUS benchmark).
255. Haltiuk, M., & Smywiński-Pohl, A. (2024). LiBERTa: Advancing Ukrainian Language Modeling through Pre-training from Scratch. In Proceedings of the Third Ukrainian Natural Language Processing Workshop (pp. 120–128).
256. Dorenskyi, O.P., Ulichev, O.S., Zadorozhnyi, K.O., Kovalenko, A.S., & Dreeva, G.M. (2024). The conceptual model of the information counteraction system of the coordination center for national security and defense issues. Central Ukrainian Scientific Bulletin. Technical Sciences, 10(41), Part 2, 23-31.
257. Lozynska, O.V., Markiv, O.O., & Vysotska, V.A. (2025). Method for detecting sources of disinformation based on ensemble machine learning models. Bionics of Intelligence, 1(102), 11–19. https://doi.org/10.30837/bi.2025.1(102).02.

FSC
www.fsc.org
MIX
Papier | Fördert
gute Waldnutzung
FSC® C083411

Kolibri 360 GmbH
Ferdinand-Jühlke-Straße 7
99095 Erfurt, Deutschland
produktsicherheit@kolibri360.de

Druck:
CPI Druckdienstleistungen GmbH
im Auftrag der
Kolibri 360 GmbH
Ferdinand-Jühlke-Str. 7
99095 Erfurt